A PEDIGREED JEW

A PEDIGREED JEW

Between There and Here – Kovno and Israel

Safira Rapoport

Translated from the Hebrew by Pamela Hickman

AMBERLEY YAD VASHEM

Language Editor and Managing Editor: Fern Seckbach

© First published in Hebrew 2004 and in English 2010 by Yad Vashem
This edition published 2016

Amberley Publishing
The Hill, Stroud
Gloucestershire, GL5 4EP

www.amberley-books.com

British Library Cataloguing in Publication Data.
A catalogue record for this book is available from the British Library.

ISBN 978 1 4456 5875 9 (print)
ISBN 978 1 4456 5876 6 (ebook)

Typeset in 10.5pt on 13pt Sabon.
Typesetting and Origination by Amberley Publishing.
Printed in the UK.

To my beloved sons, Elad and Ariel,
and to Oded, my constant companion,
all of whom are the reason I return Here
from my travels and wanderings There.

I wish to thank Timorah Perel for her insightful and helpful comments upon reading the manuscript and give special thanks to Fern Seckbach for her work.

Contents

Introduction

During the first half of my life, with mandolins playing strains of sad Russian melodies, it was as if I were trampling over endless plains of snow, a fur hat covering my head, my nose reddened by the cold, my eyes dancing with the laughter and wholeness of joy. My window looked out on the yard of the Russian embassy, where my first friends, Ivan and Natasha, the children of consular staff, were doing gymnastics under an asbestos roof: "ras, dvi, rish, ti."[1] I would exercise together with them on our kitchen balcony, "*one, two, three, four,*" and sometimes Nina, their teacher, fixing her eyes in my direction, would very patiently demonstrate how to stretch one's muscles more tautly, cheering me on in Russian chatter interwoven with a few encouraging words in Hebrew.

In our yard there was a pine tree whose trunk and roots were in our ground but whose branches, collapsing under the weight of clusters of needles and pinecones, faced the direction of Russian territory. A rusty, spiked barbed-wire fence seemed to divide the tree, which stood diagonally, into two distinct beings. There, right on that border, with both sides guarding their own pedantically, we exchanged stamps and colorful ribbons, offered each other sticky sweets, conversed in a

---

1   Russian: one, two, three, four…

childish mixture of Russian and Hebrew, and bursting into peals of raucous laughter, our cheeks blushing, we would match up couples: Tammy with Andrei, Kookie with Natasha, Natti with Raya.

I am a first-generation Israeli and, as if still at home in Lithuania, my hair is braided in two plaits tied with huge butterfly bows of red ribbon; I am wearing a wide, flounced lace dress, tied at the back with a broad sash. *Oy gevalt* (Heaven forbid)! The house in Lithuania, however, had been destroyed, thirteen generations' roots severed from the Slobodka quarter of Kovno. I, a young, feeble seedling in virgin clay soil, am scattered through the winds of time, a time when "strength" was gauged by the number of years you had been in Israel and "prestige" by whether your parents had belonged to the "Palmach"[2] or the "Haganah."[3] But as for me, *nebekh* (Yid., alas), I represented the "triumph over Hitler" as my mother used to refer to me. Hitler had commanded my life!

I have Jewish eyes, their dreamy gaze wandering, sailing into the distance, searching for signs of bygone times. I carry a burdensome yearning for my mother's unknown home in Kovno: a yearning for the wooden bridge that had joined both sides of the town, a yearning for times when one gathered mushrooms in season in Kroki, for the basement in the wooden house laden with small bottles of jam, smoked meats, and pickled cabbage.

First, the Lithuanians had gone from house to house "cleaning out" the Slobodka quarter of its inhabitants; following that,

---

2 Hebrew acronym for *Plugot Machatz* (Strike Companies), the regular fighting force of the Haganah.

3 Hebrew: "The Defense," the unofficial army of the Yishuv (Jewish community) from 1920 to 1948 during the British Mandate of Palestine created by the League of Nations after World War I.

there was the rounding up of intellectuals, the killing at the Ninth Fort, then—the rounding up of people in the Small Ghetto and afterwards—the *Selektion*[4] at Demokratu Square. In the last blow before the ghetto was liquidated—referred to as the Children's *Aktion*[5]—Grandma Tzipora, dressed only in her pink robe and slippers, had gone out into the forbidding cold of −30°C (−22°F) to accompany the children being taken away. The children had been in her charge each day when their parents would go off to forced labor. There was a great deal of music playing. Loudspeakers were turned up to full volume, blaring out the song "Lili Marlene"[6] to stifle the children's screaming as they were thrown onto trucks.

After that, Mother, Aunt Leah, and Uncle Shlomo had crowded onto the bridge over the Vilija River and were loaded onto sealed, marked cattle wagons on their way to Tigenhof in eastern Prussia, and from there, to Stutthof and Dachau. That was the end of the Lithuanian home.

So, I actually have no real home. You might view my house in Ramat Gan as an outer layer, a covering for nothing inside of it. All the other children have real homes—homes with easy chairs on which aunts and uncles, grandfathers and grandmothers are comfortably seated; and in our house, the only family members alive from my lost home, their footsteps echoing from out of Europe—they, themselves, have gone to dust.

---

4 The process of selecting from among ghetto Jews those who were to be used for forced labor and those who were to be killed immediately or deported to Nazi camps.

5 *Aktion* refers to a raid against ghetto Jews to gather victims for extermination.

6 A famous German love song written by Hans Leib; it became very popular on both sides (German and Allied soldiers) during World War II.

PART I

There
1925–1946

Nechama

The Nemunas River winds and twists, flowing lazily along its wide river bed, its tributary, the Vilija River, emptying into it. How peaceful, cooling, and pure its waters are! The banks of both the river and the stream are high and crowned by green forests. The townspeople used to go there on festivals and holidays.

There, on the right shore of the Nemunas, surrounded by the river and its tributary, in the long, narrow valley from south to north, lies Kovno with its new town's wide roads and the narrow lanes of its Altstadt. Green mountains ring the city, with ruins of fortresses here and there—forts left from the Russian Tsarist rule. These had been erected from 1879, in a period of mounting tension between Russia and Germany. The Russians ruling Kovno began building a stronghold around the city, this being constructed from nine fortresses, becoming the strongest bastion in all of Russia. Between 1882 and 1890 eight forts were built in the environs of the city. In 1909 the ninth was constructed and, with that, they had completed a stronghold whose area was 65 square kilometers (16,000 acres), surrounded by three rows of iron fencing as well as water canals.

Beyond the Nemunas's other bank, on green-covered hills, one finds the suburb of Aleksotas, while situated on the banks of the Vilija opposite Kovno is Vilijampole, known by the Jews as Slobodka, with its narrow lanes, a suburb of Kovno that is older than Kovno itself.

Compared to Kovno's bustling center, the Slobodka suburb is backward and neglected: its houses, in effect, old, ramshackle, wooden, mostly single-story shacks, their walls crooked, and lacking the most basic of comforts. Walking its narrow alleys, only some of which had footpaths and most of which were unpaved, was exhausting.

Kovno was known for its large yeshivas: "Knesset Israel" (familiarly called "Slobodka"), named after Rabbi Israel Lipkin, founder of the Musar movement—"the morality movement"—familiarly known as Rabbi Israel Salanter,[7] and "Knesset Beit Yitzchak,"[8] both in Slobodka itself. Spiritual

---

7   In the 1840s Rabbi Israel Salanter (1810-1883), whose name indicates he had settled in the city of Salant, founded the movement in Vilna and furthered it in Kovno. He claimed that the Jew was becoming a valueless vacuum, his spiritual wholeness depleted, his innocence blemished, and that the Jew must be spiritually educated and trained in good attributes, mitzvot, here meaning good deeds one performed for others—in theory and practice. Moral teaching advocated memorization and practice and was designed to promote education and training in morals, these to be carried out both in seclusion and in group-learning—probably done within the confines of the "Musar Study House." For that reason, in 1882, Rabbi Israel had set up the Slobodka yeshiva, where his supporters were educated according to ideas and his teachings as well as those of his disciples. The yeshiva was named after him and produced generations of rabbis and sages.

8   Named after Rabbi Yitzchak Elchanan Spektor and founded some ten years after Knesset Israel, it was a counterbalance to the increasing influence of the Musar movement.

teaching within the yeshivas was well known in the Jewish world.

My father, Rabbi Yitzchak Baruchson, was born in Balta in the Ukraine and came from a long line of thirteen generations of rabbis. He had studied and received his education at the Knesset Israel yeshiva in Slobodka and served as the spiritual leader of the Or Israel yeshiva,[9] adjacent to the Knesset Israel yeshiva. He was endowed with noble, impressive looks and the strength of his position and reputation was respected and admired by all. Yet his strength was not in his pocket, for money was always scarce at home. Father was the more dominant and important figure at home: when he walked in we were expected to rise in his honor, offering him the chair kept only for him. Everything revolved around the father figure: "Father is studying, Father is resting, Father is preaching Torah to his students, Father is discussing matters with members of the yeshiva."

My mother, Tzipora (Feige), born in Ponevezh, Lithuania, to Shmuel David and Malka Chayet, was the daughter of an affluent family. My grandfather's family owned a factory producing absorbent cotton in Ponevezh, and they lived in a brick house (a *moyer* in Yiddish!). Mother was a clever woman, wise and dignified, and an exemplary housewife. Our home was as scrubbed as a pharmacy and Mother's cooking was very tasty home cooking. She made preserves and pickled cabbage and cucumbers.

As the daughter of a family of means, Mother found it difficult to reconcile herself to the austerity that came with the life of a rabbinical family. One facet of that way of life

9   An institution preparing outstanding young men from small yeshivas all over Lithuania who wanted go on to learn at the renowned Knesset Israel yeshiva.

Rabbi Yitzchak Baruchson,
Nechama's father

Nechama with her mother, Tzipora

was attending the weekly town market where Lithuanian country folk gathered, their horses harnessed to wagons, to sell their produce to the city Jews. There, Jewish women pushed their way in, examining woven fabrics, fingering chickens, and adopting a manner of lively bargaining with the Lithuanian farmers. The Jews' roofed stalls were set up on the sidewalks, scattered in a long line along the road. At the entrance to his shop, the Jewish grocer, rubbing his blue hands together to warm them, proudly displayed his produce: pickled fish, legumes, spices, sacks of sugar and salt; glass and china crockery, sewing needs and writing utensils. And then there were the Jewish craftsmen's shops: the shoemaker, the tinsmith, the carpenter, the watchmaker, the hatmaker, the pharmacist, the saloon keeper, and the innkeeper.

I remember Mother preferring not to buy anything she saw that had a defect, however small it was to the eye. She was not one for compromise, wanting only the best and of the highest quality. For example, she would say, "I won't buy this tablecloth unless this stripe here is red rather than yellow." She always claimed that "in the long run, cheap goods were expensive and expensive ones—cheap."

My parents married in Russia. I was told that my grandfather, my mother's father, who was of a modern religious bent, ascribed much to the fact that his daughter was marrying a rabbi, the son of a line of rabbis, and therefore provided his daughter and son-in-law with a respectable dowry and financial support. For a while my parents lived in Onikshty in Lithuania, after that (until the Russian Revolution) in Ponevezh, finally moving to Kovno. We lived on the second floor of a wooden house at 9 Paneriu Street in the Slobodka quarter. The lavatory was in the yard. For heating we used a large, round metal stove into which we loaded wood and coal. We had a maid called Yuszia, a Polish gentile with a good

A childhood photo: Shlomo, Nechama
(seated), and Leah Baruchson

heart. Mother would converse with her as did my sister, Leah,
who spoke Polish and sometimes chatted with her.

Besides Leah and Shlomo, my older sister and brother, a
beautiful little sister was born when I was twelve years old.
She was called Rachel. She was only six months old when she
came down with dysentery and died. When that happened,
I was sent away from home but I clearly remember Mother's
sadness.

My best friend was Chayena Averbin. We were in the
same class in secondary school and went to the same youth
movement. Her family was wealthy and I remember they had
a real bath inside the house and running water! Also Miriam
Grodzinsky and Nechama Farber, whose first name was the
same as mine and who left for Eretz Israel (Heb., Land of
Israel) before the Holocaust, were good friends of mine.

The languages spoken at home were Yiddish and Hebrew.
Mother spoke Polish with Yuszia the maid and Russian with

the farmers and peddlers in the market. Although we were expected to know Lithuanian, Mother did not know the language: she considered Lithuanian an inferior tongue of an inferior people; we, the other members of the family, spoke Lithuanian only when necessary. The year before the 1941 Russian invasion, at a time my parents made the decision to immigrate to the United States or to Eretz Israel, we had private English lessons at home. Despite our poverty, an English teacher would visit our home once a week to teach us, the children; even Mother joined in the lessons and studied together with us.

Upper class families would take their summer vacations in one of the resorts outside of Kovno. As my parents did not have the means for that, they sent us—only the children—there or, at least, made the effort to send me off with another family. Mostly I joined Miriam, the daughter of Rabbi Avraham Grodzinsky,[10] the spiritual leader of the Knesset Israel yeshiva in Slobodka, and her family. They spent their vacation in a boarding house in the town of Kroki located some 40 kilometers[11] northwest of Kovno, on the left bank

---

10 Rabbi Avraham Grodzinsky (1884-1944), a man of high ethics, an educator and teacher, was born in Warsaw; he went to Eretz Israel in 1924 to assist in the founding of the Hebron Yeshiva and in time returned to Slobodka. In the first three years of German occupation, he gave emotional support to yeshiva students who were left behind. They would gather to hear his discussions on Musar. He was an admired personality, with a strong influence on religious life in the Kovno ghetto. On July 12, 1944, when the ghetto was liquidated, he broke his leg and was hospitalized; the next day (22 Tammuz 5704) he was burned to death together with other patients in the hospital.

11 One kilometer equals six-tenths of a mile.

of the Nemunas. It was a country house with a farmyard and huge grounds bordering a forest. There, the homeowner Musha, a kind Jewish woman, usually plied us with food and tempted us with cream and butter. Miriam and I shared the same room. Miriam suffered from a lung disorder, and her doctors had ordered her to leave the city every summer. Each morning we would wander lazily through the forest picking mushrooms, raspberries, and blackberries, tie a hammock between two tree trunks and discuss all subjects of the world. We even spoke about sex. Miriam was a very close friend. She and her family perished in the Kovno ghetto during the Holocaust.

In the Lithuanian Jewish community, and in Kovno in particular, a widespread educational system had developed in accordance with the national autonomy given to Lithuanian Jews at the time of independence; this was based on the Lithuanian government's declaration that private schools for national minorities should be absolutely legal, and they were given the right to teach in the pupils' own language. The educational system included three different streams: Tarbut (Heb., culture), secular education in which the language of instruction was Hebrew; Culture League, secular education with Yiddish as the language of instruction; and Yavneh, religious education, taught in Hebrew.

My brother Shlomo was educated mostly by private teachers but was also sent to study at a *beit midrash*[12] and at respectable yeshivas. Leah and I studied at the Yavneh girls school in Kovno, which had four classes in its primary school

---

12　Hebrew: "House [of] Learning," refers to a synagogue, yeshiva, or *kollel* and, specifically, to a central "study hall" dedicated to Torah and Talmud study. It is also often used as an alternate name for a yeshiva.

and eight secondary school classes. Like most other general schools, this was also private, its budget financed mainly from tuition fees paid by pupils' parents. I remember each month, when tuition fees were due, there was much talk and discussion of the matter at home—but, in the end, money was always found for education and learning!

As fitting for any organized school on a high scholastic level, the institution was housed in a modern building and was equipped with the best up-to-date facilities: libraries, laboratories, workshops and gyms, teaching aids, and modern furnishings. Discipline in the school was strict, a lot was demanded of us and the standard of studies was very high. The syllabus included Bible, Mishnah and Talmud,[13] Greek mythology, Hebrew language and literature, Jewish and general history, mathematics, geography, nature, physics, chemistry, drawing, handicrafts, gymnastics, German (we learned Gothic script, Goethe, Schiller and Heine; we could recite Schiller's ballads by heart), Lithuanian (the compulsory language), and Latin. A Lithuanian Gentile taught us Lithuanian and a Lithuanian church minister taught us Latin. Both were excellent professionally but we sensed the difference between their mentality and ours, even in the classroom. The main language of instruction was Hebrew for all subjects—including geography, history and mathematics. Starting from third grade, language classes were offered, given in the language being taught. Of our Hebrew literature and poetry lessons, the works by Bialik[14] were most deeply embedded in

---

13 The basic rabbinic collection on Jewish civil and religious law.

14 Hayyim Nachman Bialik (January 9, 1873-July 4, 1934), a Jewish poet who wrote in Hebrew, is considered one of the first, and certainly the most influential, of modern Hebrew poets. He is called Israel's national poet.

my memory: he was our idol. We learned many of his poems by heart. What is stored in my spiritual memory from over a decade of studying Bible is the Book of Jeremiah—both the philosophical arguments regarding its content as well as whole sections of text still come to mind.

Both religious and secular studies were infused with a love of the People of Israel and the Land of Israel, with belief and with God-fearingness. All the teachers were Zionists (apart from the Lithuanian and Latin language teachers, of course). I so clearly remember the Hebrew teacher with her especially impressive personality. She had the gift of teaching us Hebrew with soul, not just the language—but with Zionism and a love of Israel. Moreover, our Jewish history lessons were also spiced with a yearning for Zion.

To reach the gymnasium (the secondary school), we had to cross the bridge which spanned the Vilija River that joined Kovno to Slobodka. We usually walked: Leah with her girlfriends and I, with mine. We all wore the uniform typical of the general school (a brown jumper with a tightly pleated skirt, a blouse with a round, white collar, and a black butterfly tie; over the dress, a black chiffon apron with a large, round opening at the neck, wide-open kimono sleeves and tight over the hips; a purple, velvet hat with two white stripes and a black peak). In winter, when the river water was frozen, we would cross the river making our way over a layer of ice; very occasionally, when the cold became insufferable and when a few coins could be found for such pleasure, we would take the public bus—you paid twenty cents for a bus ticket (the currency at that time was the lit (plural, litas) and the smaller coins—the cent). We would sit on the seats in the black bus, wipe the steam off the window with the gloves we wore, and enjoy the superb, clear, pristine view of Kovno, then the capital city of independent Lithuania.

I remember my years of study at the gymnasium as a time of great happiness. I had a lot of friends; I was popular and respected among my friends owing to my father's standing in the community. And yet, there were differences in status and gaps deriving from the various financial situations: whereas we were sent off to school usually provided with a cheese sandwich and an apple, and once a week with some sausage, other girls would peel an orange and slowly bite off one segment at a time. That was something! Citrus fruits were imported from overseas, and only rich people could afford to buy them. There was also a cafeteria at the school, but, again, only wealthy girls would buy their food there. I would stand and watch them from the side. But in most ways I was like the other girls.

We occupied ourselves with sports but very much with Zionism. We mainly dreamed of Eretz Israel. Our whole way of life, the festivals, everything, in fact, was linked with the love of Eretz Israel and a yearning for the country. We sang songs then such as "*Anahnu Sharim Lakh Moledet*" (We Sing to You, O My Country), "*Moladeti Eretz Kena'an*" (My Motherland Is the Land of Canaan),[15] "*Havu levenim*" (Bring Bricks; words by Alexander Penn), "*Techezakna*" (Be Strong).[16] From an early age I dreamed of leaving home and going to Eretz Israel. My girlfriends and I would talk among ourselves; we would plan how we would run away from home, steal into the hold of a ship and, on arrival in Israel, be pioneers. That was our ideal.

---

15 *Kena'an*, an ancient biblical term for Eretz Israel.

16 The poem, actually titled "*Birkat Am*" (The People's Blessing), was written by Bialik to encourage the pioneers of the First Aliyah, who were going through a period of self-doubt and needed moral support.

Sometimes we would sneak out of the boundaries of the school, go off to the Yavneh boys school, and meet with them in secret.

As the daughter of a religious family and as a pupil at the Yavneh Hebrew Girls School, I was a member of the "Batia" youth movement—the movement for girls of the "Achdut" (under the auspices of Agudath Israel).[17] Neuhaus, the leader of the movement, was a charismatic Jewish refugee from Germany, and I suspect many of the girls thronged to the movement because of him...

At the beginning of 1939, the author, Zionist leader, and founder of the Revisionist movement Ze'ev Jabotinsky visited Kovno for the last time. On the day of his arrival, three of us pupils decided to risk being suspended from school, running off to the airport in the Aleksotas suburb in the middle of the school day. We ended up walking a very great a distance in cold, dry weather, trampling through snow. But we managed to get there and had the honor of shaking the hand of the

---

17 Soon after Agudath Israel was founded in 1912, a branch was established in Kovno, at the head of which were Rabbi Shimon Merkel and Dr. David Levin. At the end of World War I and close to the Balfour Declaration, the Zionist press in all parts of the Jewish world attacked Agudath Israel, so when youth members of the movement organized themselves in Vilna to renew activities after an extended hiatus (owing to the banishment of Jews from Lithuania at the outbreak of World War I), it was done under the name of "Youth of Israel." Most of the Youth of Israel's activity was educational—the founding of Yavneh institutions and the Yavneh Teachers' Seminary; publication of the weekly *Yiddisher Leben* (Jewish Life), and the dissemination of spoken Hebrew. Within a short time, the Zionist press again accused them of being an "Agudah" in disguise and they were obliged to change their name once again—"Achdut."

Betar[18] leader upon his descending the stairway of the airplane. I so well remember his brilliant, polished speech in Russian-Hebrew spiced with colorful Yiddish, whereby he called on local Jews to "disband the Diaspora or the Diaspora will disband you." He ordered us to pack our bags and go to Eretz Israel. Actually, he was warning us and predicting the Holocaust, but he was, nevertheless, received coldly and with quite some skepticism on the part of community leaders and official Zionists.

As a result of the meeting with Jabotinsky I began to stray from the Achdut movement framework and to identify with Betar's ideology. Like many others who were won over and carried away by the fervor of his words, we were convinced by the veracity of his words and his awakening of new ideas. Despite remaining religious, I did leave the Batia movement, never really becoming a member of the Betar movement as I no longer had the opportunity to do that...

And so we remained in Kovno, our city in Lithuania, delighting complacently in the richness of Hebrew studies and religious life as well as being open to the experiences of the secular world; we lived the daily routine of our active lives confidently in public and in vulgar blindness, sensing neither the danger hovering above our heads nor the threat that was taking on reality and approaching. It was as if we were not on the verge of annihilation—despite testimonies of Jewish refugees who had indeed come from Poland. In 1939 and 1940 we were still toying with the hope that the waves of hatred flooding Europe would pass us by and that Lithuanian Jews would continue to enjoy prosperity, a rich, Jewish public life and intellectual vigor.

---

18 Revisionist Zionist youth movement founded in 1923 in Riga, Latvia, by Ze'ev Jabotinsky.

On June 15, 1940, Russian forces invaded the major towns of Lithuania—Kovno, Vilna, and Ponevezh—and Lithuania's president, Antanas Smetona, escaped to Germany. As the Soviet troops entered our town, many Jews stood at the roadside, clapping enthusiastically at the Red Army convoy, thus angering Lithuanian nationalists.

Within a few days, with the swift and sudden pace of events, a new government was quickly established, the "People's Government," run by the Soviet regime, and Lithuania became a part of Russia. All social organizations and political parties were dissolved and their properties confiscated; national, cultural, and financial institutions were closed; a large number of arrests were made; the heads of the Jewish community and editors of Zionist journals were taken to Kovno's central prison, the "Yellow Prison," with its boarded-up windows. Important activists disappeared into Siberia as "dispatchments" and fear reigned under Communist rule.

It was then that the period of Sovietization of financial life began; big industrial plants, banks, commercial concerns and shops were nationalized, as were buildings and apartment houses. Many businesses belonging to Jews were also nationalized, and in addition, a decree was imposed on them ruling out the Sabbath as a day of rest. The Jews were forced to go to school and to work on the Sabbath and on Jewish holidays, shattering the values and the traditional frameworks of the Jews.

After all "harmful" books in the Jewish libraries had been burned,[19] these libraries were forced to merge with general

---

19 The libraries destroyed were the Mapu Library and the Science Amateurs libraries (Liebhaber fun Wissen); among the newspapers silenced were the *Yiddish Stimme*, *Folksblat*, *Das Wort*, and *Moment*.

municipal ones. Editors of the Jewish press were replaced by government supporters. Within a short time Jewish newspapers were abolished and only *Der Emes* (Yid., The Truth), a Soviet Yiddish-language newspaper, was allowed to appear.

Zionist schools of the Tarbut network and religious schools of the Yavneh group were abolished. Teaching Hebrew was forbidden and Yiddish became the only instructional language. The teaching of the Torah and the rest of the Bible, history of Eretz Israel, and Jewish studies ceased. Teachers remaining in the other Jewish schools took intensive summer courses intended to imbue them with the principles of Soviet educational methodology.

When the Russians invaded, I was in the tenth grade. As all the schools had been closed for ideological reasons (apart from the Communist school), most of my girlfriends had gone on to study at the Russian state school. But my parents decided it would not be suitable for me to be at a Communist school, so although I had only two years of school to complete, I was taken out without having finished my studies. In secret and with the help of private lessons, I was able to continue and progress in various subjects. For example, together with Rochele Friedmann, I would often go to different teachers' homes to keep up with English-language studies. At the same time, I was forming a more practical and purposeful attitude to life. I neglected Bialik, Schiller, and Goethe and learned to type in Lithuanian.

While the traditional leadership was abstaining from secret organization and activities, and most of the adults were involved in procuring exit visas for themselves and their children, the Hebrew youth were beginning to recover with typical Lithuanian persistence and were showing signs of heading toward a "return to the sources" of nationalism. Young people congregated at youth group meetings in secret, spoke Hebrew, discussed the ideas surrounding Zionism, and experienced vehement nationalistic agitation unlike any that had occurred prior to the Russian annexation. At that time, that is, at the end of 1940, two Zionist organizations came into being: Herut (Heb., freedom), a Lithuanian Zionist youth movement, and Irgun Brit Zion (Association of Brit Zion [Covenant of Zion]; ABZ). After I joined the ABZ, five of my girlfriends did the same (among them Chayena Averbin and Raya Beyerk), thus leading to the founding of the religious nucleus within the movement. After that, my friends and I in the movement spoke only Hebrew among ourselves. Activities took place in small groups of three to five members who had been accepted into the movement on the basis of personal acquaintance and mutual trust.

ABZ was in favor of uniting all political party streams siding with Zionism, holding onto cultural and nationalistic values together with curbing Sovietization. At meetings we studied history, Hebrew, and Zionism. All organization activity was carried out in strict secrecy, complete with classified passwords, disguised nicknames, and a roster for guarding the gatherings taking place in any of our hidden places. At the end of 1940, by which time ABZ had become firmly established, the first edition of the movement's journal was published underground; it was called *Ha-Nitzotz* (Heb., The Spark) and was based on a poem of Bialik, "Being abandoned has not granted me light."

By the end of the first year of the Soviet regime a detailed program, including lists of specific names, had been prepared for the purpose of sending anti-Soviet elements to Siberia... Jews whose names appeared on those rosters were included in a category known as the "Jewish national counter-revolution," among them religious and spiritual individuals, those declaring themselves as Zionists, those suspected of being "bourgeois" and "capitalists," and, indeed, community leaders.

We were in a constant state of anxiety. There was much fear. Life at home, and much more so outside it, was carried on in an underground manner for fear of our being identified as religious. We read the Passover *Haggadah* in a whisper, lest we be heard, and we lit Sabbath candles clandestinely.

From one of the Jews employed in the Soviet administration, a person who had managed to get hold of a list, we were told that we, the Baruchson family, were about to be deported to Siberia. In addition to the fact that my father, Rabbi Yitzchak

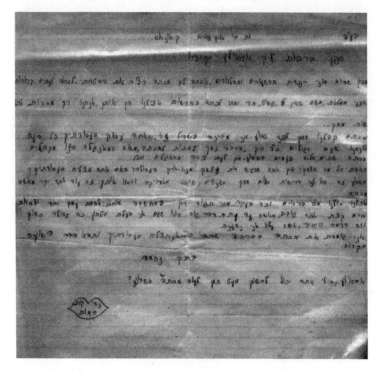

A Hebrew letter Nechama wrote to her father, who had traveled to the United States on a mission for the Slobodka Yeshiva to collect funds for the new yeshiva building

Baruchson, served as the spiritual director of the Or Yisrael yeshiva and that we had studied at a religious Zionist school, the authorities were notified that Father had been to America (to the Ner Yisroel yeshiva in Baltimore) representing the yeshiva in 1939 and had sent us immigration papers from there, a bourgeois and capitalistic center...

Early on the morning of June 14, 1941, after a surprise search and mass arrests, tens of thousands of Jews, anti-Soviet elements, and others from all over Lithuania were sent off in trains and exiled to work camps in the most remote regions of Soviet Russia under unbearable conditions. We, for some reason, were not exiled to Siberia in the end but continued to live in constant fear. Nonetheless, according to the Soviet doctrine which supported equality, Jews were officially granted the same status as that of other Lithuanian citizens and previous restraints and discriminations were cancelled. The Soviet government, however, gave preference to Lithuanians or Russians when it came to senior positions. Still, they made use of the knowledge and aptitude of Jewish intellectuals in all fields in the people's government, in internal security matters and institutions and more; Jews even rose to top officers' ranks in the militia and their participation in cultural matters was increasing. Either consciously or not, Jews were taking an active role in the Sovietization of Lithuania, and this angered nationalistic Lithuanians.

With the winds of war blowing in from the west and the Soviets ruling us, the general tendency was to get a visa to any country willing to accept Lithuanian Jews. But, in accordance with regulations determined by the government, only refugees were entitled to receive a visa. This was the way that most of the Polish Jewish refugees managed to get out of Lithuania; also Jewish refugees with German citizenship, a comparatively large group, left. Neuhaus, who headed the Batia movement, himself a German refugee without Lithuanian citizenship, was among the people fortunate enough to receive a visa to Japan; the Batia movement was gone forever.

A few days before the Japanese consulate was closed in Kovno and transferred to Koenigsberg, crowds of desperate and exhausted Jewish refugees from all parts of Lithuania collected at its entrance, pleading to receive transfer papers to Japan to proceed from there to the United States, South America, or Eretz Israel. The Japanese consul, Sempo Sugihara, motivated by humane considerations and the love of humanity, confident that his standing in the Foreign Ministry was firm, totally ignored urgent telegrams arriving from Japan, aggressively demanding he stop issuing visas as he produced transfer papers to Japan for hundreds of Jews—documents that were to save them—for the price of two Lithuanian litas per visa.

The Slaughter Begins

In the days of Soviet rule, Jewish-Lithuanian relations were beginning to sour. The Lithuanians had been hoping the Germans would conquer Lithuania, saving them from the Soviet burden and thus helping them rebuild their independence; the Jews were keen to help establish Soviet rule, seeing it as the lesser of two evils—the other being Nazi Germany. The Lithuanian hatred of the Jews was igniting and becoming stronger by the day, and their drives found a vent for this from the moment Germany attacked the USSR on June 22, 1941—to be accurate, from three o'clock in the morning on that day—when the German airplanes first bombed Kovno.

Messerschmitt planes dropped bombs on Kovno all day and large fires raged in city streets. Following a day and a half of war, the whole "mighty" Russian army, which was totally disorganized, collapsed. In the afternoon Soviet officials began leaving the town. Some of us were pleased about it as there was much fear of the Russians, and people used to say it was "better to die at the hands of the Germans than live with the Russians." They did not believe stories we had heard of what the Germans had brought upon the Jews of Poland. Many Jews were concerned that the Germans would separate the men from their families and take them to forced labor camps.

And so it happened, the day after the invasion, that the Lithuanians began plundering the Jews. The more violent they became, the more we panicked. The anarchy that suddenly prevailed in the void left behind by the Russians in their retreat had knocked the ground from under our feet and exposed us to a terrible eruption of accusations and violence. World order had changed overnight, and we were left with neither government nor law. With the rise of the pogroms, Jews left their homes and began to flee in the direction of the Russian border—not from the Germans but from the Lithuanians.

So there was an endless line of refugees, all surging forward, most on foot (as the Russians had confiscated all manner of transport to get themselves over the border) with the intention of getting to Russian territory. We also took what we could carry and left home, roaming with the throng in the direction of Russia; overnight, we had become refugees. Hungry, thirsty, and exhausted from the exertion of walking, we wandered many kilometers eastward in intolerable, oppressive heat. Animal carcasses were scattered along the way, bodies and burnt-out tanks… we finally managed to reach the border but Russian officials would not permit us to cross over and blocked our way. Only the privileged were allowed to cross: communists or supporters of Communism. Trapped like animals and pursued from all sides—with the Russian border blocked on one side and bloodthirsty Lithuanians on the other—we had no choice but to retrace our steps and return to the home from which we had fled…

Toward evening, on June 24, 1941, the first platoons of the German army entered Kovno to the cheers of Lithuanians who were welcoming the German soldiers with flowers, cigarettes, and candy.[20] "Long may independent Lithuania live," a

---

20 On June 25, Einsatzgruppe A (a mobile killing task force) entered Kovno at the same time as the advance formations of the army, consisting of Sonderkommandos SK1A and SK1B; also Einsatzkommandos EK2 and EK3. Einsatzkommando 3 was

hysterical announcer blared out of the radio. The Lithuanian flag once again fluttered in the wind above the military museum, the national anthem of independent Lithuania was played again after a year of Soviet control, and the names of ministers of the new Lithuanian government were announced.

On the second or third night after our return home from the failed flight attempt, "partisans" entered Slobodka—Lithuanian university and high school students—carrying out a horrific slaughter of Jews. They went from house to house shooting whole families. Slobodka Jews shut themselves in their houses, crowding into small spaces, clinging to each other like frightened animals, and waiting for what was coming their way.

We were waiting in the Grodzinsky family's attic. Hidden there, we watched the goings-on through cracks and slits: Lithuanian partisans were moving from house to house, raiding homes, murdering all their inhabitants, venting their anger on the household and all its contents, destroying and plundering properties. By word of mouth the news spread of acquaintances, relations, and friends who had been brutally slaughtered. Among those murdered were our wonderful dentist, Dr. Shifra Yatkonsky, and her family—my friend Chayena's neighbors. Their Lithuanian maid was the one who admitted her drunk relatives to the home of the small Zionistic family—they had only one child; he, Gaddy, was my age and had always spoken Hebrew—and they cut the bodies of the whole Yatkonsky family into pieces.

We knew our turn would come, and I so distinctly remember some of the feelings surging up in me in the echoing sound of the Lithuanians' approaching steps. I remember my stomach cramping when told that they were three houses away, that

under the command of SS officer Karl Jager, who was responsible for the annihilation of the Jews of Kovno.

soon they would come for us, and I remember my thoughts, "Anyway, in the end it happens very quickly." We hid in the attic—Mother, Shlomo, Leah, and I—and we talked about the time it would take to die and about the pain that might be involved in dying. Mother was very serene and did her best to keep us calm, claiming nothing would happen to us and asking us not to cause undue panic. For, she said, we hadn't done anything bad; that was the criterion, it was naïveté—it just wasn't possible…

To our great fortune, we were saved thanks to the mother of one of the Lithuanian partisans who were on their way to kill us. For years she had worked for the Grodzinsky family, and she prevented him and the rest of his gang from climbing up to our hiding place.

After a week or so, Leah was standing in the bread distribution line (food was already rationed), when all those waiting in line were taken to the Seventh Fort, they disappeared and were never seen again… We already knew there was no returning from that place. From time to time, the Lithuanians would remove a few hundred people from the line or just grab them off the street, claiming they were needed for work, they always called it "work," but those people never returned… When Leah did not return we thought the very worst had happened. But after three or four days she came back to us, telling us that the entire time she had been hiding under a pile of suitcases belonging to those who had been taken from their homes to be killed at the Seventh Fort; she only managed to slip away by a miracle.[21] The destruction machine was not yet

---

21 The Lithuanians used the Seventh Fort as the main location for killing people during the first two weeks of the German invasion. Thousands of Jews from Kovno were kidnapped by Lithuanian partisans from city streets and from their apartments, transported to the Seventh Fort, and brutally tortured and murdered. Around

oiled... guarding was not efficient and one murderer of Jews knew nothing of the iniquities of his comrade...

After each such wave of killings—it was horrific—we were given a little breathing time, they would take a break, making it possible for us to collect the dead, bury them, and calculate how many had perished. Among the dead were several of my school friends as well as neighbors who had lived near us... and we quickly got back to our daily routine life. Did we have any other choice?

After a fairly short while, with the waves of Lithuanian pogroms ebbing somewhat, the Germans began to inundate us with edicts and commands: we were forced to wear the yellow star and were prohibited from walking on the sidewalk—an order I remember well. Jews were only to walk in the middle of the street or thoroughfare like horses and other animals. I remember walking in the middle of the road with a group of girlfriends in those days as was demanded of us, speaking only Hebrew in display of our awakening nationalist feelings, wearing our yellow stars with pride—one on our back and one on the front of our clothes, at the side of our chest.

Daily, on every wall, some new order would be posted, yet another decree. And next to it, details of the threat to anyone who would defy it—his destiny was to be shot dead. The most stringent order of all decreed that all the Jews of the town must move to the ghetto in the Slobodka suburb by August.

That was the beginning of chaos. It was common knowledge that living space was insufficient in Slobodka

---

6,000 Jews found their death at the Seventh Fort from June 24 to July 8. Many women were raped and shot dead afterwards ("going to peel potatoes"— that is how the Lithuanians referred to the acts they carried out on women in the Seventh Fort) and the men were murdered en masse and buried in large ditches.

and all the Jews, from every part of town, rushed to get there as soon as possible and grab apartments for themselves and their family members. I remember the lengthy line of horse carts carrying furniture, carpets, chests of drawers, washing tubs, pots, bundles tied by rope, the many possessions hanging down and dragging behind the wagons. The carts scraped along behind horses, and the people—behind the carts. It also happened that people without horses hitched themselves to wagons, pulling their meager possessions along by themselves.

Everyone found consolation in the fact that at least behind barbed-wire fences and under strict German surveillance, we would finally be isolated and cut off from the Lithuanian murderers and would, ultimately, have some peace of mind. Actually, the Germans led us to believe rumors to the effect that now, at long last, we would be able to live autonomously with our own leaders. All Kovno Jews were hastening to flee the terrible city down whose streets Jewish blood had flowed.

At first the entire area of Slobodka was allocated for the ghetto but, following the Kovno municipality's intervention, the ghetto area was reduced and certain streets were eliminated from it prior to the final closing of the gates. And that was not all: two days after the ghetto was sealed another area was removed from it—by German order—thus sentencing the 30,000 or so surviving Jews (after the rioting Lithuanians' eradication campaign) to squeeze into the narrow ghetto zone, an area into that had previously held only around 7,000 people (Jews and non-Jews) in close quarters.

The Kovno ghetto was situated between Gestapo headquarters and the Seventh Fort and was composed of two quarters—the "Small Ghetto" and the "Large Ghetto"—divided by Paneriu Street; a high wooden bridge built above the street joined the two. Paneriu Street, aside from a few wooden huts on both sides, was out of ghetto bounds because it served as part of the road connecting Kovno to the northwestern province of Lithuania, Samogitia. The whole ghetto was surrounded by barbed wire, and it was absolutely forbidden to be found in the "death region"—a distance of three meters either side of the barbed wire—forbidden both to Jews in the ghetto and to Lithuanians outside it. That is how the Germans sought to avoid "transactions" between Lithuanians and Jews, to totally cut Jews off from the outside world, and to isolate them from their Jewish brethren in other cities and countries. Armed German and Lithuanian sentries patrolled along the fence, frightening ghetto dwellers with frequent shooting. Ghetto inhabitants were also prohibited from sending letters, even within Lithuania, and the telephone line between the ghetto and the city was disconnected. Only a few telephones remained in the ghetto headquarters—and those were solely for the use of Germans. The ghetto could be entered by five gates that were strictly guarded by German and Lithuanian military policemen.

Slobodka was a poor suburb with narrow, unpaved lanes, a few footpaths, and dilapidated wooden huts. In the large ghetto there were three new, big, four-story stone buildings known as the "Large Blocks" and a number of small stone buildings—the "Small Blocks." Buildings within the small ghetto were a little more modern, and therefore housed some of the ghetto institutions: the surgical hospital, the hospital for internal and infectious diseases, the children's home (orphanage), and the old age home. The ghetto looked "pastoral"—built mostly of wooden huts with plots of land interspersed between them on which vegetables could be cultivated; there were several areas in which one could take walks.

Whole families ended up wandering the streets and yards, waiting for the Ältestenrat[22] housing committee to find them some kind of living arrangements, the people happy to find temporary shelter in a deserted pig sty, a basement, or an attic. Consequently, a number of families lived in each apartment; five or six tenants—men, women, and children—crammed into one room. Families, removed from their apartments owing to the ghetto area being reduced and for whom no dwelling could be found, were placed in the "Reservath" (communal dormitories)—public buildings such as Torah study halls, a movie theater, and schools—where there were no kitchens, furniture, or running water.

Because of the terrible overcrowding and poor sanitation, the danger of infectious diseases spreading increased (a risk that worsened after the Germans had burned down the infectious diseases hospital in the Small Ghetto).

During the first winter within the ghetto fences, with temperatures falling to –30°C (–22°F), the problem of heating the houses worsened. Except for the supply of wood for heating and the few articles of furniture evacuated Jews had managed to bring with them, which anyway ran out within a short time, there was no material to use as heating fuel in the ghetto. On cold, dark nights one could hear ghetto dwellers, amid much cursing, destroying the wooden fences around huts in which they lived in order to have wood to burn for heating, cooking, and drying the wet clothes worn in the various forced labor jobs. The cemetery was left inside the ghetto—in the vicinity of the garbage pits—but Jews were forbidden to erect gravestones or even wooden signs to identify graves.

---

22 The Jewish council created by the Nazis to administer the internal life of the ghetto. It was referred to as the "Council of Elders" by the Germans or "Komitaet" by the ghetto public.

We, living on Paneriu Street, the line separating both parts of the ghetto, belonged to the Small Ghetto. Unlike a large group of Kovno Jews who were forced to move from Kovno to Slobodka, leaving their homes and moving their few possessions to an apartment allocated to them by the Ältestenrat housing office—we, to our great fortune, remained in the same place; however, now we were obliged to share our flat with another two families: the Kaplan family—father, mother, and three beautiful girls; and the Isserlis family—he was a policeman in the ghetto and had no children. The four of us. Mother, Leah, Shlomo, and I, crammed into one room. We were very crowded there but, despite that, managed well: we did not fight at all and everything was peaceful and quiet among us.

The Ältestenrat was established at a directive from the conquerors. Among its functions was the carrying out of the Germans' orders and dealing with the Jews' internal issues in the ghetto. In addition to the Ältestenrat, a Jewish police force was set up: its members carried clubs and wore dark peaked caps and white armbands. The carrying out of the Germans' commands became a most difficult moral dilemma: how was it possible to distinguish between implementing enforced commands which were, even so, to the good of the ghetto, and collaboration?

The Ältestenrat was flooded with decrees, orders, and edicts that the Jewish Police had to carry out: to order us all out of our homes and gather us together in the central square toward a *Selektion* or an *Aktion*, to arrange us in straight rows before we set out for forced labor; to guard the ghetto gate... there were policemen who screamed at us and even displayed violence when Germans were in the vicinity, but all in all, most were perfectly decent... they were no less unfortunate than we were, perhaps more so...

The organizational and institutional infrastructure of the Kovno Jewish community had already been dissolved during Russian rule, and it was now up to us to quickly reorganize and set up local leadership under German directive. Luckily for us, central elements of all parts of the communal spectrum still existed, and most members of the Ältestenrat had been key figures in the Kovno Jewish community before the Holocaust: they were respected and well-known public figures, intellectuals involved in the cultural and spiritual life of the Kovno Jewish community, doctors, lawyers, rabbis. They behaved nobly and were supportive of us despite the terrible moral burden they bore.

My memory of Dr. Elkhanan Elkes, head of the Ältestenrat—the Oberjude[23]—remains engraved on my heart to this today as an extraordinary Jew: fatherly, moral and proud, his personality contributing much to the relaxed feeling of solidarity that prevailed in the ghetto. His job was difficult and thankless, sometimes bordering on decisions regarding the death sentence of one Jew in order to give others the chance of living a little longer. He was a distinguished doctor and a keen Zionist; we had complete trust in him and his power of judgment, and we were sure he represented us most faithfully in the face of the German tyrants.[24]

---

23 German: chairman of the Ältestenrat.

24 Elkhanan Elkes (1879-1944) was born in the small town of Kalvarija, close to the German border, and received a traditional Jewish and Hebrew education. He studied medicine and by the beginning of the 1920s was already head of the internal ward of "'Bikur Cholim," a Jewish hospital in Kovno; he became known as one of the best doctors in Lithuania. He was a Zionist, was involved in cultural and Jewish life, and was close to the Hehalutz movement. After Lithuania was occupied by

Despite the horrific reality of the ghetto, the Ältestenrat still attempted to function as a communal umbrella organization, to supervise and support the various activities in the areas of culture, medicine, and social welfare.

Occasionally, with no prior warning, there was a roundup of Jews, after which there was a *Selektion*. A number of trucks carrying Germans would arrive, immediately making it clear to us that disaster was at hand. The Germans would move around ghetto areas with loudspeakers announcing that all should leave their houses and collect in the square (each time a different one, but most often Demokratu Square) and that whoever stayed home would be shot. Everyone would go out of the houses and the Germans would go from one to the next checking basements and attics in case anyone had remained there. They ordered us to form rows, four people in each. All told, we were supervised only by four Germans with their dogs. They cast penetrating glances our way, summing us up from head to foot with their eyes and moving us to the left or to the right.

---

the Germans and following the murder of thousands of Kovno Jews, he was unanimously elected, on August 4, 1941, by the key people from all echelons of the Kovno Jewish community to head the Ältestenrat. With a heavy heart he agreed to do so. As chairman of the Ältestenrat, he was impressive in his outstanding moral values, his dedication to the Jewish cause, his courage and integrity, his simplicity of manner and modest lifestyle. He also sympathized with the anti-Nazi underground organization in the ghetto and even assisted it. With the destruction of the ghetto in 1944, along with the remnants of his people, he was transported to the Landsberg concentration camp, where he was put in charge of the hut housing the sick bay. After becoming direly ill there, he passed away some months before the camp was liberated.

From the outset, we never knew which side was considered the "good" side—left or right—we never had any idea what the criterion was for selecting one or the other: men/women/ young people/old people/children/sick people/ intellectuals. Sometimes it was an advantage to be old as they actually took away the young people; once they took 500 men from among the intellectuals to the Fourth Fort and they never returned.[25] On October 28, 1941 (7 Cheshvan [second month of the Hebrew calendar]), occurred the most extensive *Aktion*, initiated by Helmut Rauca,[26] a ruthless Gestapo officer in charge of the ghetto. During that *Aktion* some 9,200 Jews were taken from the ghetto to the Ninth Fort[27] and, there, all were shot to death (this was the Great *Aktion* that left ghetto

---

25 On August 14, 1941, the Ältestenrat announced to the public that the Germans wanted 500 young, intellectual, "well-dressed" men to put the city archive in order. Only 200 turned up by the ghetto gate in the morning. The Germans and their assistants from the Lithuanian police hunted down men from the streets and houses until they had collected 534, put them on trucks, and transported them to the Fourth Fort to be killed. The Fourth Fort was occasionally used by the Lithuanians and Germans as a place for killing Jews; in 1941, the Nazis and their local assistants murdered around 4,000 Jews there.

26 In May 1983, Gestapo Sergeant Helmut Rauca was extradited to Germany by the Canadian government and, within a few months, died in a Frankfurt prison.

27 The Ninth Fort was constructed approximately six kilometers west of the city of Kovno—it was the main center of annihilation of the Jews of Kovno and the surrounding region; there, joint units of Germans and Lithuanians slaughtered 50,000 Jews from Kovno and western Europe (mainly Germany, Austria, Czechoslovakia, and France).

inhabitants stunned and despairing). Once they sent whole families to Estonia.[28]

The Germans cried "Left," "Right," and simply with the flick of a finger determined the fate of human beings, whether they should live or die. Once the people in the back rows understood what criteria was being applied—if, for example, they took, more of the older people and those who did not look especially good, people would immediately work to improve their appearance a bit and try to make themselves look younger to seem to be fit for work: they put stones in their shoes to look tall and strong, they rubbed their cheeks with red paper to give themselves red cheeks and a healthy look… there were several methods like those… Whole families fell apart when some family members were forced to the left, with others to the right. There were families who did not agree to separate, and all were sent to the bad side.

Most victims of the roundups were taken to the forts to be killed, mainly to the Ninth Fort—this being the "Valley of Death" near the Kovno ghetto! Everything was carried out in a very mechanical, orderly, organized fashion: from *Selektion*, going to the Fort, "take off your clothes," "stand in a line"— they were then shot and the people fell into the pits, were covered with lime and that was all, it was over and done with. Until today there are images that remain engraved in my mind… of expulsion… the suddenness of it… the laconic way in which things were done… the fear on the faces of those exiled… the abandoned possessions left behind in the

---

28 In October 1943, Germans and their assistants entered the ghetto, snatched 2,700 Jews, and carried out a *Selektion*—they sent old people and children to the Auschwitz-Birkenau extermination camp, the rest were put in cattle cars and sent to Estonia.

ghetto square... the sadness and heaviness of heart that would descend on the whole ghetto following the procedure...

The Lithuanians would stand at the side, watching, outside the ghetto fence: some laughed, others wept... However, despite the guarding over the ghetto, they carried on a brisk business with the Jews. There were Lithuanians who knew Jews, and for those of us who had contact with the Lithuanians—their fate was better. From their gentile friends they received food or, at a later stage, they handed their babies to them over the fence in the hope they would look after them until the end of the war.

Not long after the ghetto gates were shut, we received a new order—to give up all our gold, silver, jewelry, silverware, musical instruments, and even stamp collections—in short, anything that was of value at home. The Germans went from house to house, confiscated whatever articles grabbed their fancy, and took away whole carts and trucks overloaded with the countless spoils—the property, now plundered, that had been collected and amassed over the generations by Kovno Jewry. Despite German threats that anyone who did not give up all his possessions would consequently be killed, along with his family, Leah and Shlomo went out in the middle of the night and buried a few articles in the yard, near one of the lavatories: Mother's silver Sabbath candlesticks, gold rubles, and a watch Leah had received as a bat mitzvah present from Father when he had returned from one of his overseas trips. It was a very small parcel, but the risk of being caught was great. I was afraid. I did not want to endanger myself and get killed. I chose not to know anything about it. And, indeed, the Germans passed by later, checking, looking around, searching, and if they found valuables that had not been handed over to them in time, they did indeed kill people since it was forbidden to be seen with the smallest article of jewelry, even a ring on one's finger.

On Saturday, October 4, 1941, at seven o'clock in the morning, German and Lithuanian soldiers surrounded the small ghetto and placed a guard armed with a machine gun on the wooden bridge above Paneriu Street. People without a Scheine,[29] sick people from both hospitals of the small ghetto, elderly people from the old age home, and children from the children's home were taken out of the ghetto to the death parade and transferred to the Ninth Fort for annihilation. The rest of the Small Ghetto dwellers were forced to move immediately to the Large Ghetto via the wooden bridge and were not allowed to take any of their possessions with them. Only after a number of days were the Small Ghetto dwellers permitted to return to their homes for just two hours to collect the most basic articles. This was the *Aktion* taken against the Small Ghetto, after which it was removed from the Kovno Ghetto zone, the wooden bridge joining both parts of the ghetto was destroyed, and the people of the Small Ghetto went to live in the Large Ghetto.[30] We moved to an apartment right opposite the Jewish police station on Linkuvos Street, and

---

29 German: certificates. This refers to the 5,000 certificates SA Captain Fritz Jordan, superintendent for Jewish affairs in Kovno on behalf of the German civil authorities, had issued the Ältestenrat and which were distributed to laborers in the ghetto. These precious certificates, showing that one was a "useful" worker, were known as "Jordanscheine" (Jordan Certificates) and also as "life certificates."

30 On October 4, 1941, the Small Ghetto was wiped out: most of its inhabitants (1,608 people), including 180 children from the ghetto orphanage, were taken on foot to the Ninth Fort, where they were shot and killed. The Germans burned down the Small Ghetto hospital with its sixty people, including a doctor and a nurse. Only those holding a Jordanschein or who had the money to buy the certificate were taken to the Large Ghetto.

I remember so well how I shook with fear every time I left the house in secret to go to an ABZ meeting, lest I should be seen by one of the Jewish policemen... We shared the flat with the Kagan family. To this today I remember the sisters, Rivka and Freda, and their brother Srulik...

In November 1941 this series of *Aktionen* ceased in the ghetto, which was now emptied of around half its inhabitants, and a "period of stabilization," as it was called in ghetto terminology, prevailed from autumn 1941 to autumn 1943; it was relatively peaceful... Both Jordan and Rauca visited the Ältestenrat offices, and in their pleasant, sugary manner, assured the people there that the rounding up had finished, that life in the ghetto would return to its former routine—promises made on condition that the ghetto dwellers fulfill their work duties, mainly at the airport.

The Airport

The demands for manual labor were indeed a burden weighing on members of the ghetto during the period of stabilization and embittered their lives more than all other decrees. Every day the Germans raised the quota of laborers, and the Ältestenrat had to impose forced labor on all men between the ages of fourteen and sixty and on all women between fifteen and forty-five.

Hardly had we become accustomed to our new situation—densely crowded living conditions, being surrounded by barbed wire, and hunger too—when we were sent to forced labor. The general atmosphere in the ghetto became one of a work camp entirely aimed at serving the German war machine. The Ältestenrat Labor Office, together with the ghetto police, became the most important ghetto institutions and their function was to make sure Jews carried out their duty punctiliously. Jews worked for the Germans in building the airport in the suburb of Aleksotas, in Kovno factories and workshops (the "city brigades"), in workplaces far out of Kovno, in large workshops, in workshops outside ghetto precincts—in Paneriu Street—and as ghetto laborers.

Jews whose fate was somewhat less kind were sent to forced labor at the *Flugplatz* (Ger., airfield)—the Aleksotas airport (that is where I, as a schoolgirl, met Ze'ev Jabotinsky).

Chayena and I were among them. The Germans had planned on converting this outdated airport into a modern, extensive military airport that would serve the eastern front of the Third Reich forces. German contracting companies were busy planning how to expand and construct it, and by the beginning of autumn 1941, were already required to estimate the number of workers needed for carrying out the large job. The Kovno ghetto had to supply the laborers for the work, which would proceed twenty-four hours a day—the night shift, the morning shift, and the day shift. The Germans made sure the required number of laborers for the airport would present themselves every day—that was without taking into consideration the Sabbath, festivals and even the *Aktionen*—which led to immense depletion of the number of forced laborers. They threatened more *Aktionen* if the number of laborers was below that required. At the appointed hour, the German foreman would announce the number of workers needed. If the designated number of workers did not turn up at the main gate of the ghetto, members of the German Air Force would burst into the ghetto like some terrifying tidal wave, randomly grab whoever crossed their path, beat them—sometimes to the point of death—and drag them to the airport. As the result of all of that, a special system was established to deal with the quota of workers for the airport.

Following the confiscation of the Jews' possessions, ghetto inhabitants had ended up with no clocks or watches, so the Jewish police were required to walk through ghetto lanes early in the morning, knock on airport workers' windows, and wake them with loud cries, "Rise for work at the airport!" The Germans repeatedly emphasized the fact that the Kovno ghetto existed only because the airport needed workers and only thanks to Jewish forced laborers was the ghetto still surviving, rather than being totally destroyed.

We were all well aware of the fact that work at the airport was some kind of guarantee that the ghetto would continue to exist and, therefore, the call of Jewish police ringing in the ears of airport workers was like the familiar cry before morning prayers, "Jews, get up to serve the Creator" and became part of the gloomy existence of ghetto life. Each worker, whether old, ill, or feeble, was concerned not to miss his regular shift, regardless of bad weather conditions or hunger. In the early morning hours, in frost and rain, swaddled in our ragged coats with the yellow star attached front and back, we would all hasten in the direction of the main gate. The Jewish Police would urge us to form lines of four people per row, the Lithuanian guards outside the gate usually mocked us and beat us on the back with truncheons, and the Germans would count us, load us onto trucks, and transport us to the airport. It did not take long for the Germans to decide that it was not worth their while to transport so many Jewish workers to the airport, and we were forced to pound our feet day in, day out, several kilometers from the ghetto to the airport and back again on a road strewn with stones, trudging over sand dunes and through swamps, at a military pace and under heavy German surveillance.

Work was carried out over a huge area, outside under all weather conditions—with nowhere for us to take shelter from rain or snow, from the cold or the heat—and it was intolerably difficult: we worked with picks at digging and reinforcing, carving trenches, carrying sacks of sand and cement and wooden beams, mixing cement with manual cement-mixers or with the help of spades. We also worked at flattening the area: we were commanded to get rid of the stones and level the ground. We needed to load the stones onto wheelbarrows, dragging them from place to place; clearing one area and tipping the stones onto another, all this under the watchful eye of military sentries. Supervisors, representatives of the various contractors, and German foremen kept track of us, making sure we did not escape or make contact with farmers from the neighboring villages. They kept tally on our productivity; strictly prevented us from resting for a moment, supervised us with lashings and German shepherds, and tyrannized us mercilessly with beatings accompanied by vulgar, cynical remarks and humiliation.

We worked from sunrise till darkness fell. The food we received was very meager: we got 250 grams of bread and a little soup, which was literally hot water with pieces of horsemeat or pork and half-rotting cabbage floating in it—*yushnik*, as it was called in the ghetto, a term for pig swill. We sometimes also received half a potato. Once one of the German soldiers supervising our shift approached me, offering me a sandwich, saying I did not look Jewish. Without much of a thought I answered him spontaneously in German—*Ich bin eine echte Jüdin* (Ger., I am a pedigreed Jew). Immediately, he struck me hard with his fist. The blow broke some bones in my jaw, my teeth loosened, and my mouth bled profusely. It was enormously painful. People merely said, "Stupid girl. You could have had a sandwich and you could have saved yourself the injury if you hadn't answered like that... "

Many workers were injured while working or were killed in work accidents. Many of the others developed tuberculosis, pneumonia, chronic rheumatism, and heart disease, especially in winter as the direct result of work conditions at the airport—from standing continuously in knee-high mud and mortar for twelve hours at a time and from deficient nutrition.

From day to day we worked on, our legs weakened from exhaustion and hunger, the sweat mixed with trickles of blood streaming down from the blows and slaps we received, just waiting for the shift to end. But, because of the Germans' "rules regarding shift changes," meaning workers from one shift were not to be released before people for the next shift arrived, we were sometimes forced to stay and continue our work for two consecutive shifts— because fewer than the required number of people for the next shift had presented themselves or none at all.

After the sign was given to finish work on any given shift, we would be left standing for more long hours waiting for German sentries to collect us together with all the other forced laborers from all parts of the airport, have us stand in military file, count us again and again, finally ordering us to "Go!"

The guards escorting us would march us back "home" to the ghetto, urging us to run down the slopes of Mt. Aleksotas— they called it the "Carnival of the Jews," forcing us to cross the bridge over the Nemunas river at a fast trot and within a few short minutes.

We would return to the collection point by the municipal building and form lines, be counted once again, and then be led back to the ghetto.

On any days off I had, I would go out to work instead of Chayena. First they had killed her father in one of the roundups; then after that, they took her mother and one of her brothers—and Chayena was left alone to look after her three surviving younger siblings. They suffered terribly from hunger, and I think I once saved them from death by bringing them some carrots and potatoes.

Just as we, the airport workers, were obliged to present ourselves each morning in the yard by the main gate, so were the "city brigade" people collected by that same gate each morning—at the "gate of freedom." Thousands of people on their way to forced labor crowded into the yard near the gate, the location becoming known to many as the "slave market"; people from the Ältestenrat employment office and the Jewish police would arrange us all in lines before delivering us into the hands of the Lithuanians and the German sentries. After that we would go off in groups to our various work places. As we walked through the gate, men had to take their hats off in respect to the German ghetto leaders posted by the gate, and all of us were marched down the middle of the road, under heavy security, just like dangerous criminals being escorted from one prison to another. The passersby walking along the sidewalk, as fitting the freeborn, would eye us with contempt and animosity, happy at our misfortune.

Work conditions for the "brigades" were enormously better than those at the airport: the distance from the ghetto to work places in town was much shorter than that to the airport; brigade laborers worked inside buildings—not like we who worked in the open in all weather conditions; and those directly responsible for them were Jews. There were places of employment in town where Jews could take off for a short while to make contact with Lithuanians and do business with them: getting food in exchange for clothes and other possessions still left in the ghetto after all the *Aktionen* and German confiscations. This, in ghetto idiom, was called *machen a paeckele* (Yid., making a parcel). "City brigade" workers did not experience all the violence, beatings, and humiliation that were our lot. Neither were they searched, counted, or sorted, nor were they watched as strictly as we were.

It was no wonder that almost everybody tried to elbow their way into the "city brigade," as only there was it possible to have contact with Lithuanians in order to procure a little food. Many people, therefore, tried their luck in the employment office of the Ältestenrat to change from working at the airport to the city work force; but only those with inside influence, "vitamins" in ghetto language, those belonging to the privileged with contacts in the Labor Office—only such people had the luck to move from the darkness of the airport to the bright lights of the "city brigade."

Thus, two classes formed in the ghetto: the airport workers, who were unfortunate, miserable, and lowly, and the other workers, the privileged, who got what they wanted through bribes, inside influence, and plenty of good luck. And then there were also, of course, those working outside the ghetto. They, for example, worked at digging peat and preparing stones for building, at tree-felling and laying telephone cables.

There were Large Workshops, which functioned day and night, where trained people working at producing things the Germans lacked, such as clothes and leather goods, shoes, underwear, hats, gloves, and more. As time went on, the Ältestenrat managed to pressure the Germans into opening additional departments such as laundries, welding shops, carpentry shops, smithies, a sewing workshop, brush shop, soap and candle shop, wool-shearing shop, sock-knitting shop, knitwear factories, factories producing toys for the children of influential Germans at the front or in the rear, and so on, thus granting the ghetto the image of a "productive body" in the eyes of the Germans in an effort to prevent the ghetto from being wiped out. In all, these workshops provided work for nearly 4,000 of the ghetto's inmates.

Moreover, Jews were employed in Small Workshops, which the Ältestenrat had also established, to supply the needs of the ghetto itself: renovating apartments and buildings, repairing clothes and shoes, and producing wooden clogs for airport workers. Among the *ghetto Arbeter* (Yid., ghetto laborers) were people who were still obliged to work by age but who were unable to work outside the ghetto owing to poor health. They were employed in lighter jobs and in cleaning yards and public institutions for fewer hours and for only a few a days a week.

Only after we had all returned from our various workplaces could we once again become socially equal. We would all stand around for hours on end in a long line that wound to the main gate, the luckier people carrying small bundles of wood and twigs on their shoulders for home heating, the men removing their hats in respect for those in command, waiting for those Germans and Lithuanians guarding the gate to finish rummaging in our satchels and pockets, handling, beating, and abusing us.

In the first period of the ghetto, there was still some contact between the Large and Small Ghettos, and it was possible to cross the bridge joining the two quite freely. German sentries did wander around within the ghetto, but it was possible for us to organize life there under the Ältestenrat's directives. At that time there were various kinds of Jews: there were those involved in helping others, supporting their Jewish brethren, one example being Dr. Elkhanan Elkes, who was most prominent in the ghetto from its very first day to when it was liquidated and who stood out for his moral stature. No less commendable and outstanding was the behavior in the ghetto of most of the representatives of the Ältestenrat in the face of the Germans—Moshe Levin, chief of the Jewish Police; his deputy Ika Greenberg;[31] and Yehuda Zupowitz[32]—who did whatever they humanly could for the good of the ghetto.

---

31 Ika Greenberg, a member of the "Young Maccabee" movement and a reserve officer in the Lithuanian army, served as first lieutenant in the Jewish Police; together with commanding officer of the ABZ, Yitzchak Shapiro, and with other members of the command, he was in activist headquarters or, as it was known, "Shalhevet headquarters" (named after the Shalhevet [Hebrew: flame] journal they published under the slogan "If he comes to slay thee, slay him first"). At the time people were being rounded up, Greenberg tried to organize an anti-Nazi underground movement in the ghetto, developed a strategy for rebellion in the case of a destructive operation, and trained youth groups in the use of arms with a gun bought with funds by the Ältestenrat.

32 Jewish Ghetto Police deputy chief.

They were active in the Zionist underground and in teaching its members how to use firearms. Generally speaking, almost the entire Kovno Ghetto Jewish Police can be characterized by its extraordinary attitude to the cause of human and Jewish dignity. This police force can be held only in the highest esteem for its involvement in smuggling fighters out to the forests and for hiding a group of prisoners, which had been responsible for burning corpses,[33] that had escaped from the Ninth Fort in December 1943. Despite being caught later and taken to the Ninth Fort, where they were tortured, the Jewish policemen did not break down and did not inform the Germans of the underground hiding places in the ghetto, which we called *malines*,[34] nor of where Jews were concealing themselves—and in the end, they were shot to death.

---

33 To disguise the signs of murder, the burning of corpses of those murdered was implemented in autumn 1943. As in the camps and other extermination locations, Jewish prisoners were employed in the Ninth Fort in jobs involved with the annihilation and covering up evidence of the murders. This shocking job of theirs meant extracting corpses from huge mass graves and burning them on enormous bonfires. The prisoners were even forced to remove gold teeth from the mouths of those murdered. After being taken out of the pits, the corpses were left on stretchers, placed on a layer of planks and burned. After that prisoners had to crush the charred bones and scatter the ashes. Sometimes, in this work, they would chance upon bodies of relations and friends. All sixty-four prisoners, who were watched carefully and bound by chains after work, still managed to escape from the fort in an operation organized on Christmas Eve, December 24, 1943. Nineteen of them reached the ghetto—where they were hidden with the knowledge of the Ältestenrat and the Jewish Police.

34 Yiddish: bunkers; hiding places within the ghetto, created by ghetto inmates.

Even Eizik Serbenitzky, the dour manager of the pharmacy under the patronage of the Ältestenrat, was one of the ghetto heroes. He would leave ghetto precincts, as if for professional reasons—in order to purchase medicines—and return with a load of political information, which he would transfer to the underground. Later on, a secret radio was installed in the ghetto so that obtaining news from the outside would be more systematic and organized. Eizik Serbenitzky was put in charge of monitoring news broadcasts from London, Amsterdam, and Moscow. After noting down the main news items in Yiddish, he would pass them on in total secrecy to members of the underground.

Yet, in contrast, there were Jews, few though they might be, who sold their souls to the devil. Among them were people like Caspi-Serberovitz, a Zionist activist who, even before the war, had been expelled from all the parties owing to his unstable character and undisciplined behavior, and who was appointed to work for the Gestapo. He and his family were allowed to stay in the city, outside ghetto precincts, and exempted from wearing the yellow star; he would turn up almost daily at the Ältestenrat offices and those of the Jewish Police, interfering in matters and advising them boastfully as to how to run matters. Sometimes he threw ostentatious parties in his city house to which he invited the "gang"—Gestapo people—those directly responsible for the annihilation of Kovno Jews. Another Jew of the same ilk was Liptzer, a simple, uneducated man with a terrible need for respect and an insatiable desire to be the ghetto leader; as time progressed, he became trusted by top Gestapo people and was appointed head of the Brigade of Jewish Tradesmen who worked for the Gestapo. After that, he was appointed supervisor of the Jewish Police as well as of the Ältestenrat employment office. The policeman Tanchum Ehrenstamm also joined the ranks of traitors in the ghetto.

He was in the habit of physically and verbally abusing Jewish forced laborers, and unlike his colleagues, he broke down when the police were interrogated at the Ninth Fort, revealing the *malines* and their residents to the Germans.

There was organized activity, the early signs of rebellion, some more or less successful attempts to break free of the chains of Nazism, on various scales—personal, family, group, or organized movement.

Ghetto inmates knew there was no relying on the meager quantities of food allocated by the Germans (horsemeat, potatoes, and rotting vegetables unfit for human consumption, black bread, ersatz tea and coffee, grits, broad beans, salt, a little jam), and for this reason, each of us was forced to fend for himself and his family. The only solution was to buy food from Lithuanian city dwellers, paying with money, clothes, the few possessions left with us after we had been forced to "turns things over," or to make deals ("transactions") either at the ghetto fence (the traders were called *Zoimhendler* [Yid., fence-traders] in the ghetto) or in "city brigade" workplaces visited by Lithuanians coming to trade with Jews, a life-threatening move as ghetto people were prohibited from having any contact with non-Jews.

Because of stringent inspection at the ghetto fence, it was not easy taking articles out of there to town, but it was infinitely more difficult to bring into the ghetto food products received in exchange for those items. Lithuanian and German sentries catching people smuggling things in often beat them cruelly and confiscated the food products. Sometimes the people were arrested and handed over to the Gestapo, but when smuggling food into the ghetto was successful there was great joy.

My brother Shlomo was a genuine hero: risking his life he would secretly leave his workplace, remove his yellow star, collect food remnants—mostly potatoes—stuff them into the double lining he himself had expertly sewn into his coat and by evening join people returning from work assembled at the ghetto gate. He miraculously passed the stringent inspection of the Lithuanian and German police and reentered the ghetto with food. In this way he managed to smuggle in many kilos[35] of potatoes.

Also Leah, my devoted elder sister, always burdened with a sense of responsibility to help support the family, secretly managed to trade with Lithuanians at her workplace. Day after day she would take some item—a dress or underwear, some of the few remaining possessions we had, personal belongings and things of value she had managed to conceal from the Germans during *Aktionen* and at other times when they had come to confiscate possessions—and exchange it for bread and carrots, smuggling the food back into the ghetto at the risk of her life. That is how we procured a little more food and were saved from starvation. Both my siblings were heroes, both courageous. Shlomo would always laugh at me, saying "It would be so nice if you could actually return with the empty backpack…" I was very naïve and fearful and certainly not good with business deals.

We kept our family unit together; our daily routine was humane, cultured, and stable. Each of us carried out our duties zealously: we went to work and Mother stayed home, managing to create a sense of there being a home and a warm, domestic atmosphere: cooking from what little there was, gathering twigs for heating, drawing water and washing our clothes (all this happening before she was ordered to go out to work at a later stage since she was forty-seven). The narrow, little room inhabited by the four of us was always aired, clean, polished, and scrubbed and this really helped us to understand that at the end of every day of backbreaking

---

35 One kilo equals 2.2 pounds.

work, there was a place to which to return. In her own quiet, tranquil way Mother inspired us with a great deal of hope and optimism throughout that period. She did not sink into a state of bitter despair, and she bore the burden of daily distress with supreme fortitude. She was continuously comforting us, saying the situation would not remain this way for very long and that we should not worry, that we were to do what was demanded of us and try to get through this time. She would constantly say to us, "This period is going to be behind us; this is a difficult time and we must be strong."

As a group, our resistance found its expression mainly spiritually. There were secret synagogues and *minyanim*[36] in private homes in the ghetto; schools functioned, there were orchestras, children's choirs, a drama group, literary and poetry reading evenings, lectures and symposiums; there were Purim and Chanukah parties; poems were written and a kind of ghetto folklore developed as well as a specific brand of ghetto slang.

The Kovno ghetto underground consisted of two movements—the Zionist and the Communist. During Soviet rule, a few months before Nazi troopers entered the ghetto, both movements had been rivals, and much animosity had prevailed between them owing to differences in ideology and mentality. But with the closing of the ghetto gates, a feeling was born of togetherness, cooperation, and solidarity.

The essence of the leftist camp's doctrine, led by the Yiddish writer Chaim Yellin,[37] was active partisan fighting outside the

---

36 Hebrew: prayer quorums; in Judaism, the number of people (at least ten men) required to hold a communal Jewish prayer service.

37 Chaim Yellin (1913-1944), writer, organizer, and leader of the Kovno Ghetto partisans' movement. On April 6, 1944, while

ghetto in cooperation with Communist elements, while the Zionist camp focused on the spiritual-political struggle within the ghetto. At first my girlfriends and I had absolutely no knowledge of the active partisan camp or about their exiting the ghetto! We just had not imagined that such heroic acts could go on under our noses... all was shrouded in secrecy, each person was wary of the other inasmuch as you could not know who might be a traitor or who might be weak enough to break down under interrogation and torture and inform of the existence of the *partisanka* (Yid., partisans).

In the first weeks of the setting up of Nazi control, contact was renewed with ABZ activists—pupils, students, and others who had been close to it even before Russian rule. New members joined from Bnei Akiva, a large religious Zionist youth movement, and even from more religious streams—former yeshiva students and girls from the Batia movement—and the organizational and ideological foundations for ABZ were established in the ghetto. We joined such a group—it was a national Zionist movement— and it greatly helped our morale and spirit. More than anything else of that time, I remember our highly intensive spiritual lifestyle.

Shortly after the establishment of the ghetto, ABZ was functioning; it numbered some 150 to 200 members. Its first underground activity was to transfer to the ghetto (before the final closing of the gates) the large library of Kanterovich, a teacher from the Kovno high school. He had been exiled to Siberia during the time of Soviet rule; his library contained over 1,000 volumes, and it constituted the central ABZ library

---

on a mission outside the ghetto, he was ambushed by Gestapo agents and later executed.

of Block C[38] in the ghetto. Indeed, we were imprisoned behind barbed wire, all had been taken from us, they had tried to crush us physically and emotionally, but the yearning for freedom, hope, national pride, fraternity, and solidarity still burned within us; it was that which gave us strength, courage and... the audacity to aspire to freedom and to believe it would surely come.

The ABZ organizational structure was similar to that of a strict army framework: at the top was the organization commander, Yitzchak Shapiro, and, at his side, three to five other people—most of them regiment commanders. There were five or six regiments in the organization, each regiment made up of three to five companies with five or six members in each. Despite rigid compartmentalization and hierarchy, what characterized the movement was its great openness and the comradeship between members and commanders, known as *geduda'im* (regiment leaders) or *pluga'im* (company leaders).

I belonged to the Ma'apilim regiment,[39] which was young in spirit, vigorous, imbued with ABZ ideology and the highest motivation. We all very much appreciated and admired the regiment leader, Chaim Shapiro, Yitzchak Shapiro's younger brother. He inspired us with a lot of courage, energy, and optimism, and made a point of running all our meetings only in Hebrew. Chaim was killed tragically in the ABZ *maline* upon the liquidation of the ghetto.

---

38 One of three large, unfinished Soviet-built apartment houses in the ghetto, Block C housed the underground fighting organization as well as the illegal library where the ABZ youth movement functioned.

39 Hebrew: term for "illegal" Jewish immigrants to Palestine during the time of the British mandate.

Chaim Shapiro, commander of the Ma'apilim regiment, and company leader. Nechama Baruchson (seated on the left, in the second row) with ABZ members

We would meet in small groups, cells, or companies—with one company unaware of the existence of others. At the head of each company was the company leader. Later on I became a company leader in the Ma'apilim regiment and when the Herut regiment was formed, made up of two companies— one of young men, the other of young women—I was appointed company leader for the women. We took lessons in defense, in digging quarters for creating hiding places and for concealing books; we ran training days, seminars and parties. The Ma'apilim regiment even produced a wall newspaper called *Emek Habakha* (Heb., Vale of Tears; the Exile) and the booklet *Almanakh* in which we wrote down all regiment activities. And did we dance?—That I don't remember; we did not dance in the ghetto, but I do so well remember our bursting into song: Zionist songs, songs of yearning for Eretz Israel—and all this in Hebrew. We did not speak one word of Yiddish.

We studied and practiced self-defense, Morse code, and the theory of clandestine activity but we mostly studied topography. We learned the topography of the area so we would be able to leave the ghetto. We had to remember details about the ghetto streets and to recall them accurately. In other words, we did not waste our time, and we discussed the possibility of escape!

Our meeting place was in Block C in a room adjacent to the library. As fitting for a secret underground movement, the place was properly protected and only members knew of its existence and how to find it. There were a number of such undisclosed sites and we used them for meetings. We had discussions about "the unique character that the State of Israel would have when established," and we discussed moral dilemmas in the ghetto (favoritism, corruption, disruption of the family framework). All discussion was carried on in Hebrew. With everything around us crumbling and falling apart, we were preparing ourselves for life in Eretz Israel. We learned the language well and we learned about Israel's heritage and culture. Our belief in the future gave us the strength, the energy, and the desire to go on living; we knew that some of us, at least, would realize our dream to immigrate to Eretz Israel.

At meetings we read poems by poets who were ABZ members—Shraga Aranowitz (a former Betar member in charge of culture in the ABZ) and Yitzchak Katz. An especially striking impression that has stayed with me is of Shraga

Aranowitz's poem "The Sicarii[40] with the Yellow Star," written after the Great *Aktion*, in which he appeals to young people to keep up their morale, to rebel in case of another *Aktion*— for, he claimed, Jewish history was bloody and strewn with obstacles, yet paved with heroic deeds, despite all. This was a horrific and magnificent slice of history all in one...

The ABZ operated in absolute secrecy. All was conducted according to principles of clandestine activity, and each person was aware only of the existence of his own cell. Activities proceeded solely within companies and members were commanded to keep their ABZ membership strictly secret. Mother, Leah, and Shlomo did not know that I was active in the ABZ and that I was going to meetings; I had to keep this secret even from the family. It would be dangerous for them to know of my involvement with the ABZ although they did suspect I was busy with "romantic, Zionist nonsense," as Shlomo put it.

My friend Layala Finkelstein and her family lived opposite us and her parents were not Zionists: they were Communists, kept their distance from Judaism, and were very much assimilated. Both parents had been well-known doctors before the Holocaust and still practiced medicine in a small way in the ghetto. Layala certainly would not be allowed to join such a movement—any hint of it at home would have been perilous. I remember her jumping out of the window, avoiding her parents' interrogating look, and frantically running off, petite and short as she was. When I saw Layala going off,

---

40 A term applied, in the decades immediately preceding the destruction of Jerusalem in 70 CE, (probably) to an extremist splinter group of Jewish Zealots, who attempted to expel the Romans from Judea.

I knew that I could also leave, and we would meet at the street corner.

Walking to Block C, where meetings were held, was dangerous although there were actually no Germans in the ghetto itself: there were only Jews. But, unfortunately, there were those who informed the Germans of all unusual activities. We were anxious about some of the Jews, namely, collaborators and informers. Yet, it should be understood that our activities did actually endanger the whole ghetto. Among those who knew of our existence (hypothetically), there were those who vilified us, threatened us, and accused us, claiming that it would be our fault when all ghetto residents would be taken off and killed. They maintained that they did not want to die because of us. We understood that our very existence was a danger to the entire ghetto, but we felt this was one of the most important things—to hold onto the spiritual content of life; for, without this spirit, nothing of our inner selves would be left.

These impassioned meetings stirred our emotions. I needed to prepare myself at home for two hours before each such gathering. A different subject was discussed at each meeting. I would be given a book—a real BOOK—from the books left in the hideout! And I would carry out my preparations, later giving a talk leading into a comprehensive discussion. Everyone was bright and clever, so I had to study every aspect of the topic and know an enormous amount to be able to answer company members' questions. The arguments were vehement: about the king versus the prophet in the time of Jeremiah, about Isaiah the Prophet. In the ghetto, I intensively studied in depth all the writings of Herzl,[41] history according

---

41 Benjamin Ze'ev (Theodor) Herzl (May 2, 1860—July 3, 1904) was an Austro-Hungarian Jewish journalist who founded modern political Zionism.

to Graetz,[42] and also the geography of Eretz Israel—all things to do with Israel.

When the period of stabilization began, giving us a routine that enabled us to gather new strength and relative constancy in the ghetto, headquarters began making it possible for us to get together as a regiment for special occasions (such as festive parties on Passover, Chanukah, and Purim). Each was a stirring experience. We were always surprised to discover that this or that person was also a member of ABZ. And so our activities took on a different character—they became festive and more ceremonious. Each cheerful, moving get-together of that kind ended with our singing "*Hatikvah*" (Heb., The Hope), now the national anthem of Israel. But most of our activities continued to take place within the company framework, and we kept our vow of secrecy punctiliously.

In the summer of 1943, German nervousness was clearly felt. It was then that the Soviet Red Army began its massive offensive. Russian airplanes were circling around Lithuanian skies, and the echoing din of their bombs exploding carried a long way, reaching our ears too. The Eastern Front was beginning to move closer and closer in the direction of Lithuania.

During all that time, the Germans and their assistants were constantly taking people out of the ghetto to be killed. People were disappearing—they were going off to work and not returning. Families were losing their loved ones without ever knowing what had happened to them, and the ghetto population was thinning out. Many signs indicated that the period of stabilization had ended. The gradual elimination of the Ältestenrat began then, and the authority of Jewish

---

42 Tzvi Hirsh (Heinrich) Graetz (October 31, 1817–September 7, 1891) was among the first historians to write a comprehensive history of the Jewish people from a Jewish perspective.

A Pedigreed Jew

representation in ghetto administration, even when dealing with internal ghetto matters, continuously declined. In the meantime, another terrible blow had been dealt to the ghetto inmates in the form of the Kasernierung decree:[43] a large part of the ghetto population would be forced to move with their families to permanent housing in barracks built specifically for them at workplaces.

SS-*Obersturmbannführer* Wilhelm Göcke, who had been appointed commandant of Concentration Camp Kauen,[44] was responsible for putting these changes into practice. And, indeed, in November 1943, a significant number of the ghetto inhabitants forced to work at the airport, together with their families, were housed permanently in a large army building near the airport at Aleksotas; and, with that, the first stage of implementing the decree was completed. In the second stage, during the first half of December 1943, we, as one family. Mother, Leah, Shlomo, and I, were ordered out of the ghetto, with another 1,000 people, to a work camp on the outskirts of Schanz. That is when we, the core of ABZ activists, were separated from each other; though a number of ABZ members did actually move with us, the organization's intense activity, as we had known it, ceased.

We took the move to Schanz with complete indifference, accepting our fate. The Estonian *Aktion* on October 26, 1943, in which 2,800 ghetto inhabitants, among them neighbors and good friends of ours, were tricked into being taken away did, however, manage to break us and plunge us into bitter despair. As after each *Aktion*, also after the Estonian roundup, the ghetto area was reduced and housing difficulties increased. We

---

43 On November 1, 1943, after SS-*Obersturmbannführer* Wilhelm Göcke officially reclassified the Kovno Ghetto as a concentration camp and most ghetto inhabitants were transported to satellite labor camps.

44 Kauen: German name for Kaunas (Kovno).

came to believe that it was better to live in barracks in a work camp than to continue crowding into the limited area of the ghetto, even though we were suffering from hunger and from poor sanitary conditions. What else was there left to lose?

The Schanz labor camp, under the command of SS *Lagerführer* Bruno Banzke, had been established on the outskirts of Schanz, southeast of Kovno, not far from the Panemunis bridge over the Nemunas River. The ghetto Jews who had been moved there were housed in five wooden blocks (barracks).

We lived under concentration camp conditions: we were in an area surrounded by barbed wire, guarded on all sides by sentries and SS soldiers. We were housed in horribly cramped conditions such as we had never experienced before in the ghetto; we were in a large barrack, a huge place with triple bunks, *nares* (Yid., benches or shelves) on which we slept. We—Mother, Leah, and I—slept on the second tier; here, men were separated from women, so Shlomo was kept in another barrack away from us. But we could still see each other and have a more-or-less normal family life, relative to the situation. At the back of the barrack were some wooden shelves for storing the possessions we had managed to carry with us from the ghetto—a few clothes, blankets, and some kitchenware.

Azriel Berkmann, who had become known for his initiative and as someone who was able to make contact with the Germans when he was still head of the ghetto workforce, was appointed by the Ältestenrat to be deputy of the camp; altogether, the Ältestenrat made sure that each new camp would also have people from the original ghetto Ältestenrat staff and from its institutions in order to establish a fast and efficient system of services for camp residents. Three policemen and five supervisors, all from among Jews in the camp, helped with keeping things organized. A few Jewish women worked in the camp kitchen.

Jews in the Schanz work camp toiled in one of four large workplaces designed to serve the German army: the army building unit, the army supplies office, the army clothing office, and the regional fueling station. I worked in the army supplies office.

Early morning we were commanded to present ourselves for roll call and to get ourselves into straight lines. The minute we heard the order over the loudspeaker, "All workers of the military supplies office must immediately take themselves to the left corner"—we would stand in rows of four people; and Hermann Berkovitch would gather us in our lines and take us to our workplace shouting: "*Los, los* (Ger., get moving)... move forward." The atmosphere was not heavy with tension or fear of the unknown, so we left for work aware that we were really going to our workplace. For ten hours a day I worked sorting food items for the army, among them carrots, potatoes, and onions. During that period, we were not left hungry: a number of us women prisoners would sit in a row in front of huge cases of vegetables to sort the produce—we would throw any damaged or rotten vegetables to the side to later be cooked in the central camp kitchen and that was our food.

Leah worked as a secretary in the army supplies depot in an office run by a man by the name Miller; he was the office manager of military food provisions and a declared anti-Fascist in his views. Miller behaved quite humanely toward camp internees, and because he really liked Leah, she was sometimes able to return home with leftovers, this being a help to the four of us. In the same office, there was a German woman called Martha working with Leah. This woman really disliked her, or perhaps she was jealous of Miller's supportive attitude toward Leah, and she made life very difficult for her.

Mother served as a kindergarten teacher and was in charge of small children (up to about ten years of age) whose mothers were sent off to forced labor day in, day out. Ghetto children were outstanding in their maturity, wisdom, and ability to survive and endure. They almost never cried—as if they understood it was forbidden to do so. There were cases of seven- and eight-year-old children who already knew how to steal food in all sorts of sophisticated ways.

Mother got the job of kindergarten teacher through inside influence— by virtue of being the wife of Rabbi Yitzchak Baruchson from the Or Yisrael Yeshiva. We saw that as a great privilege.

I remember the winter of 1944, a season that happened to be especially cold, as a time of increased suffering from freezing weather and terrible hunger. Trading with Lithuanians had been reduced due to more stringent guarding. The Lithuanians themselves had just about nothing to eat and were forced to supply German military forces from the meager yield of their fields and the agricultural products they had managed to grow and produce.

One morning, March 27, 1944, we awoke and began getting ourselves ready to go out to work. It was horribly cold and there was a white blanket of snow covering everything outside. I, however, was full of warm, good energy... Mother was lying next to me without a blanket. At night, it turned out, she had wrapped her blanket around me, covering me with it well so I would stay warm... I asked her, "And where is your blanket? Why did you do that?" She did not answer me. She was amazing in her tenacity in the face of suffering and she never complained... Like a soldier, she quickly got up, dressed and washed in freezing water; it was, literally, icy water... that is the last memory I have left of my mother.

At seven o'clock we went off to work as usual; on our return we confronted a horrific tragedy—there were no children and Mother was also gone.

The Children's and Old People's *Aktion*

Two witnesses, women who, by chance, had not gone off to work that day, told us what had happened. They had been concealed when the Nazi troops invaded the camp, armed as they always were, as in every *Aktion*, with cudgels and German shepherds. "Your mother should never have gone!" the women said. When the Germans began looking for those children who were still in the camp, all of whom were below the age of twelve, and loading them onto trucks, Mother had come out of the building in her pink robe and slippers, running toward the Germans, saying she could not let the children out on their own in such cold weather, that she must be there to look after them. The Germans—there were all-in-all only two Germans overseeing the *Aktion*—were standing at the side watching the Lithuanians and Ukrainians carrying out the job with immense cruelty, venting all their anger and hatred of Jews on those small children and the elderly. They told Mother she did not need to join the children, but she insisted and answered, "I have to keep my eye on the children; they can't go alone... they are too young." The Germans did not argue with her too much and said, "Very well, get up into the truck." That was around eight o'clock in the morning. Loudspeakers were blaring out the song "Lili Marlene" as well as melodies by Wagner and Strauss so the children's screams would not be heard, and that is how they were taken... They were stealthily taken out of the camp precincts at a time when adults were at work and in trucks covered on all sides by tarpaulins to hide from view all that was going on; they were put into railway carriages and, from there, taken to be killed. We never saw them again...

The *Aktion* against the old people and children was carried out that day at the Schanz labor camp in the same way as in the central camp and in the rest of the work camps populated by survivors of the Kovno ghetto, under the direct command of SS *Scharführer* Bruno Kittel.

On our return from work we threw the barrack door open and went inside, only to discover that no one was there. Mothers were rushing around the camp streets in a frenzy, looking for their children; and three other children—Shlomo, Leah and I—were looking for their mother, but in vain.

No words can describe the shock and pain of those mothers making their way back toward evening, having not found their children. I will never be able to forget those scenes. The mothers began tearing out their hair and their screams rose to the heavens. Until today, I still see Eisele's mother. Eisele was a child of about three, a beautiful, blond child with a ready smile. When his mother became convinced that he was not to be found, it was awful. Mothers could not find their children... I remember all the mothers' pained voices merging into one mighty lament; you could not hear individual voices. Overwhelming depression, heavy mourning, and a sense of bereavement settled over the whole camp. We thought that would be the end of us, that there was no longer any reason to live. But very gradually the lamenting subsided, people calmed down little by little, routine was restored, life went on, and people went out to work. Parents could not observe *shiva*,[45] as they were not sure if it was correct to do so. They did

---

45 Hebrew for "'seven"—the seven ritual days of Jewish mourning.

not think about death, preferring to hold on to a sliver of
hope, and gave in to thinking that the Germans would not
have taken away small children to be killed. Perhaps they
even hoped that children taken by the Germans would have
better conditions... so we went on imagining the children were
possibly alive and just somewhere else...

It seems reasonable to think that the children (and the
elderly) had been taken off to Auschwitz[46] in railway carriages,
but historians are not unanimous on that; they cannot be
certain as to where victims of the "Children's *Aktion*" from
the Kovno concentration camp and subordinate work camps,
including that at Schanz, were taken. It is said that on the first
day of rounding up, the victims were taken into town to the
railway station, and from there, were probably transported
to Auschwitz and killed in the gas chambers. On the second
day of the *Aktion*, however, those caught were taken directly
to the Ninth Fort, where they were killed that same day and
their bodies burned. The fate of the victims of that *Aktion*,
which took place on March 27 and 28, 1944, is concealed in
a haze of uncertainty. The Germans made sure to cover up
any signs of the killing, so to this very day, we are left with
no information about the execution of Mother or the children
and the old people.

At night, I think of Mother being taken off "there" to the
unknown, wearing only a robe, in a cold so intense it could
freeze your bones. In my mind's eye, I see her trampling
through the snow in her slippers. All those years I have been

---

46 Auschwitz-Birkenau: the largest Nazi concentration and
   extermination camp; located in southern Poland, it was the
   largest graveyard in human history. The number of Jews
   murdered in the gas chambers of Birkenau must be estimated
   at 1.1 million people.

plagued by the fact that, in the last moments of her life, she must have suffered so terribly from the cold…

At the end of June 1944, everyone knew that within a number of days, or at most, weeks, German control of Kovno would come to an end: Soviet airplanes were showering bombs non-stop over Kovno every night, the echoing sounds of shooting and explosions and the clatter of German armored vehicles retreating from the East were drawing closer, reaching our ears, and the hope began beating in our hearts that a miracle was coming our way, and that, within a few days, we would be saved from our terrible torment.

Witnessing the chaotic evacuation of German institutions in town and the retreat of the defeated German army forces, with their many companies stretching in a line many kilometers long, and in light of rumors gleaned from newspaper fragments, broadcasts heard on the radio concealed at great risk, and empty boasts made by Lithuanian passersby about the impending start of the Vilna Campaign (Vilna is separated from Kovno by only 100 km), we impatiently anticipated our long-awaited release. Mysterious smiles started to show on our forlorn faces. Between the blocks, on heaps of ruins and by the barbed-wire fences, far from the eye of German sentries, there were so-called "military commentators" impassioning their listeners assembling around them, a sparkle in their eyes; these commentators were explaining in great detail to the crowds about the unavoidable overthrow of the Third Reich and about the Russian victory. A refreshing breeze of freedom began winding its way through the muddy, contaminated, sooty lanes, giving people, their bodies covered only in rags, dragging themselves sluggishly due to hunger, the will to hold onto life. Now, with the Russians advancing with giant steps and, with them the approach of the yearned-for victory, the desperate attempt to survive and to cling to the glimmer of life within us suddenly seemed worthwhile.

With the will to live, people suddenly began looking after their health— taking breaths of fresh air and warming themselves in the sun to gain strength, gripping life, lest they miss out on being freed... more women refused to abort despite the order decreeing that ghetto women should not become pregnant. "All will have passed and be over by the time to give birth," they would say...

In early July 1944, Göcke informed the Ältester, Dr. Elkes, that the Kovno camp and its satellite labor camps were about to be eliminated, and all of their inhabitants sent to East Prussia to work. When the Jews in the main camp learned of this, their cautious optimism was shattered, replaced by panic accompanied by a slew of suicides (which until then had been rare). At the same time, two desperate rescue attempts began to be organized: escape from the ghetto to the city of Kovno or toward the villages in the area, and the construction of additional *malines* while awaiting the redemption by the Soviet army.

On July 7, 1944, Göcke told Dr. Elkes that evacuation of the ghetto would begin the following day. That very day they liquidated the labor camps in the Kovno area, and by evening, internees of those camps began to arrive in Slobodka—to the main camp—except for the prisoners of the Aleksotas and Schanz labor camps.

Sunday, July 9, passed peacefully, with no activity on the part of the Germans. This fact led many Jews into firmly believing that the nightmare was finally ending. Quite a few of us continued to hold onto life at all costs. But suddenly, as if out of deliberate malicious intention, Russian airplanes abruptly ceased flying over Kovno, and we found out that the Red Army's offensive had been slowed down and that Vilna had yet to be taken.

From Monday to Wednesday of the same week it rained with a vengeance. We wallowed in mud, still hoping that it would not occur to Göcke to obtain the freight cars necessary for removing the Jews—for, anyway, there was a shortage of railway wagons and other vehicles, and they were needed for evacuating German troops from the Eastern Front. And even at the cost of being proven wrong, we wanted to believe that the Red Army would eventually arrive and free us before Göcke managed to implement his scheme.

But what could be more astonishing than the announcement of Wednesday, July 12, 1944, that Göcke had succeeded in getting the rail wagons necessary for transporting the Jews in the direction of Germany. On that morning, all the Jews who had been brought to the central camp were ordered to organize themselves into lines—five people in each row—there in the clearing between the Large Blocks, and they walked from the ghetto toward cars awaiting them on the platform of the railway tracks at Aleksotas. We, the internees of the Schanz camp, were not returned to the central camp at Slobodka as were Jews from the remaining work camps from the Kovno region, but rather on the same day, we were taken directly to the railway platform at Aleksotas.

Row by row, surrounded by heavy German guard, with the troops holding cocked rifles and closing in on the convoy on both sides, we marched with the bags of provisions we had received for the journey. We were bombarded with shouts of abuse and hateful glances from the crowd of rejoicing Lithuanians gathered there in tense expectation of the leaving of the last of the evacuees, so they could finally break into the camp area and steal whatever was left in deserted buildings.

Leah, Shlomo, and I walked together and, joining us was Dvorele Friedmann, the girlfriend of Mikhel Itzhaki (Gelbatronik).[47] By then we knew what the Germans

---

47 One of sixty-four prisoners of the Kovno ghetto who were forced to take part in the burning of corpses of victims of the mass slaughter in the Ninth Fort; see above, "The Airport," p. 58, n. 33.

had been wreaking upon the Jews and, as a result, we did not believe we would subsequently be taken to East Prussia to work. We imagined our fate would be like that of all the people who had been taken away and killed in all previous roundup *Aktionen*. I went off wearing clothes with the yellow star attached front and back, and in the small parcel I was carrying, I had another dress and a slice of bread.

We walked from the Schanz camp in the direction of the trains. As we were crossing the Schanz-Kovno Bridge, which was extremely narrow, lines were broken up and for a short moment as we walked, we mingled with the Lithuanians. Dvorele and I had agreed we had nothing to lose, and with that, we both threw our personal belongings into the water of the Nemunas, removed the yellow stars we had been wearing, put scarves on our heads in an attempt to look like gentile country women and left the line in the hope that someone would take pity on us and allow us to wait out the period in hiding. Dvorele succeeded: she managed to escape. A Lithuanian family took her into their home and she lived with them until the end of the war; and as for me—after only 200 meters, two Germans approached me and took hold of my arms. They beat me in no uncertain way, gave me yellow stars and ordered me to wear them again, sending me straight back to the line—and that was the end of that; there I was without my few belongings and a veteran of a failed escape attempt, too. Yet, in my heart I said, "At least I tried." That was how I felt about it; it had not succeeded but at least I had tried. I went and found Leah and Shlomo in the line. I don't think they even knew of my attempt to flee as they hadn't been looking. Whoever could try anything…

At the Aleksotas railway station, there was absolute chaos. German army personnel were rushing around at their wits' end, trying to track down train carriages and other vehicles on their way west, so they could get away from the front which was moving closer. Even now, there were a few Jews who still believed a miracle would happen, that the roads and rail tracks would be cut off and that there would be no way to travel westward...

They crammed us all into ten, sealed freight cars with barred windows, accompanying us with shouts of "*Los, los, schnell, schnell* (Ger., Quickly, quickly)!" Each wagon was guarded strictly by the Germans. And on that very day, those cars packed with Jews set off toward Germany. We took one last look back toward the ghetto in which we had suffered for three years, only to see it going up in flames—the ghetto area had been set alight from all sides to prevent Jews from trying to hide there to find refuge; houses were blown up and burned down, and many people in hiding were burned alive. Clouds of black smoke rose up from the familiar and beloved neighborhood that had once been so dear to us and which had also been a witness to the illustrious history of hundreds of years of Jewish life in Slobodka.

The journey in cattle cars, in awful crowding and exhausting heat, with neither light nor air, was a harsh experience. We were squeezed so tightly into the wagons that there was absolutely no space: fifty people in each wagon, with almost no room for us to stand. In the corner, there was a bucket to be used as a lavatory and it gave off a stench. On our way, we passed by wide, open fields and familiar villages, but the moment we crossed the border into eastern Prussia, we no longer believed or hoped for a miracle, and we were engulfed by a grave sense of our imminent end. By that time we had already heard about Auschwitz and other concentration and extermination camps to which Jews had been taken in trains, so we were absolutely certain that we were also being brought to our deaths. We were sure we were being taken to the ovens, that we were on the way to some crematorium. That was indicated simply by the way we were being transported, which matched the rumors we had heard as to how people were driven to their deaths and how nobody in those transports was left alive except by chance. The atmosphere in the wagon, as I remember it, was very bleak: silent and introverted; we wondered how long we had left to live and how long the journey was going to take.

There were a number of attempts at escape, since no one still believed we would survive. Many with us in the carriages endangered their lives and jumped from small slits in the wagons; some of them did, indeed, manage to save themselves, going to some house where people agreed to hide them. (It should not be forgotten that by then, the Russians were not far away and local people—mostly the Volksdeutsche among them, the ethnic Germans living outside the Reich—wanted to show their goodwill.) There were people who broke arms and legs, while others were shot then and there upon being caught. I was not among those who leaped from the train: after having tried my luck at getting out of the line on the Schanz-Kovno Bridge and not succeeding, I had decided that this would be my fate; and as such, there was no point in trying to escape.

On the following day, Thursday, July 13, the freight cars stopped at Tiegenhof—a small railway station in eastern Prussia, not far from Freie Stadt Danzig.[48] Among terrible

---

48 German: The Free City of Danzig was an autonomous Baltic port and city-state, established January 10, 1920, in accordance with the Treaty of Versailles of 1919. It ceased to exist after 1939 when it was occupied and annexed by Nazi Germany. After Germany's defeat in 1945, Danzig became part of Poland, under the Polish name, Gdansk.

commotion, men and boys were separated from women and girls—boys and girls who had miraculously escaped from the children's and old people's *Aktion*. The women thought they were being assembled to be taken off and killed and were stricken with despair. Some women doctors injected themselves with poison in an attempt to commit suicide.

From that day on, Leah and I did not see Shlomo again. Parting from Shlomo was a second farewell for us. After four months without Mother, who had been taken in the March Children's *Aktion*, we were now also forced to leave Shlomo, following the separation of men from the women.

Immediately after the men's transport left Tiegenhof, the women and girls set out in open carriages—the latter were some kind of tall wheelbarrows hitched to each other like railway carriages. The narrow train crossed green fields, entered a dense forest, cleared its way between birch trees and approached its destination, all this while encircled closely by SS black-uniformed soldiers. After half an hour, the train stopped.

We did not know where we were headed, nor did we know where we were. We saw barbed wire, electricity poles, a tall chimney with dark smoke rising out of it, guard towers surrounding the camp on all sides, and sentries, their weapons held ready, encompassing us from all directions. All we knew was that we were at some kind of Lager (Ger., camp), a Konzentrazionlager (Ger., concentration camp). The black-clad SS soldiers welcomed us with shouts, beating and pushing. They dragged us out of the cars as one would cattle—with whips, sticks, and cudgels. This cruel reception with blows and swearing was a gentle hint of what we were to expect.

On our arrival, we were still wearing our ghetto clothes with the yellow star. I had torn off my yellow star in my attempt to escape on the Kovno–Schanz Bridge, and after I had been caught, was forced to reattach it; it was not sewn but pinned on to my clothes. And as to my personal belongings— they had long since reached the Nemunas river bed... so, I was "exempt" from carrying things.

But not to worry; whoever arrived there without possessions, as I had, was not going to miss out on anything; everything was being taken away from us. From the minute we arrived, with our passing through the "Gate of Death," we were admitted to buildings—just as we had heard from stories of Auschwitz—and the soldiers informed us that we were in the Stutthof concentration camp close to the village of Sztutowo, not far from the harbor city of Danzig. We were ordered to strip and place our clothes on separate piles: dresses on one and shoes on another. Were they perhaps meant for the transports arriving after us? All of this was carried out, among other reasons to check for papers, jewelry, and money in the lining and pockets of our clothes.

We stood there almost naked. A lot of SS officers and soldiers wandered around, sizing us up with their eyes. We felt so degraded. It was our luck that this was July and the weather not yet cold.

While we were still waiting for the shower, German soldiers walked around among us with baskets, commanding us to put any valuables we had into the basket: jewelry, watches, paper money, and gold rings. And the basket was, indeed, filling up... Some women suspected the showers were not really showers but gas chambers, and, yet, they held out hope that, after the shower, they would be fortunate enough to return to where they had entered, would dig up and retrieve what they had buried in the ground. Those women tried outsmarting the Germans and did not give up their possessions. They tore up the bills, quickly buried rings and gold coins under mounds of earth and in sand pits they had formed with their feet, marked the place, smashing and crushing their watches with their feet. Certain women had some bread and sugar left from what had been distributed before we left Kovno; they devoured it quickly, stuffing as much as they could into their mouths. There were women who tried valiantly to hold onto pictures of loved ones—the pictures were usually grabbed from them, torn up in front of their eyes or thrown into flames. Leah and I miraculously managed to hold onto pictures of those closest to us by folding them and hiding them in our brassieres.[49]

After that, we were taken to a large building (the Zauna[50]) from which floated the smell of Carbol,[51] and there we were told we would be washed and disinfected. All those signs, as well as the dense soot constantly rising skyward from the chimney maw in front of our eyes, unceasingly attested to what we had known from hearsay—that we were going to die. We could not believe there was any other possibility (that is, that the showers were, in reality, showers…).

Yet, in the end, they really were showers! Water and not gas! There was only cold water though, not much of it either and, after a few minutes, we were sent out of there; but, to our amazement, we found ourselves alive and were as happy as if we had been born anew.

After the showers, we underwent gynecological examinations under the supervision of a Polish gynecologist. The doctor inserted a finger into our vaginas. They probably wanted to check if there were pregnant women among us and send them to the ovens, or perhaps they were searching women's bodies for any valuables they might be hiding.

---

49 The pictures are now in the archives of Yad Vashem.
50 German: sauna, baths. In some extermination camps, this was the place used for the mass gassing of prisoners.
51 Carbol-fuchsin, used as an antiseptic.

The stage of showering and the gynecological examination was only the first shock in our admission to Stutthof and the processing continued on into the night. To break our spirit, hits and blows accompanied everything. One group of fifty women would leave the showers as the next group was called to enter, and so on. Out in the open air we sprawled on the ground in the yard, where bits of grass sprouted here and there, waiting, naked and shivering with cold, for the last group to exit the showers.

Later on, they threw us some clothes—garments belonging to others, to people who were no more… ragged clothes that were worse than ours had been. I was given clothes that were too small for me, despite the fact that I was narrow and very thin. It was all, after all, a matter of luck that we had left the showers alive and I had underwear and a dress. It was a blue, checkered dress. On the front, at the side, and on the back as well, there was a red emblem in the shape of the Star of David printed on the garment.

After that, we were given numbers—numbered tin tags that were pinned onto the emblem. They, "the supreme race," were filled with scorn and megalomania and, in all cynicism, wanted to instill in us the understanding that "from now on you are no longer human beings but merely numbers. From the moment you passed through the gates you lost all your rights. You have only one right left and only one possibility: to go up to heaven through the chimney." That declaration was accompanied with a finger pointing in the direction of the crematoria.

I remember having a pair of shoes thrown to me. They were small shoes—surely those of a girl younger than myself, a girl who had been burned to death in the crematorium, poor, miserable child—and they were not the right size for me. That is when my problems with shoes began. Mostly, even when very cold, I preferred walking and running even in the dead of night to the Appel (the daily head count) not wearing the ill-fitting shoes. And so I said to myself that if I managed to get out of there to freedom, the first thing I would do would be to write about "the value of shoes in one's life"... There was a lot of suffering—from the cold, from corns, from cuts that did not heal and from festering sores caused by wearing shoes without socks and their pressing on one's big toe and aggravating the sores. A lot of women suffered from their icy, cold feet—but I did not. I don't know whether I was just lucky or if it was that my feet did not freeze since I would hop up and down; I realized that I had to increase the blood circulation in my feet. Generally speaking, the extent of one's survival depended quite a bit on one's own intelligence and in the way a person coped with the fear of extermination. Later on, one of the shoes became quite worn, those shoes that I hated and that made me suffer, and there, inside it, I found a gold ruble[52] coin some mother had apparently put into her daughter's shoe. As you will see, that coin helped me a great deal...

The intake process also included a number of formal steps: clerks of the political department wrote down all our personal data and interrogated us; cards were made up for us by the work authorities to assign us to labor categories at a later stage.

With the showering process, the distribution of clothes and shoes, registration and receiving numbers completed, we were ordered to form groups of five in the camp yard, where we were surrounded by machine guns and SS soldiers on all sides. Later, we found out that this was the Old Camp. It had eight blocks for living quarters, a workshop, a supply building, a bathhouse, and a sick bay as well as two buildings which housed the camp offices; there were also a headquarters building, dog kennels,

---

52 Unit of currency in Russia and states of the former Soviet Union.

rabbit cages, and a small grove. Beyond the wall we could see the camp commandant's home as well as residences for personnel. We were counted, each of us was given a tin bowl (*Beklaschke*, as we called it in Yiddish) with a wooden spoon to eat with, and then a German soldier took us off along gravel paths lit by spotlights. We were able to see veteran prisoners from earlier transports, men and women alike, with shaved heads, all wearing uniform clothes—blue and white striped suits. Our luck was that they did not shave our hair off—they only cut long hair shorter—and they did not order us to wear those striped clothes; so we were still somewhat "human beings" and had a little of our personal dignity left. All this constituted a sign of life… an indication that we would stay alive!

The Stutthof extermination camp[53] was spread over a huge area and divided into sections. Each such site was fenced off and guarded stringently by sentries in tall watchtowers. And each group of sites was encompassed by rows of electrified barbed wire. A silence of death enveloped the camp. In each section there were long lines of barracks, and each section was designated to house a specific group of prisoners. The people from new transports were brought to them according to countries of origin, the crimes they had committed, and their ethnic identification. Professional criminals were indicated by a green symbol with a down-pointing arrow, political prisoners with red, Jehovah's Witnesses with purple, homosexuals with pink, social deviants with black; an up-pointing green arrow was ascribed to prisoners under heavy police supervision, and prisoners who had tried to escape from the camp wore what

---

53 At the end of 1943, gas chambers were built at Stutthof, after which it served as an extermination camp. In June 1944, the gas chambers were first used for extermination, mainly of Jews. In December 1944, annihilation by gassing ceased.

was called "the escape mark"—a red spot in a black circle. Initially, Jewish prisoners wore the yellow star, but with the accelerated rate of huge transports arriving from all parts of Europe in the summer of 1944,[54] their clothes were marked, back and front, with a red emblem that actually made no reference to the people's country of origin.

We walked through a gate guarded by a German sentry and were taken into a barb-wired zone separated from other parts of the camp. The part of the Stutthof extermination camp where we Jewish women were housed was referred to as the "New Camp." In adjacent sections, separated by barbed wire from the women's camp, there were men—but it was forbidden to make contact with them. At a distance of a kilometer and a half west of the New Camp was the Sonderlager (Ger., Special Camp)—among the special inmates housed there were German officers who had vigorously opposed the Reich as well as those who had taken part in the assassination attempt on Hitler on July 20, 1944, with their family members imprisoned too. Between the New Camp and the Special Camp stood some buildings surrounded by high walls, and these served as a kitchen, a laundry, disinfecting rooms, and storerooms.

We knew there were also Polish and Austrian political prisoners; Russian prisoners of war; English people and others; Danish communists; Belgian, Czechoslovakian,

---

54 The year 1944 constituted an extraordinary chapter in the history of transports to Stutthof. After the Stalingrad victory, the Soviet offensive began. The Germans were forced to vacate their camps in the east and destroy them. Large transports of Jews from Riga, Kovno, Königsberg, Bialystok, and Lublin arrived at the Stutthof site. The largest transports came from the Auschwitz concentration camp, which could not keep up with the mass extermination of Jews from southern European countries.

French, Greek, Spanish, Dutch, Romanian, Serbian, Croatian and Italian prisoners... but for us, Jews from Eastern Europe and the Baltic countries who constituted the lowest echelon, there was no contact with them. Barbed wire separated us from other blocks and we were forbidden to talk to the people living in them, men or women.

There were thirty, large, gray barracks in the New Camp— twenty of them designated for housing prisoners, with the remaining structures being used for workshops and for the German DAW ammunitions factories; from afar, the latter looked like summer bungalows in some spa town. Beautifully manicured flowerbeds with a rainbow of blooming color adorned the plots between the huts filling the air with an intoxicating perfume. On barrack No. 18, where German and Austrian women were housed, a sign read: *Eintritt fuer Ostjuden streng verboten* (Ger., Entrance to Eastern European Jews strictly forbidden). These German-Jewish women wanted to keep themselves separate from us and they themselves, at their own initiative, had put up the sign at the entrance to their building. They, as it were, belonged to the upper class— and we, as Ostjuden (Ger., Eastern European Jews) to the lower. This hurt us a lot. For weren't we all in the same boat? They had been in the camp for a while by then, while we had come in a later transport. The Germans were happy about this—enjoying rift and racism within the Jewish people, between Jewish women and their own sisters.

Our barrack was an immensely wide hall with a long corridor dividing it into two sections, referred to as Block A and Block B. Each block was intended for 250 women, but actually housed 500. Each of the dormitory cubicles (Stube; Ger., barrack room) had room for one woman, but we had to lie there packed in like sardines, stressed and cramped, four or five women to a pallet. I was on the second pallet—the middle one—and that was the worst, like some overstuffed drawer: one could not sit on it for fear of bumping one's head on the board above, which was just over us; and one could not get off it without disturbing women lying on the lower shelf. When we had to dash out to assemble for Appel, "residents" of the upper pallet would jump on our heads. Squeezing our way through the dense overcrowding to get to the middle board to grab a short rest until the next parade summons or getting down quickly when nature called—these in themselves were acrobatic exercises...

At each end of the building there were doors—one led outside, and the other was the entranceway to the adjacent room of the Blockälteste (Ger., block elder) and her two deputies—the Stubendienst (Ger., room servant). Those three were Ukrainian prisoners. Their heads were completely shaven; they wore the striped uniforms and were very vulgar and cruel. And, into the bargain, they were lesbians and would force Jewish women to help satisfy their sexual needs. They would curse us, calling us "Jewish pigs" and "garbage animals"—and they would wake us with spine-chilling screams ordering us to roll call a few times each night: we would have to run as fast as we could to get to the Appel-Platz in time to organize ourselves, four women per row. We were very fearful: my personal dread was that they would separate me from Leah, my older sister. For me, she was a support and a mother figure as she was five years older than I, and not too long ago, Mother had been taken from us in the ghetto *Aktion*. I was very naïve and childish, much the younger daughter of the family, and I really felt I was not able to do anything on my own, not even launder a handkerchief.

If, in the ghetto, we were still "human beings," riddled with tensions and fear, who, despite everything, continued to look for ways of being saved from the talons of a bitter enemy, here in the camp, we became, in time, apathetic, devoid of any ambition to keep on going or of any reservations. In certain ways, by the flick of a wrist, we had been transformed from human beings into some other kind of creatures. All at once, we had been robbed of our names, our possessions, and our clothing—all the elements that provided us with a sense of identity that distinguished us from each other and enabled people to preserve human dignity. We had become one single, ragged, numbered mass. We realized that, in order to survive bodily, we needed to abandon our cultural and spiritual background, our social status, our past, and our customs—and draw upon our last bit of strength to stay alive: always ready to receive orders, fearfully awaiting the next blow, learning to interpret the smallest nuances in camp routine as hints of what was to come, lustily drinking sour soup from our bowls, greedily chewing on our daily slice of bread… with the one and only aim for all this, to live through one more day, and then another, to remain alive!

All the "good things" to which we had been accustomed in the ghetto, such as toilets or the possibility of washing—were no more. The toilet, which was no more than a large crate put together with rather strong boards, was always full to overflowing and stinking with human secretions and fluids; we were permitted to use it only at certain times. All in all, that meant two to three times a day, for five minutes at a time. To look after bodily cleanliness, to freshen up a little and to avoid body and head lice, we were forced to go to the Waschraum (Ger., washing room), half immerse ourselves in icy water and again put on our one dress. Before getting onto the pallets to go to sleep, we did not undress, needless to say, as we had no change of clothing; and even if we might have had, we would not have not taken off clothes because of having to get to Appel on time.

The Hangman of Stutthof

Apart from several Appels throughout the day and night, we neither worked nor did anything else at Stutthof. We were free to do whatever we felt like—after roll call—even lying around in the yard, warming ourselves in the sunshine. But these long, boring days heightened our sense of hell and life in the shadow of death, and the fact that everything was commanded—rising, sleeping, eating, bodily functions—the nerve-wracking Appels, the need to avoid beatings and, particularly, the constant fear of being selected to go to the gas chambers. A week after our arrival there, the first *Selektion* took place: from among the women who had come from Kovno and Shavel (Lith., Šiauliai), the elderly, the frail, and the ill were sent off. The Stutthof extermination camp was, indeed, a kind of living hell. There was no real chance of escaping from the camp, which was surrounded by water, located on swampy ground in an area sectioned off by a network of water canals amid the dense population of the German enemy.

In Stutthof, intimidation of the inmates never ceased. The Lagerälteste (Ger., camp elder; camp supervisor) of the New Camp, the person in charge of the Jewish women's barracks there, was the Ukrainian, Max Musolff—"Max the Devil," "the Monster," "Max the Terrible," "Satan Max," "The Stutthof Hangman," as all called him. A prisoner himself, he was of slight build, wore a black satin shirt, and carried a thin whip that never left his hand. With jocularity and glee, he would beat women to get them off the sleeping pallets, lashing out precisely, his reign of terror threatening all the women there.

When we heard that Max was in the vicinity, we were all struck with fear. He was most ruthless: at 2 a.m., every morning, they would wake us over the loudspeaker for roll call; we had to go through the only exit, an especially narrow door, and we were warned that whoever did not get there within two minutes—would be shot on the spot. We would all crowd together and push our way through the exit in order to run at full speed to get to the lineup in time, and Max would be standing in the middle of the passageway, his skinny whip in his hand, blocking the exit, cursing and swearing and hitting out at anyone passing him. He cursed in garbled German: "*Ihr verfluchte Judenbande*" (Ger., You despicable band of Jews), "*Ihr verdamtes Sauvolk*" (Ger., You damned pig-folk), "*Ihr Schweine*" (Ger., You Swine), "*Euch freshen geberi?*" (Ger., Do you need [an animal] feeding?) I so clearly remember these words as he would repeat them morning after morning. Several times a day, with no warning or reason, Max would suddenly appear in the building and mercilessly beat some of the women: he would hurl his fist into their faces, kick their stomachs, and pull out their hair. He would finally leave his victims dripping with blood and run off, seething with wrath and enflamed by his wild attack, into the next block. At night, he would derive perverse sexual satisfaction in the barrack where he resided—he would get drunk and flog naked young women—usually Jewish women, especially young, beautiful Hungarian women who had arrived on transports from Auschwitz. For years I dreamed of him being caught and tried and that I would have the privilege of testifying against him; to this day, I still see him so palpably, as if he were standing here in front of me right now.

At first Leah and I would run off to Appels hand in hand; but after a while, friends, with our best interest at heart, told us that we must not reveal that we were related as the Germans were known for separating mothers and daughters, siblings and even good friends, for the sake of keeping them apart. We understood that they might separate us if we kept together too much. Even if we were to keep our distance, however, there was still the possibility that they might separate us; we decided not to stay together all the time, only to be in the same place. So, in effect, we were together and we were not together; sometimes we stood in line next to each other, and at others, we stood in different lines so they would not suspect us of being sisters. Every time we assembled for the Appel, I was afraid that this time they would take Leah from me.

German soldiers and senior-ranking officers would be present at Appels; they would stand there peering at us penetratingly. It was very frightening. We were terrified that one of our faces would appeal to them, in which case they would remove the owner of the face from the line and take her away. German shepherds lay in wait in every corner, ready to pounce on us and tear us to pieces with their jaws.

In addition to mental and physical torment, we were constantly under the threat of "special treatment"—being shot in the neck, the gas chambers, the crematorium or the pyre. Executions and killings took place publicly "in the name of the law" and usually before lunch...

Selektionen were made daily during roll call, and women were taken off to the crematoria. A woman with a rash on her face, for example, or one who looked a little feeble or too old—any of these would be taken to the other side of the camp, to the Old Camp, to the gas chambers. The wind would scatter their ashes and the smell of burning human beings was intolerable. That is what it was like day after day, night after night. And not one of us could ever forget the words of welcome on our arrival at the camp, "You have but one right left to you—to reach heaven by way of the chimney."

Our worst hours of suffering were in the evening. After the morning Appel, which could sometimes go on for a long time, finishing no earlier than 4 a.m., they would distribute coffee and a slice of bread. We were expected to march up in pairs to receive a bowl of coffee; and if a woman moved slightly clumsily, for fear of being beaten, they would resort to pouring the boiling coffee over her.

If someone were to flinch at the sight of the food or was not standing straight when servers were taking food from the huge vat, Max would take her portion, throw it over those standing near her, and say, "Today you won't be eating." That was one way we could miss out on our daily ration of food.

The ration consisted of 200 grams of bread per day, a bowl of black rye "coffee" for each two women in the morning, and soup for lunch. And all that was dished out with terrible beatings. At first, only the Ukrainian women were in charge of the food, although, later on, some of the Jewish women were appointed "Kapos."[55] One of them was my friend, Luna Rosenson. Her job as a Jewish Kapo was to call us to meals and to distribute our portions. Each Kapo was responsible for a group of twenty women; she would receive a loaf of bread, and it was her job to divide it up into equal portions, as best she could. They would work it out "to the last millimeter." If a woman was lucky and she had an in with the Kapo, she might get a few extra crumbs. The Jewish Kapos were also responsible for arranging us in rows at roll call. They behaved well. They did not have the same authority as the Ukrainian

---

55 German: foreman; a term used for certain prisoners who worked inside Nazi concentration camps during World War II in various lower administrative positions.

Kapos, but they were able to help us women and they did their utmost. As far as dishes were concerned, there was a small tin bowl for every two women, and this bowl was used for both the coffee and the soup that were dished out; each woman had her own wooden spoon. At a later stage, the Kapo would collect the bowls the minute the meal was over as they were needed for distributing food in other parts of the camp.

Hardly did we have a moment to find a peaceful corner to concentrate on our daily portion of bread, when, yet again, the whistle would sound and, immediately after that, the call to go "Outside, and get ready for the Appel!" And, so, to another roll call. An Appel under a blazing sun, standing there motionless, with no possibility of using the toilet—and, anyway, the lavatories were locked during the day. That is how we were forced to stand until noon. Whoever's strength failed them sat down for a moment, hidden among the other lines; some women passed out. For hours on end we would wait for the SS officer, with his polished boots and spotless, well-ironed uniform, to take count of us; on his reaching the end of it, we would hold our breath, standing there tensely without batting an eyelid, waiting for the moment roll call would end, and all would be over without a hitch. To the number of prisoners lining up in the field, they would add the number of women who had died that day, giving them the total number of women in the New Camp. If the sum did not match their calculation (for example, it sometimes happened that they had included a sick woman standing in an Appel among the list of those who had died; or the number of a prisoner who had died had been added to the list of the ill), we ended up—thousands of prisoners— standing in the same place, stuck in deep mud or sweltering under a burning sun, until the discrepancy had been resolved.

Even for us, we who had been used to working all day in the ghetto, standing like that for so many, long hours was terrible.

At noon, we had to pair up once again to get our bowl of soup—mostly soup that had been made from beetroot and cabbage leftovers or gruel—eating it together, two women from one bowl, using our wooden spoons. The only good thing about the soup was that it was hot; but its shortcoming was in the meager portions. Apart from that, they did not give us enough time to eat it. The minute we found somewhere to eat and sat down, there was the whip raised above our heads and backs lest we dawdle over our food. And again, with the meal just over, beatings included, we were taken outside, opposite the block, and forced to stand once more in Appel. There was a morning roll call, "the coffee Appel"; the afternoon roll call, "the soup Appel"; and more Appels designed to entertain the soldiers and to drive the prisoners crazy. In time, the Appel became a sort of ritual to which we related with awesome respect, without batting an eyelid: it was the main focus of daily life in the camp, the one and only basis for counting hours and time. The Appel was the framework for calculating the concept of time: "before the Appel," "after the Appel," "the next Appel"…

We were in Stutthof during the summer months of 1944. It was a very terrifying time, and yet we were somewhat encouraged by rumors of an assassination attempt on Hitler, for those accused of having connections to it had been arrested and brought to a certain camp adjacent to our New Camp. In addition, rumors had it that the Germans were losing the war, the Russians were approaching, and the Nazis had put an end to their extermination policy.

Hope had begun to throb in our hearts; and, at the same time, we understood that in the Stutthof concentration and extermination camp, it would mean the crematorium unless we were able to go out to work—for they would not keep even one of us alive just like that, without any benefit to their war efforts. And, so it was, one fine day, that they began talking about sending us off to work. I remember everyone pushed to be included in the list of those going out to work, Leah and I no less. The older women, the ill and the exhausted were sent to the left, while the rest of the women—those younger and healthier— were moved to the right. Leah and I were lucky enough to be put in the right column—the one for those destined to work. Women standing on the left side were sent to the crematorium.

We caught no sleep the night before the day we were to set out for work. Those murderers had made sure to lecture and warn us that whoever did not work would also not continue to exist… In the middle of the night, with the waving of cudgels, we were sent out of the barracks, and shivering with cold (despite the days of intolerable heat, the nights were freezing), we each had to wait for the distribution of a blanket, a bowl, and a wooden spoon.

After long hours of waiting, at approximately 4 a.m., we began to march out of the camp. Just as we were beginning our trek, there was yet another, heartbreaking selection process in which they separated older as well as much younger women from the rest. Those of us who remained continued walking in the direction of the unknown. The main thing was that we had managed to leave Stutthof!

To get cheap labor for places far away, the Germans had formed dozens of secondary labor camps that were affiliated with Stutthof, constituting an extra link in the death chain of the Stutthof extermination camp.

Those forced labor camps, which were in the Danzig Corridor, were also under the administration of the SS. The supervisors of the women prisoners were Lithuanian guards, Latvians, and sympathizers of the Reich regime who had been drafted from among the local people. The camps were between eight and twenty-five kilometers from each other, and there was no consideration whatsoever for the lives of the women prisoners there. In most cases women from Kovno and Shavel, as well as women from Hungary, Czechoslovakia, and Poland, worked in them at hard labor. In each camp, anywhere from 700 to 1,700 women were packed into abnormally crowded conditions; there was filth and hunger; the little food offered was substandard and created havoc in our intestines. It was cold, work conditions were degrading and intolerably difficult, and there was a general poisonous sense of being in some kind of a hell. It did not take long for those conditions to cause skin and intestinal diseases, pneumonia, night blindness, recurrent urinary tract infections, chronic weakness and total exhaustion, with a failing of the body ending in death.

We, the women prisoners of these labor camps, had a daily routine as follows: at 5 a.m.—to a shrill voice calling "Everyone up!"—we were ordered to wake up, "Get your coffee!" (another order) and, fifteen minutes later, to stand in front of our quarters in lines of five women to a row to wait for camp officers and for those supervising the Jews to count us again and yet again, until they would finally say, "The numbers match."

Every morning, we were also to line up with our spades, bowls and blankets. If, for example, there were blankets missing, we were interrogated; and as a punishment, a number of prisoners were taken back to Stutthof, to the central camp, the number of women taken being equal to the number of blankets missing.

After that, each of us would be equipped with a spade from the pile of spades, and we would be joined by armed guards; off we went to the work site a few kilometers away from the camp.

It was intensely cold in the mornings in the fall but, as the day wore on, the sun would occasionally peep out, turning the snow into muddy slush, making the ground soft and boggy.

And then, when darkness fell, as we returned from work, the quagmire in the forest would freeze.

On our return to the camp, we were once again ordered to stand in rows of five and await senior camp staff officials who were coming to count us.

Following the end of roll call and the hurried daily portion of soup, we would curl up among piles of hay and straw for a night's sleep, wrapped in thin blankets, bundled in worn-out, old coats, warming ourselves with our own breath and shivering with the cold.

All in all, over a period of some six months I was in seven work camps affiliated with Stutthof.[56] I was in each camp for three to five weeks. In those work camps, they mostly put us up in stables, barns, silos, and tents, all substandard structures; most of the work meant digging *Bau der Fortifikationen* (Ger., building fortifications). We dug deep canals for protection from tanks and armored vehicles, we dug trenches and pits, we built shelters and fortifications, we paved alternate passage and escape routes for the Germans so they could get away in time, and we worked on various construction jobs. We had to dig down to a depth of three meters and, with all the strength we could muster, tip the muddy soil up onto the canal bank.

Armed SS soldiers in black uniforms oversaw the first journey from Stutthof; these soldiers belonged to the Totenkopf[57] units. They took us to the river, where we were ordered to get into boats; they packed a few hundred women into each one; everyone had to stand, there was nowhere to lean and no

---

56 The camps I was in were Rehberg, Stoboy, Brosen, Niederworben, Hoheneck, Hecht, and Strasburg.

57 German: Death's head. Adapted by the Stabswache (Adolph Hitler's bodyguard unit) and later by the Schutzstaffel (SS) with their military insignia featuring a skull above crossbones.

rail to grab onto. After a trip of some four hours, we reached Elbing; we left the boats, and after a long and exhausting walk, came to the first labor camp by evening.

The moment we arrived, each of us had to be equipped with a spade from the pile of tools and quickly eat her daily portion of soup. They put us into a horse stable, on whose floor was a bit of straw full of horse droppings; they told us that these would be our living quarters. We slept on the prickly straw, here and there "stealing" a bit of straw from each other in order to pad our bed… It was the end of summer and the weather was still warm, so we could tolerate living in a stable. They would wake us at 5 a.m. and stand us in rows of five for roll call. There were twenty officers there, and we were forced to stand on our feet for many hours at a time. They would count us several times to be sure nobody was missing; they gave us a little bitter coffee, divided us into groups, and off we went to work with spades over our shoulders, escorted by SS guards. Our job was to dig, constantly carrying a prayer in our hearts—that this pit would be used as graves for the Germans. Curfew began at seven o'clock in the evening. Buckets for use as chamber pots were put into the stable at night, and we were then locked into the stable. That is where Leah and I became covered with lice. We were extremely hungry. Only occasionally would the Poles throw us something to eat, and we were jealous of the dogs that were well fed and humanely treated by the Germans. While what was called meat in our soup was horsemeat, the dogs were lucky enough to get real beef and bones.

When we had finished digging in one place, they would collect us and march us some eight kilometers under strict guarding to the next digging site. The guards, their guns held close and ready for any incident that might arise, would lead us there like cattle and house us once again in some filthy stable.

After a stay of four weeks in Rehberg, they took us, once again on foot, to the next camp—Stoboy—yet another place riddled with filth and lice. We were there for a month and a half. Winter had now arrived. I remember how very cold it was (−35°C [−31°F]). We would leave for work before sunrise in total darkness, walk a very long distance to the site where we were digging, trampling through the snow in our wooden shoes—the snow would stick to the soles, making walking extremely difficult—and there we would dig the frozen earth for ten consecutive hours, which was very tough. With daylight fading, we would return, our limbs frozen, a long line of women walking in single file, once more plodding through the snow, surrounded by massive forces guarding us on all sides. Many women died on their way back to the camp, and it was our job to carry them back with us so that the number of women who had died plus those who had remained alive would match the number of women who had set out to work earlier that morning. Despite the cold, we would strip off our clothes: Leah would take off her clothes and I would put on her dress to air it; later, I would strip off and she would put on my dress to air it. We had a horror of the lice swarming over our bodies, mainly a fear of typhus which was transmitted by them. Typhus, reinforced by hunger, was a mortally dangerous combination. We tried to see to bodily hygiene, no easy task whatsoever: for months on end, we wore the same dress and the same filthy undergarments, with no possibility of a change of clothes, and we were forced to sleep on straw saturated with animal excrement.

In most of the camps where we stayed, they did not supply us with any water for washing. With our own hands we had to melt snow: we would take a fistful of snow in our hands and rub our faces and hands; that was how we washed. Sometimes, a woman would try to wash her hands, giving up on some of her coffee for that. After that she would have to dry her hands on her filthy clothes. This was all merely a symbolic gesture of bathing. Not one woman menstruated, thank God. That was a miracle from heaven, as we would not have been able to contend with that in the conditions under which we were living…

The most degrading thing was the latrine. At a distance of 150 to 200 meters from the camp, we had to dig various pits in the earth, sitting on the edge of the pits to move our bowels. Many of the women, ill with dysentery and suffering from terrible stomach cramps accompanied by watery diarrhea containing mucous and blood, simply could not make it to the latrines; and, so, each morning we ended up cleaning the paths of feces and blood. Leah also took ill with dysentery at Stoboy. She had always suffered from a sensitive stomach and intestines. She had endless diarrhea. Eating frozen potatoes, uncooked meat leftovers and rotten vegetables took their toll.

At that time, our work digging at Stoboy finished and we were about to move on to the next camp to take up work there, digging and building fortifications. Poor, sick Leah was very weak, verging on total exhaustion; she was shaky on her feeble feet and could hardly stand up. Then, one day, she was no longer able to walk one step further. We knew too well that they would take the ill and weak out of the line, that they would disappear, never to be seen again.

We walked from Stoboy to the Brosen Camp (a distance of ten to fifteen kilometers). We walked through forests, on side paths, the soldiers making sure local folk would not see us and would have no contact with us. There were horse-drawn wagons on the path and whoever could not walk and was in need of help was put onto the wagons. Leah could not trudge on, and they put her into one of those wagons, together with other sick and weak women. The last time I saw her there she was wearing a brown coat with a cross-weave of brown and white stripes creating a checked effect, with a hood and the stamped red Star of David back and front. I, myself, had a blanket. Lying in the wagon, Leah took the blanket from me to save me carrying the weight of it. It was terribly cold. We walked in single file, and time and time again, I would look back in the direction of the wagon that was behind us; they just must not take Leah from me. I could not walk beside her as we were forced to proceed in a certain order. We were constantly guarded by soldiers with guns cocked and, for simply no reason whatsoever, they would strike us with rubber cudgels. I kept turning my head to keep my eye on Leah. When I turned around again, the wagon had suddenly disappeared! It was as if the earth had swallowed it. There must have been a bend somewhere on the path, at which the wagon suddenly turned off. Of course, they knew there were relations, friends, and acquaintances lying in the wagon, and to make the business of our parting from each other easier for themselves, they, quickly, in the blinking of an eye, had diverted the wagon of sick women from the path and it was gone... as if it had never been there! It was all done swiftly and efficiently, as in the *Aktionen*. I was sure that Leah was no more, that they had taken her off. I did not know to where, nor did I know whether she was dead or alive; I knew nothing. I just kept thinking to myself about how I, of all people, was the sole survivor of the family.

I became filled with a terrible sadness. Mother was no longer alive, Shlomo was gone—as far as we knew and could understand—and, now, Leah, my sister, had been taken from me. Now I remained alone in the world. Father, who had been sent as a representative of the Slobodka Yeshiva to the Ner Yisroel Yeshiva in Baltimore, America, belonged to another world and I did not believe I would ever be lucky enough to be reunited with him. And, anyway, Father had become a distant dream, totally disconnected from reality. I had the feeling, once again, that I had no responsibility toward anyone to live, for, indeed, everyone was gone. Nothing mattered to me any more. I became indifferent to everything, ready to die. There was no reason left for me to go on living.

My blanket had also disappeared together with Leah. No words can describe what it meant to lose one's blanket in these conditions… The blanket was the most valuable item: it served as a rain cape, a skirt, and a scarf in which to wrap oneself… Some women cut strips off the material and sewed protective head-, arm- and leg-coverings for themselves to keep out the freezing cold; with these strips they lined their wooden shoes and bandaged their wounds. Despite the Germans' frequent threats ("Do you know what punishment you deserve for vandalizing army property?"), the hobnailed soldiers of the Reich were not able to eradicate common practices such as these. A woman whose blanket had remained intact, or almost intact, was considered rich and she would zealously look after her "treasure."

Following a long, difficult journey on foot, we got from Stoboy to the Brosen Camp, where we would stay for three weeks. There, as in both former camps, we were put up in a stable: and again there were the same, familiar piles of straw, poor lighting, dirt and stench. As time went on, dampness coming through the roof and the secretions from sick women became mixed into the bottom layers of straw to become an amalgamation of stinking sods. Only the top layer, having dried out during the day, was somewhat suitable as a place to sleep. Any small move or contact with the pile of straw, even to the depth of just a few centimeters, increased the degree of the stench. Possessions women tried to safeguard concealed in the straw quickly fell apart and absorbed the smell. Under those conditions, there was no place for hygiene. At the end of a workday, we had to put our tools back in a certain order.

Whoever did not do so, simply throwing her hoe any old way, ended up being beaten mercilessly on the head with that hoe... so there were many women who had been wounded by hoes...

From there we were transferred to the Niederworben Camp. With winter approaching, the cold was intensifying and bladder and kidney infections became common. One could not be cured of any sickness, as on their way to the latrines at night, women would again catch cold, bringing back the infection. There was a *Selektion* at Niederworben and dozens of women were sent to Stutthof for extermination.

A few weeks later, we were sent from Niederworben to the Hoheneck Labor Camp. To get there, we had to walk some ten kilometers in pouring rain. In Hoheneck, we were also put into horse stables from which the horses had been taken out close to our arrival; we were forced to sleep on straw that was filthy with horse droppings. In that camp, we suffered even more from lice, cockroaches, and mice. The horse stable was a two-story structure, and we had to climb up a ladder to get to the second story. There were holes in the ceiling through which the rain dripped. Occasionally, bowls of "soup" got spilled when women ascended the ladder to the second floor. We would sometimes fall down the ladder and get bruised. There were also some holes in the floor on the second story, and sometimes people fell through... There were approximately 200 women up on the second floor and some 300 downstairs. There was no water for washing ourselves. According to the Germans—the wells had been poisoned. Women would get tin cans ready for use as toilets, and their contents sometimes overflowed from the upper story onto the heads of those sleeping below... The ladder to the top story was small and rickety, perhaps meant only for chickens. Only one woman could climb down it at a time. And, as climbing down took time, particularly if it meant 200 women, those on the upper floor had to get up earlier, at 4 a.m., in order to make it down in time for roll call.

At Hoheneck there was another *Selektion*. I was fortunate in having three good friends: Yehudit Fein, Ira Brasner, and Bronia Borgansky. We were four girls together. We helped and consoled each other. We had known each other from Kovno, from our days in high school. For a while, Ira had been a neighbor of ours in Slobodka. Yehudit was blond and beautiful, tall and slim, with huge blue eyes, she held herself well and had a gorgeous figure. I remember Yehudit was thrown a gray coat at Stutthof; it suited her build wonderfully and she looked like a queen in it. Since she had the looks of an Aryan German, she had caught the eye of a German soldier, actually, a particularly humane soldier, and as a result, she was chosen to be a Kapo in the labor camp and to be responsible for us for a period of time; she was one of three Jewish Kapos in charge of us. Her appointment helped me a lot—occasionally I ended up with an extra slice of bread. And when Yehudit was ill, she lent me her wooden clogs.

The shoes we were issued in Stutthof did not hold out under the work conditions, with the endless tramping to and from the work site and in that climate. So on arriving at the work camps, we were given wooden clogs (*klompas*). Women who managed to get clogs in their correct shoe size were considered happy and fortunate. They looked after their shoes very well and, at night, would sleep with their shoes concealed under their heads. The clogs I received were huge, and, since we had to do a great deal of walking, from camp to camp, my feet hurt terribly. I was suffering a lot from pain and had cold feet. My feet were always swollen, afflicted with blue bruises from the cold, and full of bleeding wounds that were chafed even more by the clogs, producing foul-smelling pus. As time went on, I adopted a special posture and gait caused by a lack of coordination between my upper and lower body; and all this was in order to adjust to the shoes. I think this was one of the worst forms of physical suffering I was forced to experience. Sometimes, when I went out to work, Yehudit would lend me her shoes and I will never, ever forget that kind gesture of hers!

In the work camps, there was heightened awareness, particularly in winter, as to the need to be mobile and to work constantly as a means of preserving body heat. Hungarian women who were with us in these camps very often did not grasp this. They arrived from Auschwitz in a particular emotional state. All had prisoner numbers tattooed on their left arms. A vast number of them were unusually beautiful, but, because of what they had been through, they had lost all will to live. They ate any garbage they could find, were no longer interested in washing themselves or in looking after personal hygiene, and their bodies and clothes were crawling with lice. They would not give in to the insistent pleading of the rest of the women prisoners to place the clothes they wore day in, day out outside at night to freeze them clean and sleep naked, wrapped in a blanket; they insisted they were accustomed to a warmer climate and that it was too cold for them. Some of them, including young girls, had given birth to babies in the work camps: many of them had become deranged over time. There were those who would stop working and just lean on their hoes without moving. We tried to convince them of the importance of keeping moving but to no avail. Those in the habit of not moving were beaten, and some simply froze to death.

One day, we were taken on a two-hour walk, reaching a forest clearing in which there was a town of dilapidated, temporary buildings. This was Hecht Labor Camp, camp number six. Each of the structures had been designated to house some twelve horses, but each was used to house sixty women. Needless to say, all the buildings were exposed to the effects of stormy weather. In rain and snow, dampness came in through cracks in the wooden boards from which the structures were built. On occasion, the interior of the building would become one large puddle as there was no flooring. We tried solving the problem using our own initiative: we dug down one and a half meters to make meter-wide drainage canals and piled the soil up against the outer walls. We covered the roofs with hyssop and put woven fir branches around the buildings to keep out just a little of the dampness and cold.

The camp was situated some fifteen kilometers from the work site, and we had no choice but to make our way there and back on foot in the mornings and evenings and in terribly cold weather. We would wrap straw and rags around our legs. The work involved beating the frozen ground with a hoe. Slivers of ice sprayed in all directions, having a blinding effect. There was a great amount of work. The ruthless guards took out on us all their anger at the deteriorating situation on the front. There were women who could not take being hungry and went out to steal a little bread. Those who were caught were beaten and tortured in front of all the women of the camp; they did not, however, weep and they held their own.

Once, a disturbed, thickset German soldier was watching over us when we were at work. At noon, Assia Yoffe-Berlowitz and I went off for a quarter of an hour's break. I remember how beautiful the weather was, and I even remember what we were talking about: we were dreaming of Eretz Israel. We said to each other, "Just imagine if we were doing this work as pioneers, digging Israeli earth with our hoes." We were talking, singing, and daydreaming. Altogether, in the camps at that time, we talked a lot about Zionism, we talked a lot of Hebrew and that was what kept us going—our yearning for Eretz Israel. We were talking about the folly of our not escaping and getting out in time, regretting our foolishness. We often thought back to Jabotinsky, to how right he had been in predicting the fate of European Jewry... when we suddenly caught the eye of the disturbed German soldier breaking into a gallop, running toward us. We were startled and ran away from him. I was wearing my large, heavy, clumsy wooden clogs; of course, he had no problem catching me and, after that, he nabbed Assia, bringing us both back to the camp. A complaint was filed against us, since during our fleeing from that soldier we had unintentionally gone beyond the unfenced camp border.

We were each sentenced to five lashings. All the camp women were assembled and lined up. In the center of the yard, a stool was placed specifically for whippings. Assia's turn was first: she was ordered to bend over and the same German sentry who had filed the complaint against us had to carry out the sentence. He was holding a thick, wooden cudgel in his hand, took a few steps back, and then, swiftly and gathering all the strength he had, he lunged forward, bringing the cudgel down on Assia's back. Before each lashing, he would, once again, sprint backwards to gather momentum, increasing the force with which he sprang forward. And my fate, as second in line, was to witness it all and to know what awaited me in just a few short minutes. It was awful. Yet, I did see that Assia rose onto her feet after five lashings. Actually, she was as white as a sheet but did not shed a tear. Taking slow steps, she went back into the lineup and took her place among the other women in her line. I decided that, if she could withstand it, so could I; one must not cry... the Germans were not to be given the satisfaction of that. And the truth is that I did not weep at all.

The Discovery of the Lost Prisoner

One day, one of the women prisoners went off into the depths of the forest either to pick mushrooms or to answer the call of nature, and she lost her way back to the Hecht Labor Camp. A German soldier found her wandering around and thought she had come from another labor camp, which was some seven kilometers from our camp. Instead of sending her back to our camp, he took her to the other camp and there, in that camp was... LEAH! A few days later, the young woman was sent back to the Hecht Camp and she told me that Leah was alive! Words cannot describe the excitement that gripped me on hearing these tidings. I suddenly felt as if I had grown wings and my will to live returned. Conversing with myself I said, "Here, you see. It means that the situation is not so very bad and that there is yet hope." Hope was the most important motivation of all, immediately followed by the goal—something worth living for.

I had thought there was hope, but that did not mean that I believed there was a God. Over time, I had put aside my belief in God, not intentionally nor from any kind of rational decision, not even with any firm opinion; my belief had simply ceased to exist, had gone, totally dissipated. This had just happened on its own. It was as if God had been extracted from me. I had had a steadfast belief in God before the

Holocaust; I had been very religious. It seems to me that after the pogroms the Lithuanians carried out, after what my friend Chayenale had gone through, after the Great *Aktion* in which I witnessed how they killed all the people together with whom I had been living for years—the process of deserting God had begun within me. I could no longer talk of God nor believe in him and that is how my belief, caught unaware, had been uprooted.

And, here, this same friend who was returned to the camp, had told me that Leah was alive and she was doing the same jobs as I was—digging and building fortifications. And, to add to that, I had heard from her that Leah was "doing just fine": she had two blankets (one of which, indeed, was mine, the one I had given her when she was lying in the wagon on the way from Stoboy to the next camp) and a loaf of bread as well!

Despite Yehudit and Ira's insistent pleading, despite their repeated utterances of "Just don't dare!" I plucked up courage and asked one of the sentries responsible for us to allow me to move to the other camp. At that time, there had been two sisters with us in the camp. Both were ill. Their mother was in the other camp and they had put in a request to be reunited with her. Because of that and through them, I had been able to wangle a sort of exchange agreement: their mother would move to my camp and I would move from this one to the other.

Was there not a certain risk in asking to move? One must not forget the times: this was at the end of 1944, the Eastern Front was approaching us with giant strides and the Germans, at the same time, were losing spirit. So it was now possible to say openly, "I have a sister in the next camp and I would like to move there to be with her." I took the risk by choice. At worst, I might be beaten or they could refuse my request. Apart from that, I still had the same gold coin I had found that time in the sole of the shoe that had chafed me so in Stutthof...

I approached a German soldier, saying I would give him something valuable I had if he would be so kind as to move me to the nearby camp. At that stage of our conversation, I had not yet shown him the coin; I must have matured by now, no longer being as naive as I had been in the past. Owing to the situation I was in, I had aged and had, overnight, become an adult. The soldier approached his supervisor and they both agreed to grant my request. They told me to start walking. The same soldier I had initially approached trod behind me, and, right at the beginning of the walk to the other camp, I gave him the gold coin. The truth is that I now really wanted to be rid of it. Holding onto it had become extremely dangerous. It had become burdensome and, countless times, I had thought of throwing it away somewhere or burying it.

The labor camp where Leah was situated was on one side of the Polish town of Strasburg (Brodnica), and our camp (Hecht) on the other. To get from one camp to the other, one had to cross the town of Strasburg. And so, in daylight, I walked along the main street that crossed the town. It was in winter—at the close of 1944—and I remember it being cold; I was walking along the road together with the horses and cattle, for it was forbidden for Jews to walk on the sidewalk; the German soldier was marching behind me with his rifle ready, pointing straight toward my back. I was thin, really gaunt, and wearing a coat that was too small: it was short, with the Star of David stamped in red, front and back. Many of the town's inhabitants gathered on the sidewalk on both sides of the road. I was very surprised to see normal-looking people after such a long time. They stared at me and they were crying, tears running down their faces.

By the time I had reached Leah's camp, Strasburg, I was weak and hungry, really on the verge of passing out. She welcomed me with hugs and kisses and there was great excitement. First, she organized some hot water for me. HOT WATER! Then she covered me with two blankets to make me warm and comfortable. Thirdly, she had some bread! And that was the main thing—the bread. Until today I fail to understand how she managed to save the bread and organize that welcome...

Now that we were together, we could give each other strength. We continued to do the same work, digging and building fortifications, but now we could help and look after each other. We remained in the Strasburg Camp for approximately three more weeks.

In the meantime, the front was approaching and the Russians were drawing closer to the labor camp. At night, gripped with excitement, we would hear artillery shells exploding and air attacks from the front—and this was music to our ears. We assumed our day of freedom was near. Lithuania was already back in Russian hands, and we were so looking forward to that moment of freedom. We were now hopeful that perhaps, despite all, we would come through this entire ordeal and, somehow, be liberated. That was all that kept us alive—a thin shred of hope. Apart from that hazy fantasy, we lived like animals: we would leave for work in the morning in the dark before sunrise and work until evening, until it was pitch dark; we worked with picks or hoes all the time, digging, digging, digging, apart from a break of approximately a quarter of an hour at noon. In the evening, we were returned to the filthy stable... and started the routine again.

One morning in January 1945, the familiar whistle sounded earlier than usual and, immediately after it, we heard the following command, "Everyone up! The camp is to be evacuated. We are moving deeper into Reich territory." There was much bustling: the camp was disassembled and equipment loaded. Most of the women prepared knapsacks for themselves or sacks made of rags or paper bags for their few possessions as well as their food rations for two days (half a loaf of bread). The Kapos fetched stretchers to carry the women who were ill; the other women formed rows of five abreast, as usual, and even those unable to walk still had to stand on their feet. Escorted by armed guards and officers on motorcycles, we obeyed their command of "*Aufmarsch*! (Ger., Start marching) Leave everything and start walking." Wrapped in the torn blankets that we had, our feet bound in rags, we set off on the march today referred to in literature as the "Death March."[58] The objective of this march was to get us as far away as possible from the approaching Russian front and to bring us into German territory.

We knew the Germans were suffering defeat and needed to retreat, and we had the feeling that the orders given were again unclear to those having to carry them out. Even the guards themselves looked alarmed and nervous to the point of madness.

We began our walk at a fast pace in the snow and freezing cold with purpose written all over our faces. We walked for many kilometers, the endless hours turning into days. Very gradually, our strength began fading and our pace slowed down. One woman would feel ill, another's shoes would tear. The journey was becoming more difficult as we had to clear our own paths through snow-covered forests. We were not allowed to set foot on a road so as not to block the way for the

---

58 Ger., Todesmarsche, forced marches of long lines of prisoners under heavy guard, over long distances, under intolerable conditions, in the course of which the prisoners were brutally mistreated and many killed by their escorts. Death marches are known to have taken place, especially in the final stage of the war, when concentration camps were being evacuated.

endless convoys of armored vehicles and retreating German infantrymen.

Leah was feeling very ill on that journey. She was weak. I also felt weak but apparently had more strength than she did. I held her arm and we walked on arm in arm, leaning on each other, our wooden clogs worn down and our clothes in rags. And so we dragged ourselves on, I in my blue coat with the red Star of David stamped back and front, and Leah in her brown coat with the same stamp back and front. We had a little bread that we had wrapped in a piece of cloth and strapped to our backs. That is how we shuffled on, bent and despondent, leaning on each other, our feet trudging on, constantly under the threat of the soldiers' rifles. We begged them to let us rest in order to renew our strength, but our plea was in vain; the soldiers refused our request, urging us to keep walking. Having no choice, we continued dragging on for many more hours, using our last bit of energy; we were tired, hungry, and thirsty.

The guards were angry with us for not advancing faster, thus slowing down their retreat. They shouted, went wild, cursed; they pushed us, beat us with their rifle butts, sometimes threatening to set their dogs on us or even to shoot dead whoever was not walking in line or was lagging behind. Indeed, there were some women who were too feeble, such as those limping from exhaustion, women who had stomach and intestinal illnesses who were literally crawling, women who collapsed as they walked—these women were shot dead. Many women actually froze to death in the intense cold and were left at the side of the path.

At the end of our strength, on we traipsed through a winding path on the frozen ground, with most of the women slipping on its thin ice cover, making every effort to keep together, until we reached the thick of the forest. As we entered the forest, the Germans decided that it would be best to destroy us all there and then. We heard shots: The Germans were shooting in all directions with one aim in mind—to kill as many of us as possible. I think they got rid of them all in the forest. Perhaps one or two of the women from that camp survived. The fact remains that, in spite of my many efforts to track down traces of that camp years later, I didn't find a single woman who had survived it. For a long time I tried to find one, to clarify what had happened to another, to know something of a third woman, but to no avail—to this day I have not come across one single surviving person from among them.

In the meantime, Leah's physical condition had deteriorated badly. At the Strasburg Camp, she had saved me from hunger and total fatigue and had welcomed me with devotion and supreme self-sacrifice, a gesture I will never forget; while there, in that forest, there was a moment when I carried Leah, telling her, "We have nothing to lose; let's leave the line and escape!" By then, we were no longer part of neat lines. There was disorder, and disorder was, to some extent, a more dangerous situation than order itself.

Leah did not have the strength to object so she went with me. For two days no food came our way. We were very hungry and exhausted. We wet our cracked lips with snow, quenching our thirst. We did not talk much—at such a moment one simply exchanges a few words in Yiddish, deciding to take the risk and flee from the forest.

At one particular stage of our flight, Leah sat down on a rock in the middle of the forest. She was very tired, on the verge of passing out, indifferent and depressed, emptied of all will to continue in the race for life, and I could see she had decided to give up, to give in to fate. Leah had sat herself down on the stone, strongly objecting to pressing on in this endless flight to nowhere. "You go on. I'm staying here," she whispered, her eyes dull. And then I slapped her, I pulled her up from the stone with all the strength I had left and we continued on, running, running, running, hand in hand. We forgot about our hunger and we forgot the thirst that burned our throats. Our legs which had failed to carry us were, so to speak, disconnected from the ground and we floated on. Panting heavily, we skipped over piles of pine needles, clearing our way between tree trunks. Bursts of gunfire kept echoing in our ears, we heard the barking of dogs, screams in German, the rattling of motorcycle engines as well as the groaning of wounded women and of the dying. The smell of gunpowder became mingled with the smell of pine resin, and we just ran on and on and on. It seemed like eternity until we finally left the forest behind us.

So we really did manage to get out of the forest! We found ourselves standing at the side of a main road. We saw German army soldiers surging forward on horseback and various vehicles, going westward—in the direction of Germany.

We sat down to rest for a short while. It was cold. We took snow and drank some of it. We knew there was no chance for us to advance as long as we had the red Star of David stamped on our coats, back and front; it was a matter of a few moments, an hour at most: the first German among the retreating soldiers to see us would understand we were Jewish and would kill us. We could not remove the emblem like we had been able to with the yellow star we wore in the ghetto; however, Leah had a needle and thread hidden in the lining of her coat and, possibly, a pair of scissors as well; she cut a piece of fabric from the bottom of the coat, from the hem, and sewed the patch over the Star of David.

We had invented a story—that we were Volksdeutsche— that is, Germans from Lithuania. (We did speak German and Lithuanian, of course.) How had we come across this idea? There had been a camp of Lithuanian Germans—Volksdeutsche—close to our camp. It was a labor camp, but they had conditions much superior to ours and there was no murdering of prisoners there. Both camps had been disassembled at the same time when the Russians had begun to move closer. We decided that if we were to adopt the identity of women prisoners from that camp, this would seem reasonable. From then on, we, therefore, spoke only German and Lithuanian among ourselves and were very careful not to slip into any other language. And it should not be forgotten that Leah remembered her Polish very well; in this region—Eastern Prussia—Polish was the dominant language.

As we passed through villages, the gentiles would ask us "Who are you?" "We are Lithuanians returning home from Germany," we would answer and the older gentile women would scrutinize us, clap their hands and sigh with "Oh, Jesus and Old Mary" and they would cross themselves.

We knew the front was drawing closer, whereas we were moving in the other direction, toward Germany; it was then that we realized that we would have to stay where we were or move in the opposite direction, against the stream of people who were retreating westward—that is to say, we would have to go eastward, toward the Russians. In wintry weather, in the snow... so we continued toward the east on the main road—two gaunt, deserted young women, taking fate into their own hands—treading our way among concrete rubble on paths and trails left behind in ruins by the war. Our shoes had worn out, our tattered clothes had lost all shape and form and, in all of that time, we had not met a single Jew. It seemed like there were no Jews left in the world, and we were the only two Jewish women who had been saved from destruction. Germans kept rushing past us in their flight, advancing westward. A great many refugees were walking, and we, among them, trudging on swollen legs, hungry for a piece of bread, hiding in deserted huts on the outskirts of villages. Whoever has not walked endlessly like this will never really understand the meaning of it; and for whoever has, we are not telling them anything they do not already know. On top of everything, Leah was so very weak, barely able to carry herself on her feet. "Where are you dragging me? Who will be waiting for us?" she objected. And I did not answer her—I feared unnecessary talk would weaken me—and I was cruel to her in my silence. There was only one time when I did not hold my peace and burst out in anger, "Oh, really. As if it matters at all whether we're walking eastward, westward or to the south," for we were going to the unknown. A German threw us some tobacco and cigarettes. That was when I began smoking. I learned to roll tobacco in small pieces of paper. Anything you could put in your mouth to stay the hunger was of some help.

Somewhere the Russians were still fighting the Germans; despite hearing the thundering of cannons, we marched on. Our bodies yearned to lie down on the ground, to rest, to forget everything, but our feet continued trudging along icy fields and piles of snow; and we, hard though it may be to believe, slept as we walked. We sank into a sort of haze, but unconsciously, caution drove us on. The urge to live prevented us from sitting down for fear of not being able to stand up again and, consequently, freezing to death. And so we kept on walking, our steps getting weaker, staggering as we went. At farm entrances we pleaded for a slice of bread, we begged for charity. I remember entering a small house in a village along our way. There, on the table, was a loaf of bread and a bucket. I grabbed the bread… with the bucket. For what did I need the bucket? God only knows. I quickly ran out of there and that was the first time that Leah, who had always shared everything with me and would always let me eat before she did, grabbed the bread from me and began eating it…

We continued walking… with the bucket. It was very frightening to be plodding along the main road with all the German Army passing by and looking at us. It was also highly dangerous, but we had absolutely no other choice. That was the reality in which we found ourselves and, once again, we had nothing to lose.

It was beginning to get dark and we were beset with terrible fear. We were afraid of being raped. How does one spend the night under the stars in January? One could simply freeze to death, especially having so little physical strength, when one is so weak and on the point of total exhaustion. We were oh so feeble. We decided to knock on the door of one of the houses and ask to be taken inside. There was definitely no alternative. We knocked on a door and went inside. To our great misfortune, this house served as the… regional headquarters of the Gestapo. At that first moment our hearts sank but quick-witted Leah's initiative returned to her and, with the intuition of a person who is on the brink of devastation, she stepped forward and knelt in front of the German soldiers saying "*Gott sei Dank*" (Ger., Thank God) … finally we have met our German brothers! Who would have dreamed of that? What a stroke of luck. We are Volksdeutsche fleeing from the Poles and here luck has brought us to soldiers from the Motherland." We went on to repeat the story of our being Volksdeutsche from this or that camp, claiming we wanted to work for them and help them in return for food and a place to sleep at night. The soldiers gathered round us, speechless, not knowing what to do, finally taking us into the house. Immediately on our entering—in order to prove ourselves and make a good impression—we mended their socks, doing our best to be efficient. The smell of cooking pork met my nostrils;

it was a very strong aroma, and I will remember it till my dying day. The table was set, they were seated around it, and they invited us to join them. Despite my intense hunger, I was unable to eat the pork and I was afraid they might have some suspicion as to the reason I did not eat pork, thus revealing my Jewish identity. I tasted the pork but just could not manage it—I vomited it all. Leah, actually, did eat it and felt stronger. I think that might even have saved her. The table was laden with lots of treats, crowded with many other dishes of food, and we, who were so hungry, ate and ate, hearing them telling jokes about Jews...

With the meal over, the Germans began harassing us. They wanted to fondle us, they joked and talked obscenely. There was no alternative for us but to continue sitting in their company, trembling but laughing artificially. Except for the pork I could not stomach, I do remember how wonderfully we played our part. One of them put his hands on me, and Leah kicked me several times under the table, showing me by means of gestures and blinking, how to stop him flirting with me. Even before that happened, clever Leah took some mud and, with her great initiative, spread it over my face and hers to make us look unattractive and deter the soldiers.

While we were there, the soldiers were constantly on the army phone, receiving irritating reports as to where the border was. And, in the end, they were given the order to move. There was an alarmed-sounding "Jawohl" (Ger., Yes, Sir) and orders barked out. They began busying themselves with arranging backpacks—clear signs of retreat.

They called the Russians "*Der Ivan*" (Ger., the Ivan). And now, on the point of their departure, they turned to us saying, "It is a pity that two such young women should stay here for the 'Ivans'. Come with us to Berlin; do join us. We will take you there on horseback." Indeed, all they had left were their horses. This time Leah excelled more than ever, "Oh for the *Vaterland*! (Ger., Fatherland) Oh for Berlin!" And then she began to cry, complaining of great pains in her leg; sobbing, she said how much we wanted to go there, and really, who knows what the "Ivans" would do to us, but she could not move on because of her leg... She was actually screaming as if gripped with pain, "Oh, I can't take it any longer! Oh my leg, my leg... Take me in the wagon!" And all of this performance was carried on because we really wanted to remain where we were until the Russians arrived, but we could not say so. They tried cajoling us to join them, but in the end—hearing the shots of the Russians actually entering the village—one of the soldiers spat in our direction, and the officer cursed angrily at the sight of Leah wailing, and throwing the door shut behind him, he departed. The other soldiers hurried out after him, leaving us to ourselves.

By dawn the Germans had vanished.

As soon as the Germans had left, local inhabitants and refugees, looking for a place to hide, entered the house. Among them was one old woman, a Polish gentile, who collected the remains of food left by the fleeing Germans, crumbling dry bread into a piping hot liquid. She did not offer us anything to eat. "Go to the Germans, you wh...s! " she called out to us. We tried explaining to her, "Grandma, we are not Germans; we were only putting on an act... "

"Jews?" she questioned us. "Cursed be the Jids!"[59] But I think she knew, deep in her heart, that we were Jews and, in the end, she did give us a little food.

For two whole days we hid in that house, with streams of retreating Germans coming into it to rest, to search and

---

59 Derogatory name for Jews.

check, then moving on. During all that time, the convoy of retreating Germans passed through the village, one soldier after another, regiment after regiment. They did not refer to it as "retreating," but rather as "evacuation." In the last stage of the retreat, a particular corps went through, the rearguard, whose objective was to kill anyone left; to destroy everything so not a thing would be left for the enemy. They killed the cows and other cattle with spears and long bayonets and prodded at piles of straw in granaries and mattresses to find whoever was hiding under them.

That same Polish gentile woman hid us under two mattresses. We heard the Germans entering the house, beating with their bayonets and stabbing them into different places, but they did not discover us. After they had gone away, we emerged from our hiding place and heard that the Russians had arrived.

I remember picking a flower from the garden and presenting it to the first Russian soldier I saw as a gesture of appreciation of being freed. We were so happy then. We thought—here was the beginning of a new life.

We were not aware of the fact that the Russians walking in the lead were completely drunk, perhaps because of their dangerous mission. We realized this only later: they were so inebriated that they were literally falling over.

New problems began with our telling the Russians that we were Jewish. That was a mistake—they did not believe us! We unraveled the patches we had sewn onto our coats, showing them the Star of David stamp—and despite everything, they arrested us. They claimed that, if we had survived, it must be a sign we had collaborated with the Germans. That evening we lay down to sleep in the same house that had previously accommodated Gestapo headquarters, and we could hear how those same drunk Russian soldiers were planning to "share us"—Leah and myself—that very night. Happy to have been able to understand the language spoken, we surreptitiously crept out of the house and got away. Our luck was that they did not see us leaving. We hid until light dawned and then began walking eastward—in the direction of the region, which had already been freed by the Russians. We kept on walking. Once again, we were trampling through snow, with neither direction nor aim. We knew we had no choice but to walk on—hungry and unwashed, our clothes in tatters and our feet wrapped in rags. Night fell once again, daylight dawned anew, still many more days and many nights passed; and we continued to walk, two Lithuanian girls returning home. We passed villages and deserted towns; secretly we looked in vain for Jews, and Jews were nowhere.

As long as the Germans controlled the region, our aim had been to conceal the fact that we wanted to go eastward—to avoid arousing suspicion in the minds of the retreating Germans in light of our refusal to advance westward with the torrent of people, and yet still remain in the same place, awaiting the arrival of the Russians. Even so, to stay at the front itself would be dangerous: a battle was almost incessantly being fought there. We tried not to stand out as people who did not belong there in the area, we did not join the Germans in their march westward and we continued to be in locations the Russians had not yet reached. On we walked, treading the same territory, moving but not moving on and advancing just a little further toward the unknown.

But how many kilometers could we possibly walk in a day? If we were lucky, we would stop a cart and clamber onto it. The problem was that everyone was streaming in the direction of Germany, meaning there was little transport moving in the opposite direction, and we were forced to go on foot a great deal. We would walk a few kilometers and then get caught and we would be imprisoned.

The Brichah—The Escape

We spent time in six different prisons. We walked on and were detained, walked again and were detained once more. Every time we were caught, the Russians refused to believe that we were Jewish. They thought we were spies. Oh, the stories were endless. It would take them time to find someone who could speak a little Yiddish, the person would interrogate us—and then, the next day, we would be released but without any documentation. If they had only given us some piece of paper stating we had already been imprisoned and interrogated, we could have moved on; but no... other Russians, who knew nothing about us, would imprison us once more and, so, on it went. We were in jails together with Russian deserters, with German prisoners, and with criminal offenders. They weren't real jails, rather improvised quarters, with men and women in mixed quarters.

The Russian secret police, the NKVD, was in the habit of carrying out their interrogations at night. And we, who were not aware of that, were afraid. We were terrified of the night, still from the time of the Germans. We were mostly afraid of being raped. One night, when Leah and I were bundled up asleep, the interrogators came into our cell, they shone flashlights with strong beams into our faces and called out our names. We did not rise. Although we had been impatiently expecting that moment, knowing we would be able to prove our innocence and our Jewish identity to the interrogators, we nevertheless did not go to the NKVD interrogation because we were afraid they wanted to rape us. We had agreed to jump... we made plans for how they would have to drag us bodily... It was only the next day that we realized what a serious mistake we had made and we even tried to reinitiate the investigation—but they no longer called out our names. The Russian soldier guarding us said, "The fact you did not go to the interrogation proves your guilt! You will soon be exiled to Siberia." We had no choice left but to try to force our way into being questioned. When they returned, calling out names of other people, we attached ourselves to those people, going off to the interrogation under names we had made up. We entered the NKVD interrogation chamber; a Jewish commissar (Communist party official) was there who spoke good Yiddish, and he listened to our story with great sadness; but he told us he would not be able to do very much for us. He released us from prison and we got as far away from there as fast as humanly possible.

We ran, we walked away from there, moving eastwards. In all that time, we saw no Jews. We believed then that only the two of us, Leah and I, were the sole survivors of European Jewry. We trudged on and on. On one occasion we sat down to rest in a forest. Leah was leaning against a tree trunk with my head on her lap. We shut our eyes and listened to the forest sounds. "Nechamke," Leah asked "do you think, in spite of all, that there are Jews left in Poland and that this whole episode will come to an end?" "There will be no end to it... *Es wet nicht sein kein soff* (Yid., there can be no end).—"The end has already come," a broken Jewish voice answered from the thick of the forest. We both jumped up on the spot. A strange creature emerged from beyond a thicket of bushes: he was clothed in colored pieces of fabric, his feet wrapped in rags, a deranged look in his eyes, his hair disheveled, his beard bristly, his nails long and dirty... like a wild animal... We were more afraid of him than we were of the Russians.

"*Yiddische tochter?*" (Yid., Jewish daughters), he asked, his face distorted.

"We are Jews," I answered, "looking for other Jews."

"*Schwesters—ich bin der achron hayehudim, und ihr seit meine Gast* (Yid., sisters— I am the last Jew and you are guests in my house). Welcome." He took us with him. We knew immediately that the man was not sane, but the moment was so dramatic and the meeting so unusual, that it caused us to forget everything. He was the first Jew we had met since leaving the scenes of horror. The madman showed us heartwarming hospitality: he roasted potatoes for us on the embers of his fire, potatoes he had stolen from gentiles; and he hummed Sabbath songs; and we—our voices choking on tears—hummed along with him. Tears were trickling down our faces. We were remembering home.

Later, we met another few Jews, a few more and then a few more... little by little... people who had just emerged from the forests and from hiding places, who really looked like animals; I have no words to describe them. There were pathetic people. There were cripples. There is no describing what we witnessed! We met people who had lost their minds, who had lost limbs, who were half paralyzed; people ill with all sorts of sicknesses resulting from malnutrition, people who were totally unkempt. A rumor that the Russians had arrived had sprouted wings, and as if miraculously, these people had appeared, all coming out at the same time from their hiding places. For days on end we saw them coming forth in a rush and wandering in the direction of the same assembling point; roaming as if from some inner directive toward the same place. The stream of people grew stronger and stronger; all were walking on in silence, immersed in the silence of death, each of them sealed into the privacy of their own mind. This almost surrealistic spectacle—the sight of people bent over, trudging single file, and occasionally, taking into the line another wild-looking character who had burst forth from the edge of the path—this picture is tinted gray in my memory. It was all depicted in shades of gray: the pallor of people's faces, the dust clinging to their hair, the rags they wore, their worn-out shoes covered in mud. Some individuals still had a single, prized possession they had held onto through thick and thin—for example, the gray blanket from the labor camp. On the smoking ruins, passing by the gray armored vehicles of the Wehrmacht[60] damaged by the bombing, there we walked on and on, crushing gray thistles underfoot... a cloak of frost covering everything, and, step by step, we approached Poland which was now freed—covering some of the journey on foot, some in horse-drawn carts. And how did we manage for food? We managed: we stole some from one place, we were given some in another, we entered houses and took whatever was on the table, we begged and asked for food—we did it with no embarrassment... Soldiers would throw us cigarette butts and papers, and I would sit myself down alone in some corner, crumble the cigarette butts, chew the tobacco and spit it out, or I would smoke it after having carefully rolled it into a cigarette paper—and all in order to forget the pains of hunger.

And so, in our tattered rags, barefoot and hungry, Leah and I wended our weary way among forests and villages, through destroyed cities and faulty roads until we reached the snowy, wide open spaces of Poland, a Poland that had been liberated.

---

60 German: "defense force": the unified armed forces of Germany from 1935 to 1945.

It was at the end of January or beginning of February 1945. Chaos prevailed everywhere. Order had not been restored, no laws had been passed and borders had not been determined. Bands of murderers and robbers imposed fear on the people coming and going: they included "White Poles" opposing Soviet rule, German soldiers who had not managed to retreat in time, and criminals simply exploiting the anarchic times to plunder and rob people. What they all had in common was their abysmal hatred of Jews.

Despite the cries of suffering of millions of Jews, whose blood had saturated Polish soil, open and latent antisemitism still continued to raise its ugly head; attacks on Jews were widespread and, more than once, we came across local people who would collect at street corners, glance at us antagonistically, and murmur words of astonishment mixed with deep disappointment, "How many more Jews are there..."

Not far from Lublin,[61] some Jewish women met us, showering us with hugs and kisses and bringing us to their town. There, Chaya-Miriam Scher[62] recognized us; she had

---

61 Following the liberation of Lublin, on July 24, 1944, the city had become an assembly point for survivors from the city and its vicinity, for Jewish partisans in the area east of Lublin, and for Jews who had taken refuge in the Soviet Union at the beginning of the war. Until the liberation of Warsaw in January 1945, Lublin was the provisional capital of Poland, and it was there that central institutions of the surviving Jewish community established themselves.

62 Rebbetzin Chaya-Miriam Schulmann. She was the daughter of Rabbi Yitzchak Isaac Scher, granddaughter of the "Slobodka Grandfather" Rabbi Nathan Tsvi Finkel (a pupil of Rabbi Israel Salanter, founder of the Slobodka Yeshiva). She eventually married Rabbi Mordechai Schulmann, head of the Slobodka Yeshiva.

known Father and was aware that he had been sent to the United States on behalf of the Slobodka Yeshiva. She inserted a few dollars into a challah[63] she had baked for us. The first thing I did was to write down the poem "The Sicarii with the Yellow Star," the poem I had heard in the ghetto, by Shraga Aranowitz, an ABZ member who had perished in the ghetto when it was destroyed;[64] I also wrote a few lines about the ABZ: "Jewish endeavor in the Underground."[65] I did not know then who or what was left in the world or what the future held for me; but I had a need to put my feelings down on paper, to document something and to preserve a memory...

In those very wintry days of 1945, Lublin, which had already been liberated in 1944, was the temporary capital of Poland and a main city: the Polish government that was yet to emerge declared it as its seat; a great many Polish citizens thronged there from Russia within the political framework of repatriation;[66] under the sponsorship of the new regime, the "Central Jewish Committee" was established there with a communal kitchen and a shelter for the needy—"Beit Peretz" (Peretz House). Lublin became the place where the first of the refugees from the liberated camps congregated along with survivors of partisan units and whoever had come out of hiding after weeks and months of concealment in inhuman

---

63 A special braided bread eaten by Jews on the Sabbath and holidays.

64 This has been handed over to the Yad Vashem Archives.

65 This has been handed over to the Yad Vashem Archives.

66 "Return to the Homeland"—a policy adopted by the western armies under the command of General Eisenhower toward displaced persons, and according to which they were permitted to return to the countries in which they had resided before the war.

conditions. With no possessions, hungry, and afflicted with disease, a great many people flocked in the direction of Lublin, cramming into its filthy streets and squares.

What was that invisible strength within us that drew Leah and me, as it had motivated other Jews, and brought us to Lublin? For each one of us—of all those people who had miraculously remained among the living and had been roaming along devious paths—each had been thinking to himself that he must be the last of the Jews on the face of the earth... Was this, perhaps, some inexplicable gravitational force, some kind of intuition of all people or a latent column of fire which had led the children of Israel through the desert?[67] In addition to Beit Peretz, there were another two communal houses in Lublin for receiving refugees, both of which were financed by the Jewish Committee: one was situated at no. 8 Lubratowska Street, the other at 71 Nanartowich Street. Since I was remembered as an energetic ABZ activist in Kovno, both during the Russian regime and in the ghetto, Leah and I were taken to the home in Lubartowska Street, where they housed people who had been in the various Zionist movements and youth groups and were now designated for the "Brichah"[68] with the support of the "Brichah Center." Compared to the other two houses, in which various Jews not affiliated with

---

67 As in "The Exodus from Egypt," as described in the Book of Exodus; this was the departure and emancipation of the Israelite slaves from Egypt. Led by Moses and Aaron, the Hebrew slaves left Egypt to return to the Land of Israel where their forefathers had lived and which God had promised to them. The Exodus forms the basis of the Jewish Passover holiday.

68 Hebrew: escape. Brichah was the body for organizing "illegal" immigration to Palestine after World War II.

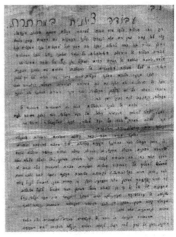

Document written in Hebrew by Nechama Baruchson, a few months after the liberation (March 1945), in which she hurried to record the operation of the Zionist underground in Kovno ghetto

any organization or movement gathered, conditions in our house were more-or-less adequate.

The Brichah movement coalesced and took shape in Lublin in January 1945 in a totally spontaneous way and in the style of an underground Zionist movement, in light of the authorities' refusal to allow Jews free movement. Survivors from among Polish Jewish fighters, including those who had taken part in the Warsaw Ghetto Uprising, joined partisans who had come out of Lithuania. After idealistic discussions between both camps—the Polish and the Lithuanian—in which various political streams and different Zionist movements were represented, it was unanimously agreed that the plan to leave Europe, the Brichah, must proceed and that ways must be found to help the remaining refugees migrate to Israel. "To Eretz Israel"—this was the slogan, and by virtue of it, the refugees were able to surmount all obstacles with unshakeable decisiveness and strong devotion. The Brichah movement was taken to be a symbol of life, a life preserver for saving tens of thousands of Jews who had survived and had nowhere to go. That is how this most wonderful vision started, a kind of Exodus from Egypt in modern garb: a large stream of people, a great multitude made up of groups and individuals, began walking with every intention of reaching the sea.

The Brichah organization took upon itself to take groups of people to the borders and have them met there, to give them food and somewhere to sleep, to advise them as to how to negotiate border crossings, to furnish them with travel documents and permits acceptable in the country taking them in, to clear escape routes that would bring the refugees close to regions occupied by the Americans and the French, and, from there, to get them to Romania (and later, to Italy), to countries with an outlet to the sea.

The method of operation was as follows: in each of the transition countries (Poland, Czechoslovakia, and Hungary) and from the countries where people had stayed, central points of escape were fixed, which were dubbed "depots." Refugees spent a number of days at any of these points, and, from there, were taken to a border area—to another transit station. In one of the border communities there was a holding point, some kind of very small escape headquarters whose function was to organize the transfer, with the assistance of local smugglers. Close to each border station, there was a person posted on behalf of the Brichah whose job was to take the group over the border, delivering it directly into the hands of other Brichah people who would be waiting for them on the other side of the border. The refugees were thus led to the border itself and handed over directly to the receiver, who would transport them in trucks or would accompany them on foot to collecting points, and from there—to a railway station.

Neither Leah nor I had the faintest inkling about the existence of the Brichah, despite the fact that Lublin had been its headquarters in its earliest days and the first point of the exhausting route of the wandering *Borchim* (Heb., escapees), up to their arrival in the Promised Land. Neither were we aware, truth be known, about the very existence of the Jewish Brigade,[69] about soldiers from the Land of Israel who had remained in Europe to help organize the Brichah, or about the British Mandate[70]... We had been totally cut off from things. Nobody had wanted us to know. Until reaching Romania we were ignorant of all this. Without our knowing what was going on, we had been co-opted to the Brichah. We had a vague understanding of what it was but without realizing who the people behind it were; we understood it was a network focusing on getting people over borders and smuggling refugees into Eretz Israel.

---

69 "The Jewish Infantry Brigade Group": a military formation of the British Army that served in Europe during World War II. Although the brigade was formed in 1944, some of its experienced personnel had been employed to act against the Axis powers of Greece, the Middle East, and East Africa. More than 30,000 Jews volunteered to serve in the British Armed Forces, 734 of whom died during the war.

70 During the Mandate period, the British government placed limitations on Jewish immigration to Palestine. These quotas were controversial, particularly in the latter years of British rule. Starting in 1939, Jews organized an illegal immigration effort, known as Aliyah Bet, whereupon tens of thousands of European Jews fled from the Nazis and headed to Palestine in rickety boats. Following the war, 250,000 Jewish refugees were stranded in displaced persons (DP) camps in Europe. Despite the pressure of world opinion, the British maintained the ban on immigration and began imprisoning illegal Jewish immigrants in Cyprus.

Semi-legally or, most often, illegally, we crossed over barbed wire, changed identities, muttered words in languages not our own, used falsified papers, and bought our way out through bribes. Any method was acceptable— provided we would be able to reach the shore from where we were to sail to Eretz Israel for which we had been yearning.

Trains were our means of transport: these were put at the disposal of our network by repatriation institutions; trucks, brought to the Brichah organization by the Jewish Brigade or purchased cheaply from the Allies, bore military license plates and their drivers had army papers. When such a truck crossed into a neighboring country, it was repainted and fitted with different numbers on the license plate and the registration papers were changed as well, totally transforming its identity.

The "Brichniks," those working for the Brichah organization who accompanied us in those trucks were uniformed, posing as American soldiers. It so happened, a few times on our crossing through borders, that border guards saluted those "American officers," the latter playing their role admirably and saluting back with intentional indifference, as if this was a daily routine...

The Brichah was extremely chaotic and totally disorganized. The activists were emissaries from the Jewish Brigade who directed the throng of people toward the sea and who gave the Brichah its unique character. The Brichah, which made an effort to post an emissary at every major transition point on our travel route, consisted of Jewish soldiers from Eretz Israel, who had been drafted in Eretz Israel toward the end of World War II and had served in the British army. They had fought in the last stages of the battles in Italy and took part in the defeat of Hitler and Mussolini. For us, they were the first representatives of the Jewish settlement in Eretz Israel, the first and just about the only people to offer us assistance—

we Holocaust survivors (or as they began to call us "She'erit ha-Pletah"[71])—and to organize our mass escape from Europe.

It was in Lublin that we first met someone from the Jewish Brigade who had the most preliminary contact with the refugees. He did not reveal to us that he was from Eretz Israel; this was forbidden as his activities were secret and dangerous. All he did was to hastily show us his identification badge—a Star of David, the symbol of the Jewish Brigade—and, from that, we vaguely began to comprehend that he represented some organization whose aim was to assist us in some way. We were greatly overcome with emotion. For us, survivors of the camps, in which we had witnessed and had experienced so much, this brief meeting served as a source of encouragement and an incentive to hold onto our will to live and to not give up. We clustered around him, we were restless and excited, finding it difficult to believe our eyes.

We stayed in Poland—only as a transit station—with the purpose of traveling further. At that time, in the beginning stages of the Brichah, the escape route from Poland was through Czechoslovakia and Hungary to Romania (from there we intended to proceed on *aliyah* [Heb., ascent; term for Jewish immigration] to Eretz Israel). The Polish authorities exerted a great deal of pressure against those organizing the escape, the latter being forced to take us through illegal exit routes. From Lublin we were taken southward, toward the Carpathian Mountains and the eastern border of Poland to the border town of Krosno. There, crossing the border was arranged by bribing the Russian soldiers. We had received transfer documents forged with Red Cross stamps and were able to cross over the border along the Carpathian Mountains.

---

71 Hebrew: the Remaining Survivors, a term used for the Jewish survivors of the Nazi Holocaust.

This was one of the most exhausting parts in the episode of our wanderings because of the steep slopes and difficulties in negotiating the passes. Gangs of Ukrainian nationals swarmed the area, carrying out surprise attacks on Jews and slaughtering them mercilessly.

On completing the border crossing, we reached Humenne, a town on the Czech border. In addition to its convenient geographic conditions, courteous Czechoslovakia was beyond wonder. In the town of Humenne, we found shelter in a hospital that a Czech Jewish doctor had established. There, despite Soviet control fraught with much danger, our hearts began to beat with the long-forgotten sense of freedom. We still felt weak, we were dressed in shabby rags, but, for a very short while, we could push away our memories of the immediate past; we forgot about our flight and about the destination to which we were fleeing and took tranquil, pleasurable walks through the beautiful and welcoming streets of the town, with joy in our hearts.

After sojourning in Czechoslovakia for a few days, we moved on to Hungary. We traveled part of the way in tarpaulin-covered trucks but some of the journey was on foot. Young men and women, people of the Brichah organization, under the auspices of the Haganah,[72] walked with us prior to our entering each new country, teaching us how to conduct ourselves and what to say in case we were apprehended. They taught us basic vocabulary in the language of that place; words such as "hello," "thank you," "please," and other expressions we might need to get along. We received guidance as to the region of that specific country: its geographical location on the

---

72 Heb., the Defense, the Jewish paramilitary organization in the British Mandate of Palestine from 1920 to 1948, which later became the core of the Israel Defense Forces.

map of Europe, its leaders, when it was captured and when it was freed, the colors of its flag, local currency... and every time we were about to enter a new country we were given "new" names; that is how we took on the false identities of people of different nationalities. For example, upon entering Hungary, I was called Mostar.

On the Hungarian-Romanian border we passed through Tokaj (a gorgeous small town in Hungary, famous for its wine) to Oradea Mare, where we returned to our real identity—that is, to being Jewish refugees—and we even had to prove the authenticity of our identity before a representative of the Romanian Border Control Authorities, a local Jewish man whose job it was to test our knowledge. On receiving his approval, we went through the routine procedures customary for all kinds of refugees at that time, with no exceptions, finally receiving permission for the convoy of fugitives to continue on its way. The Red Cross ran the refugee camp in the border town of Oradea Mare, which was situated on river banks. The local Jewish community put two buildings at our disposal and supplied us with whatever we needed. After a few days rest we proceeded to the escape point at Cluj, from where we were supposed to set sail for Eretz Israel via Constanta. We were then congregated at a "*Hachshara* Kibbutz,"[73] and in expectation and readiness, awaited the day when we would board the boat.

In Romania, the Brichah now had proper headquarters. We met a lot of survivors there, friends and acquaintances

---

73 Hebrew: the *kibbutzim* or *chavot hachshara* (training farms) were places where refugees collected, mostly in rural towns, with the population made up of various people who had been in Zionist youth movements. They were run by a secretariat elected by members at a general meeting.

from Kovno, from the ABZ and from our school, such as Sara Liebensohn. Words cannot describe the excitement and joy on meeting someone we knew... "Are you alive?" we would ask each other. Hesitatingly, we would look at and examine each other, as if not believing our eyes, as if the person standing there was a ghost that had returned to the land of the living. We felt we had reached a safe haven.

From Oradea Mare we were moved to Bucharest. The war seemed to have totally passed it by: at night, streetlights flickered in the squares and in the daytime everything was to be seen in abundance wherever you turned. We refugees were accommodated in a large house on a pleasant street near a park—no. 5 Nipon St.—and the Joint[74] provided us with a little money to buy ourselves clothes. In spite of the fact that both Leah and I were among those who been shepherded there, we nevertheless had some standing, because we spoke Hebrew, some of the people had known our parents and family, and some people knew I had been active in the ABZ. In addition, they knew we had a father in America [since 1939], so we received many marriage proposals...

As time went on, we began to realize that our hopes of getting to Israel quickly from the port town of Constanta would not materialize as soon as we had expected. During all that time there was concern that the Russians would try to thwart our plans for escaping to Eretz Israel and would bring the Iron Curtain[75] down on us. It became known that the Russians were about to reinforce their troops in Romania in

---

74 American Jewish Joint Distribution Committee (JDC), a United States Jewish charitable organization founded in 1914.

75 The symbolic, ideological, and physical boundary dividing Europe into two separate areas from the end of World War II until the end of the Cold War, c. 1945 to 1991.

order to expand their influence and complete their annexation of Romania to Soviet control. Before we might once again find ourselves under Soviet occupation, from which we had fled, it was therefore decided to evacuate us from Romanian soil, and, as quickly as possible, to cross the border in the direction of Italy, in the hope that there we would be able to realize our aspirations and board a boat to Eretz Israel. The evacuation from Romania was planned extremely efficiently and carried out in strictest secrecy so as not to arouse any suspicion in the eyes of the NKVD. We were transported in railway carriages from Bucharest to the town of Alba Iulia, close to the Hungarian border, and from there we were taken, by means of a bribe, to Budapest.

Budapest had been massively bombed during the war—mainly Buda; whereas we were accommodated in the other section of the city, in Pest. There we stayed in deserted schools or large apartments, we were served a hot meal, rested for a few days from the strain of traveling, and were able to collect our strength for the next leg of our journey.

From there we made our way to Austria. Again we were drilled in what to say should we be caught. Once more we learned a few words in the language of the country we were about to enter clandestinely. And again, we familiarized ourselves with the local currency. This whole procedure had become over-familiar, but we were, nevertheless, still afraid. We did not know who to be afraid of; we did not know who would stop us. Our fear of everyone had turned into one web of confusion: the Russians? The British? The Germans? Nothing could be clarified as far as we were concerned.

The train sped on through the Hungarian plains in the direction of Austria among wonderfully worked lands—checkered plots of golden crops, strips of green vineyards, endless squares of orchards, and fields of vegetables. Snowy white, cackling geese scampered around between sheds, and herds of sheep wandered up and down the mountain slopes to the strains of the pipe of a barefoot shepherd. Dozens of refugees like us were packed into the carriages—each person with his or her meager bundle, the only remaining luggage from one's life, and a quiver of memories… One just had to take care not to trip and fall on this shaking, rolling journey… just to be sure to hold onto any possible projection or protrusion, even to hang onto windows and door frames, just to cling for all you were worth to the carriage ceiling without looking down or to the sides—with the sole intention of getting across the border and arriving at the last Brichah stop, Italy, on the way to our yearned-for destination, Eretz Israel. The rattling of iron rings and the whistling of the locomotive aroused in us memories from the depths of the not-very-distant past. Indeed, not all transports are the same…

When our train from Budapest arrived, a problem arose as to how to get us out of the Russian-occupied zone and into one of the Western-occupied regions, so we could later get to Italy and, from there, join Aliyah Bet[76] to Eretz Israel. We traveled by train from Vienna to Semmering, a town on the border between the Russian- and British-occupied zones, walked three kilometers to the British train, and from there, continued on to Graz, which had become the first large concentration point of the Brichah in Austria.

In Graz, trucks belonging to the Brigade met us, taking us to a small house in Innsbruck, a snow-covered holiday resort high up in the Alps. We traveled in trucks accompanied by

---

76 Hebrew: abbreviation for *Aliyah Bilti Legalit*, the code name given to "illegal" immigration by Jews to Eretz Israel during the British mandate of Palestine in violation of British restrictions against such immigration.

soldiers of the Brigade disguised as American soldiers, and there were false passports ready for us in which we were defined as "former prisoners from concentration camps."

Here, in the Tyrol Mountain region, we also needed to exercise caution as the British Secret Police patrolled the length of the Austro-Italian border in order to prevent Jewish refugees from entering Italy. The Brenner Pass— the place where Adolf Hitler and Italian leader Benito Mussolini had met on March 18, 1940, to publicly celebrate their pact—had been officially closed and was being stringently guarded by British, French, American, and Italian forces; Brichah organizers needed to operate in a completely "shady" fashion (using forged papers, new names and trucks with false license plates, surreptitiously crossing borders at night, paying off border guards, etc.).

Following endless hassle and much tension, the French permitted us to cross the French barrier on the Austrian border on our way to Italy—it seems they were touched by our collective passport defining us as "former prisoners of concentration camps." But we still spent long, tense hours waiting while they checked our transit papers, with the border guards having nerve-racking telephone conversations with their superiors, for the signal to move on...

All I remember after that is that we ran as fast as we could, that it was mountainous—the Alps were covered in snow—and we were very afraid of being caught. We literally stole our way across the border. We walked along narrow mountain paths in single file; on paths permanently covered with snow; our few possessions on our backs, our cups tied with string to our backpacks. There was a steep incline and people and their luggage slipped down it... With great hardship and huge physical exertion, we made our way and entered the dense, dark, tangled forest... Branches scratched our faces and we slipped on piles of pine needles here and there. Close to the

Italian border itself trucks from the Brichah organization were waiting for us.

People from the Brichah whispered their instructions in Yiddish and in Hebrew and pushed us onto the trucks as quickly as possible. We were crowded together in the vehicles along with all the possessions that we owned... We traveled toward the Italian border; but would we manage to cross it? They concealed us in the trucks by covering us with huge tarpaulins. We drove on in absolute darkness, crammed close to each other and shivering from cold and for fear of being caught. Incidentally, the dollars Chaya Miriam Scher had given us in secret, as related above, were put into the communal pot, which would be handy to bribe policemen and border guards if we were caught.

When the tarpaulins were removed and we were let out of the trucks, we had no idea where we were. Had we been caught in some dangerous location, only to immediately be sent back to the border we had just crossed, or had we reached the country of our destination—Italy? A few long moments passed before I realized what was going on. Yes, we had arrived in Italy, in Tarvisio...

Soldiers from the Brigade helped us alight from the trucks—strong Eretz Israel soldiers wearing the Star of David, the Jewish Brigade insignia, on their khaki uniforms, not as a degrading emblem or as a sign of shame, but with a sense of pride and as an army identification badge. They carried us—weak and excited—on their shoulders, dried the tears from our cheeks, kissed us, gave us chocolate, and sang "*Hatikvah*" in our honor. That is where we first heard Sabra[77] Hebrew, real spoken Hebrew...

---

77 Hebrew: prickly pear. The sabra is a prickly fruit-bearing plant. The analogy is used to describe people born in Israel, considered to be "rough" on the outside but sweet on the inside

And that was the most exciting and beautiful moment, the one that made surviving so worthwhile.

In Italy, the final stop as far as the Brichah Organization was concerned and the main collection point for transferring the Remaining Survivors (defined from here on, according to Palestine British Mandate authorities, as Illegal Immigrants) to Eretz Israel, we turned from fugitives into displaced persons.

Responsibility for us was assumed by the Mossad l'Aliyah Bet,[78] whose job it was to obtain ships to sail to Eretz Israel, to equip them with everything that was needed, to make sure the refugees boarded them, and to bring them safely to the shores of Eretz Israel—either legally, for example by providing "certificates,"[79] or illegally, by infiltrating the "illegal" immigrants into the country, which was what happened in most cases. The Mossad L'Aliyah Bet consisted of soldiers from Jewish units of the British army and of emissaries from Eretz Israel.

Magenta was our next stop after Tarvisio. We spent over three months there at a Hachshara farm where we learned about Eretz Israel and Zionism. After that, we were moved to Milan, to no. 5 Via Unione St., a center where a large number of refugees were gathered prior to leaving for Eretz Israel. We lived there for a period of time; we were fourteen people, men and women, all sleeping in one room.

---

78 Hebrew: The Institute for "Illegal" Immigration, a branch of the Haganah that operated to facilitate Jewish immigration into British Mandate of Palestine, in violation of unilateral British restrictions. It operated from 1938 until the founding of the State of Israel.

79 Official entry visas to Israel issued by the British authorities during the time of the British Mandate in Palestine.

One day, Leah and I were sitting in the huge dining room at Via Unione when I suddenly felt someone standing behind me, covering my eyes with his hands. "Guess who it is, *wus is dus* (Yid., What is it)?" he asked. I did not manage to identify him. After my patience had run out, he took his hands away and there I saw Azriel Levy of the ABZ standing in front of me.

"Are you alive?" I asked him, our way of turning to someone we knew from before, now seeing him again after the war; and he answered "I have just arrived from Germany... I did survive... Shlomo is alive!" Leah and I heard what he said about Shlomo our brother and just sat there stunned... It is difficult today to describe what we felt at that moment: we had gone through so many hard times. Today, looking back, I would imagine our emotions were a bit dulled; for if not, there was no way we could have survived all we had suffered. We received the news and began to digest it... we did not weep. For the whole duration of the Holocaust I did not cry, not even once. To this very day, I have no tears; that is one of the symptoms of being a Holocaust survivor.

We started questioning Azriel about Shlomo. We learned that after the women and men had been separated at the Tiegenhof railway station and after they had sent the women to Stutthof, Shlomo and the other men were taken away from Kovno to Kaufering—a town in the Landsberg region in Bavaria— one of eleven sub-camps that were affiliated with the Dachau concentration camp.

Just a few days after Azriel had met us, Shlomo appeared—a handsome young man, tall and thin—and he spoke fluent Hebrew. I am unable to describe this reunion in words. There is simply something blocking my memory that keeps me from recalling what happened at that very moment. I do remember that at this first meeting he gave me a ribbon, a black ribbon that SS officers had worn as an armband. Shlomo had removed

Nechama (on the right),
Shlomo, and Leah Baruchson
in Italy, after their reunion
following the liberation

it from an SS man he had killed out of vengeance at the end of the war. Shlomo also gave me his Dachau identity tag.

Shlomo had been appointed to be a group leader for displaced persons being prepared for their *aliyah* to Israel.

In Milan, I worked in the Eretz Israel office headed by Dr. Linder. The branch was at no. 5 Via Unione St., and it functioned legally, with no need for secrecy. My job was to travel to the north of Italy, to centers where refugees were staying and to record the number of people there and their details. On my return to Milan after each of those journeys, I would pass the lists on to the relevant people so that they could plan more precisely for the *ha'apala*:[80] how many ships had to be purchased and who should receive immigration permits first—for among the many refugees there were many children, elderly, sick and feeble people who had been given second-level priority.

---

80 Hebrew, term for illegal immigration to Israel toward the end of the British mandate period.

I was living in a hotel with another friend, and, afterwards, at the house of an elderly Italian woman in the Courson da Finanza. She was constantly feeding us. The Eretz Israel office paid our rent.

It took me a month or two to learn Italian. When my elderly landlady was asked where I was, she would always answer, "She is on the trains," for that was the means of transportation I used. I especially liked spending my free time sitting in cafes with soldiers from the Brigade, and, thanks to the Italian that rolled off my tongue and my facial features, they called me "the Italian girl."

Through the Red Cross, we managed to make some contact with Father—a letter with a picture.

People wanting to make *aliyah* to Israel had to wait their turn. To expedite Leah and Shlomo's *aliyah* and enable them to receive their *aliyah* certificates faster, I decided to stay in Italy for a year to continue working for the Eretz Israel office. Apart from that, one of the three of us had to travel to America to accompany Father on his journey to Eretz Israel; age was on my side: I was under twenty-one, and that being the case, I was eligible at that time to receive an unlimited visa to the United States.

At some time between September and mid-October 1945, Shlomo and Leah were appointed to be group leaders at a *hachshara* farm of the Dror movement near the harbor town of Bari in the south of Italy. On October 16, 1945, they were taken in a fisherman's boat to the "illegal" immigration ship, *Pietro B*, and, on October 22, 1945, they reached Rishpon beach in Eretz Israel together with another 172 *ma'apilim* ("illegal immigrants"). From there they were taken the next day to Kibbutz Shefayim.

Only on May 17, 1946, was I able to sail on the *John McKay* from Italy to the United States to meet Father. Until our *aliyah* to Israel together in July 1947, I taught at the Baltimore Jewish School where Neuhaus, our admired leader from the Batia Movement, was principal... Father cried like a child when he saw the marks on my back from whippings I had received at the Hecht forced-labor camp near Stutthof and he took me to a doctor. I was fed vitamins and a variety of foods since I was weak, gaunt, and anemic; standing in front of my class of American girls, I had to wear red lipstick and hold my peace. Nobody there wanted to hear about the Holocaust...

In the meantime, Leah had married in Israel and I spoke to her by phone to congratulate her. As a wedding present, I sent her a recording of myself singing Rachel's[81] song, "*Ve-UIai Lo Hayu ha-Devarim me-Olam*" (And perhaps these things never took place), with the rolling *r* in my broken voice...

---

81 Also known as "Rachel the Poetess"; Rachel Bluwstein Sela (Sept. 20, 1890–April 4, 1931), a writer of lyrical Hebrew poetry. Most other poetry is set in the pastoral countryside of Eretz Israel.

PART II

Between Here and There 1954–1992

Here: A Half-Sabra (1954–1968)

Ramat Gan—a beautiful garden city with streets green with tamarisk, ficus, and olive trees. Spacious gardens are adorned with goldfish ponds and strewn with flowerbeds. Orchards of fruit-bearing trees abound; bees dart and sparrows fly about in the clean, azure air. You are to be my home! That is the place God had chosen for Tzipora-Feige's granddaughter to be born.

I don't exactly see myself as the result of pure love but as the integration of two lost souls, desperate to cut a path for themselves among the century's waves of fate that had been forced upon them, two souls who had attached themselves to each other and formed an alliance to stick together, jointly thrusting a stake into the ground of Eretz Israel.

In World War II he[82] fought with the Australian army against Japan, Nazi Germany's ally, in the coarse, tangled jungles of Burma; he had arrived in Israel with Machal,[83] and under the pseudonym of "Abie the Australian," was the main

---

82 My father, Abraham Simcha Kaufman.
83 Hebrew acronym for "'Volunteers from Outside of Israel" used to describe both Jewish and non-Jewish volunteers who came to Israel to fight Israel's War of Independence. Approximately 4,000 Machal volunteers took part in the war in support of Israel.

mortar man of the Irgun[84] in the occupation of the Manshiyya neighborhood on the outskirts of Tel Aviv-Jaffa.[85]

And who is she? She[86] is the descendent of a family of rabbis from Kovno, silent about her Zionist beliefs for fear of their becoming known to Soviet authorities or to her strict father, a rabbi. It is she who had relentlessly planned her escape from home and illegal immigration to Eretz Israel—however, in the end, a dreadful chasm gapes open at her feet and she finds herself wearing the yellow star, transported in cattle cars from camp to camp, finally wandering throughout war-torn Europe. Her next-to-last stop is the Brenner Pass on the Italian-Austrian border; her final stop is Italy, with the Brichah Organization.

And who am I? I am the pebble that has been thrown into the waters of the artificial lake of the National Park of Ramat Gan, scaring away the fish and creating concentric circles of identities. I am a Ramat Gan citizen, an Israeli, and a Jew, and also, just as my mother, from "There"—and the "There" is divided into "before the war"—ice-skating on the frozen river, sweet Yiddish laughter accentuated with rolled *r*s; "during the War" is time on "another planet,"[87] and "after the War"—our

---

84 Abbreviated version of "Ha-Irgun ha-Tzevai ha-Leumi be-Eretz Yisra'el" (National Military Organization in the Land of Israel), a militant Zionist group operating in Palestine from 1931 to 1948, the armed expression of the ideology of Revisionist Zionism as conceived by Ze'ev Jabotinsky.

85 The Irgun's capture of Manshiyya, following a tough battle, leading to the capture of Jaffa, took place at the end of April 1948.

86 My mother, Nechama (Baruchson) Kaufman.

87 An assertion made by Yehiel Dinur (Katzetnik) during the Eichmann trial (1961), referring to the Auschwitz extermination camp and the Holocaust in general as a "universe in which conventional rules and customs of human civilization did not apply."

sailing to Eretz Israel as numbed souls, creeping on frozen toes, bent and low-spirited from a sense of alienation and from memories; and, to make matters worse, they were called—no, WE were called *sabonim* (soaps);[88] they pointed at us with rebuke, saying "They, those people, put us to shame. They went as sheep to slaughter."

The first circle is Ramat Gan: a house where both walls and roof are whitewashed, the stairwell is a shade of pink, and the heavy, massive wooden entrance door, its gray paint beginning to peel away, is always held wide open by a small stone placed at its side. In the yard are a carob and a pine tree, small bushes, Goliath the dog's kennel, and the rusty nozzle of a sprinkler. In summer, after the yard has been raked and watered, it is shady, cool, and fresh out there; then Mother brings out a green-colored Formica table "groaning" under the weight of bowls of red plums and apricots. I am a little girl wearing very short, frilly pants made of red fabric dotted in white. I have a wooden cart Father built by himself, and in it are my dolls—Tzilli and Gilli—whom I am taking for a walk to the other side of the yard. I am stepping on concrete tiles scattered over the dusty walkway, I cross under the pergola draped with flowering oleander near a dripping tap, avoiding the pine grove, finally walking down the sloping path; I knock on Tammy's window to make sure she wakes up. Here we play at having a grocery store, just like the one in the "Rynek" (Polish/Lithuanian marketplace) that was in a

---

88 A widespread, highly derogatory slang expression used by native-born Israelis referring to Holocaust survivors, reflecting the general belief that the Nazis used the bodies of murdered Jews to produce soap and expressing the contempt native-born Israelis felt toward the survivors.

shtetl;[89] we weigh dry leaves as if they were pickled herrings and pieces of cheese and display things on the back of rough scaffolding—using medicine bottles filled with raspberry juice as if they were bottles of oil and juice.

In the afternoons, all the neighborhood children would congregate near the booth used by the policeman positioned opposite the building of the Russian embassy, from which the police keep an eye on all who enter and leave it. Wearing our blue gym pants tied with elastic, sandals, and *kova tembel*,[90] we met there to play and quarrel; we would divide into groups of boys and girls, or smaller and bigger children, or pupils from one school against those of another; and we would play hide-and-seek and a game we called "one-two-three pickled herring." I find running fast difficult. I am thin and frail, and my legs barely carry out the orders I give them. In the neighborhood I am disparagingly called "the ghetto girl."

Tammy holds my hand tightly in hers and drags me along with all her might in the direction of the hiding place, "Come on. Get a move on." She pushes me and hurls me into a spot under the bushes. I am terribly afraid and anxious of being discovered, and burst into choked laughter from all the tension. Tammy pinches me on my thighs and arms and the pinching becomes more and more painful, just as when they pinched the

---

89 Yiddish: small town with a large Jewish population in pre-Holocaust central and eastern Europe.

90 Hebrew: "fool's hat," a bucket hat that dates back to the beginning of the Israeli War of Independence. Israeli soldiers needed to protect their heads from the hot sun. At first, they used the Arab keffiyeh but then realized the importance of distinguishing themselves from Arab soldiers. They used a local heavy-duty fabric for these simple hats.

baby in the *maline* below Block C so his crying would not give away the people hiding there from the Germans. And I keep on laughing until I can no longer restrain myself and a yellow trickle of urine starts to drip down, streaming onto the earth. After the game, our heads perspiring, we sneak into Shmulik's yard to drink some water from his sprinkler. All we need now, God forbid, is for one of his big brothers to catch us...

By now I know that on Mondays Russian embassy personnel with their wives always meet together to sing songs and choral music. Apart from our radio set that is always tuned to "*Ha-Mador le-Chipus Kerovim*,"[91] we have no record player or transistor radio for listening to music. After supper and my shower, I, in my striped pajamas, would slip to the windowsill facing the embassy and listen intently to the piano accompanying the singing. The men sing in thunderous bass tones like a troupe of Cossack cavaliers galloping on horses; the women sing in soprano voices that are tender and pure, flowing and sad. And I, with tears in my eyes for no obvious reason, learn the melody and sing along in la-la-la. My eyes close. In my dreams I am floating, winging my way "There," far away and isolated... to the small town on the banks of the Vilija River, to the "bim-bam-bom" of Hasidic tunes. But even dreaming has limitations on what is permissible. I am riddled with guilt feelings mixed with a sense of treachery: I, the tall Sabra girl, trampling barefoot around the gravelly hills in the daytime, among broom bushes and prickly pear cactus, floating her way into the night, giving flight to a precious and imprisoned bird, I am roaming "There"—to 9 Paneriu St.

---

91 Hebrew, "Search Bureau for Missing Relatives," a popular radio program in Israel that assisted Holocaust survivors in their search for missing relatives.

At 4 a.m. the milkman arrives, riding his tricycle with rows
of bottles hanging off the handlebars. He will soon reach our
doorstep to deposit four glass bottles full of sweet, fresh milk.
Once they have been emptied, Mother will wash them and
they will be returned empty to the doorstep, to be replaced by
full bottles. At the end of the month, the milkman, his bristly
beard adorned with silver streaks, will come along wearing
his brown peaked cap. When he takes a seat in an armchair
in the hall, he will roll up his shirt sleeves a little, by chance
revealing a number from Auschwitz tattooed on his arm, will
take out a gold ballpoint pen refill, and will mutter the amount
owed to him in almost inaudible Yiddish. He is one of the
survivors from "There"...

It is morning. My Sabra image is aroused to the sound of
chirping birds. The air is cold and fresh; one could cut the
silence into thin slices of serenity and boast in the glory of
the *tallitot*[92] of those passing on their way to the synagogue
for *Shacharit* (morning) prayers. At exactly six o'clock Mrs.
Pollack, the Yekkete,[93] waters her flowerboxes of geranium
and turns on her radio. Aristocratic, classical strains foreign
to our ears, to us the "Ostjuden," fill the air. Music by Wagner
and R. Strauss is not broadcast...

---

92 Hebrew: prayer shawls worn by men during morning prayer
    services, at the reading of the Torah, on Yom Kippur and other
    holidays.

93 Generally jovial, somewhat derogatory term referring to Jews
    from Germany and Austria. The term "Yekke" derives from the
    German word for jacket—*Jacke*. According to what is recounted,
    German Jews arrived in British Palestine of the Mandatory
    Period wearing suit jackets and, despite the heat and blazing
    sun, were reputed to have worn their jackets, regardless.

My brown leather satchel, closed with two silver buckles, hangs on my back from two wide straps; my cloth food-bag, pulled shut at the top with a piece of elastic, has my name embroidered on it in red and yellow—in it there is a thinly sliced sandwich wrapped in wax paper, a piece of fruit, and a starched napkin; I am wearing a green school uniform, the color befitting Ramat Gan, the garden city. Mother waves goodbye to me from the balcony, blowing me kisses into the air. It is a quarter to eight and I make my way to school.

There we are welcomed by loudspeakers warming our hearts with wonderful Israeli songs: "*Shibbolet ba-Sadeh Kor'ah ba-Ru'ah me-Omes Gar'inim ki Rav*" (An Ear of Corn in the Field Bows Down in the Wind, Laden with So Many Seeds), "*Nitzanim Nir'u Nir'u ba-Aretz*" (Buds Have Been Seen, Have Been Seen in the Land), "*Sovi, Sovi Mamterah*" (Turn, Turn, Water Sprinkler). Among us there are rich and poor, Europeans and Sephardim, new immigrants and Sabras who are children of Sabras, both dark- and pale-skinned; and now we are all placed in this verdant melting-pot, blending with the closed fist of uncompromising Sabra pride. Every day we vow, we pledge ourselves anew to Mother Earth in the words of the song: "*Mah Od Lo Natamt ve-Nitten*" (What Have We Not Yet Given and We Will Give); with bright eyes we sing in Yemenite, Romanian, Polish, and Yiddish accents, "We will clothe you in a robe of concrete and cement and will sew you carpets from gardens." Again and again we give thanks, but not to God in heaven (for this is not fitting for the activist Sabra spirit) but to the daring Palmachniks (but, as already mentioned, Father was a member of the Irgun and, according to what our teacher Ruth had to say, this, unfortunately, did not count[94])

---

94 Views on the Irgun have been as disparate as on any other political topic in Israeli society. Leaders within the mainstream

and to the steadfast *ma'apilim*. However, according to Teacher
Ruth, one was never to mention "those people," the "Surviving
Remnant" who had gone "like sheep to the slaughter."[95] We
are making the wilderness bloom: using our little hands to dig
holes in the sand for dainty seedlings and inserting coins into
the white and blue collection box of the Keren Kayemet Le
Yisrael,[96] redeeming *"dunam po ve-dunam sham."*[97]

"Who is here? Father is here." We are learning the alphabet
and reading from a loose-leaf folder. And on completing the
"Aleph Bet" (the Hebrew alphabet), what did we learn to
sing? *"Oyfn pripetshik brent a fayerl"*[98] Our teacher, Ruth,
who detested the "exile mentality" of Diaspora Jews, was
daring enough to teach us a song from "There," however,
not in Yiddish—the language of "Those" from "There"
and "Then," which had existed before the Holocaust—but
translated into Hebrew, "On the hearth a little fire burns /
And the room is warm / And the rabbi teaches little children /
Their Aleph Beis… " But I could sense it was "There," in a

Jewish Agency, the Haganah, and the Histadrut, as well as the
British authorities, routinely condemned Irgun operations as
terrorist and branded it an illegal organization as a result of the
group's attacks on civilian targets.

95 For quite a few years, due to ignorance and a lack of understanding,
arrogant native-born Israelis tended to be ashamed and critical
of Holocaust survivors for not having fought the Nazis and their
collaborators. Holocaust survivors were labeled "trash" and
"human debris" by many members of the Israeli establishment.

96 Hebrew: The Jewish National Fund, founded in 1901 to buy and
develop land in Palestine (later Israel) for Jewish settlement.

97 This slogan of "an acre here and an acre there," which prevailed
during the 1940s and 1950s, spoke of the redemption of land.
(A dunam equals 1000 square meters, that is, one-quarter acre.)

98 A famous Yiddish song sung by eastern European Jews.

house above the banks of the Vilija and Nemunas rivers. I had not, however, told even my closest friends that in our home, when Father and Mother did not want me to understand their conversation, they would speak Yiddish among themselves. Oh, how un-Sabra, un-Israeli and so shameful!

A slice of rye bread with *grivalach* (Yid., goose fat), chicken soup with soup almonds, a chicken *pulke* (Yid., thigh), rice with *tsimmes* (Yid., sweetened, cooked carrots), *compote* (stewed dried fruit). I must be quick to finish my lunch. I have a ballet lesson with Helena, a Polish Jew. To the sounds of Yuri the accompanist's accordion, we assume the various positions, the splits, and half-handstands. When my turn arrives, I just stand there; but I am to make any type of half-handstand. I perform some kind of movement like someone swimming on dry land; I bend down on my knees, lean on my hands, and then—bend each leg and spin around as if I had really performed a half-handstand... and everyone laughs.

Far from Helena's deafening shrieks and the jeering of the pupils around me, the restrained and estranged laughing, as that of gentle young ladies, I am carried away on the wings of fantasy, swept into sweet illusion suggesting that here I was leaping and hovering in the air, having stood on my hands with my legs stretched heavenward like a ballerina whose shapely body wears a shimmering leotard and a short, short pink lace tutu. Like Ariella the French girl and Anat with her long, blond ponytail flowing down over her shoulders, her hair tied with a narrow, red velvet ribbon. "Then" and "There" on the *rampa*[99] they would have passed the *Selektion*... but I...

---

99 Railway platform (ramp) located in Auschwitz II/Birkenau where selections were held after people were unloaded from trains. The term was used in general for the railway platforms for trains arriving at any given concentration or extermination camp.

well, that's me... stiff and unemotional... the daughter of a "soap" and of a father who was in the wrong underground movement... I am hunched over and bent, and Helena—just like an old Kapo—screams her lungs out to the point that the veins in her neck swell up like those of an angry goose, "Stand up straight again!"

The lesson ends. Daydreaming, and cut off in my silence, I wrap myself in my gray rubber poncho on which small children holding umbrellas are printed in maroon. A hood shields my face from the pouring rain which is puncturing the darkness and has begun to beat down on us in the meantime. I am wearing red galoshes and off I dash home. Running downhill is easier...

We have a "Friedmann" kerosene heater at home; the kerosene absorbed into the wick gives off a stench. Comfortable warmth is spreading through the house. On the aluminum grid covering the wick we place a row of potatoes to roast as well as a kettle of water to keep the air from becoming too dry and, at the same time, to have boiling water ready for piping hot tea. Eventually, Mother brings me to bed, covering me with a thick quilt. "Then and There, in that world which once existed and is no more, Helena was a prima ballerina. In Mengele's[100] camp they performed experiments on her and there she died," my mother tells me and gives me a good night kiss.

It is Thursday. I am roused from sleep by Subia's voice; she is our cleaning lady and she comes to us once a week from Rosh

---

100   Josef Mengele was a German SS officer and a physician in the German Nazi concentration camp of Auschwitz-Birkenau. He supervised the selection of prisoners arriving in transports, determining who was to be killed and who was to be a forced laborer. He performed human experiments on camp inmates.

Ha'Ayin.[101] I find it difficult to converse with her as she only
has a smattering of words in Hebrew and those are garbled
in a heavy Yemenite accent. She wears traditional Yemenite
clothes, her head covered in a floral scarf. She begins with the
business of laundry. From the clothes hamper in the bathroom
piles of shirts, undershirts, underpants, sheets and pillowcases,
pants and skirts cascade down... piles of clothing just like at
the entrance to the Stutthof camp.

Coloreds are thrown into a broad, deep tin tub filled with
water in the bathroom. Subia takes a shirt out of the tub of
water, flattens it onto a tin washboard, rubs a huge piece of
soap all over it, up and down, up and down... Seeing the large
brown slab of soap my thoughts wander off to "There"—
off in the direction of barbed-wire electric fences. Goodness
gracious—could it be true that they made soap from Jews?
What is clear is that "They" were given so-called soap and
were taken naked to so-called "showers" from behind which
jets of carbon monoxide gas were emitted.

On finishing the laundry, Subia eats her breakfast in
the kitchen and chats with Mother, who is busy washing
dishes. How on earth do these two Jews, a Litvak[102] and a
Yemenite, understand each other? That is beyond me. Soon
the commotion involving major preparations for the weekly
washing of floors will start and, until that time, I am free to
put my hands into my pants pockets and make off to the

---

101 Hebrew: fountain-head, a city in the central region of Israel.
102 Ashkenazi Jews with roots in the Grand Duchy of Lithuania.
     In popular perception, Litvaks were considered to be more
     intellectual and stoic than their rivals, the Galitzianers (Jews
     geographically originating from Galicia), who considered them
     cold fish. They, in turn, disdained Galitzianers as irrational and
     uneducated.

living room to lean back in the armchair next to the side
cupboard, where the electric and water bills as well as my
report cards are filed, and to see what is on the bookshelf:
there are books of poetry by Bialik and Tchernichovsky,[103]
English paperbacks, booklets on actions carried out by the
Irgun and the Australian army during World War II, prayer
books, the Bible, and Targum Onkelos.[104] With the expertise
of a professional Peeping Tom, my fingers grope behind the
books, wanting to continue to probe between the volumes
despite the fact that I do not exactly know what I am looking
for. Wait. One moment. My fingers freeze on the spot, move
forward, stop, move back a few centimeters. It seems they
have discovered something.

I manage to pull out a faded brown envelope on which are
stains of insects squashed by the weight of the books protecting
it; a rusty staple is fastened to the folded, triangular sides. For
a split second my fingers refuse to carry on, but my curiosity
gets the better of me and I am determined to find out what is
concealed here. It is a little difficult to pull the staple off the
envelope as the rust is also stuck to the paper; but, finally, it
opens and a bundle of pictures spills out. The reddish-brown
shades tell me that they are old but their corners are incredibly
straight. It seems they have been pedantically safe-guarded. An
explanation in green ink, written with a fountain pen, appears
at the bottom of each picture; the handwriting is round and tiny,

---

103 Shaul Tchernichovsky, a Russian-born Hebrew poet considered
     to be one of the great poets of the Hebrew language. He
     identified with nature poetry and was greatly influenced by
     ancient Greek culture.

104 Aramaic translation: the official eastern (Babylonian) translation
     of the Torah by Onkelos (c. 35-120 CE), a renowned convert
     to Judaism in talmudic times.

like miniature pearls: "*Sonderkommando*[105] putting bodies of the murdered into ovens"; "gas chambers"; "Musselmann[106] by barbed-wire camp fences"; "Dispatching people by train to camps"; "*Selektion* process at camp entrance." I knew Mother was never to be asked to explain the pictures, and I never spoke to her about them.

I had one lovely Sabbath outfit: a white skirt with red pockets stitched onto it—the appliqued pockets were shaped like flowerpots from which hand-embroidered colorful flowers peeped out—worn with a striped red and white blouse. In the morning, before our Sabbath walk, I would dress up: I would put a perfumed handkerchief under my watchstrap; wear a gold chain with an azure, heart-shaped pendant on the back of which was inscribed the *Shema Yisrael*[107] prayer; and sport black patent leather shoes with white socks finished with pink lace. We would step out unhurried, take our Sabbath walk along sleepy town streets, pick yellow-weed, look in shop

---

105 Work units of Nazi death camp prisoners who were forced to aid in the killing process during the Holocaust.

106 A term used among inmates of Nazi concentration camps to refer to those suffering from starvation and exhaustion, showing chronic emaciation and physical weakness, apathetic listlessness regarding their own fate and a lack of responsiveness to their surroundings. The term possibly comes from the Musselmann's inability to stand for any length of time due to the loss of leg muscle, necessitating the person to spend much time in sitting or kneeling positions, an association with the position of the Muslim at prayer.

107 Hebrew: "Hear [O] Israel," the first two words of a section of the Hebrew Bible that is used as the centerpiece of all morning and evening Jewish prayer services, closely echoing the monotheistic message of Judaism. It is considered the most important prayer in Judaism.

windows, and find the flickering sunlight glary to our eyes. Sometimes, if we wished to visit places further away, we would take the motorcycle that had been bought from reparations Mother had received from the Germans, and we would go to the Alexander Stream, to Ha-Kfar Hayarok,[108] or to the Wingate Institute[109]—to the stone monument engraved with "We are a wall unto thee, o Motherland," and we would be moved by the power of these words each time we read them.

As we ate our Sabbath meal on the balcony, we would listen to greetings and songs on the radio program "Songs You Have Requested": "*Lipa ha-Eglon*" (Lipa the Carter), "*Shovach Yonim*" (The Pigeons' Dovecote), "*Ha-Shiryonim Yatz'u*" (The Armored Trucks Set Out), "*Ha-Tizmoret shel Rishon*" (The Rishon Orchestra)... after which, as all were drifting into afternoon sleep, I would stretch out on the army blanket spread out on the carpet in the living-room, surrounded by "Kofiko" and "Chipopo" books,[110] leaning on my elbows, pondering about how even a monkey could have had more luck than I, he being fortunate enough to live on a moshav (cooperative agricultural settlement) with his large and rooted extended family and circle of friends around him: an Israeli family whose roots had never been destroyed, never needed to move on from one house to another, from ghetto to

---

108 Hebrew: Green Village, an agricultural youth village for immigrants, founded in 1950.

109 Israel's national institute for physical education and sport, named in honor of Major General Orde Charles Wingate.

110 Israeli children's literature by Tamar Borenstein, the main characters being endearing human-type monkeys. Examples of titles in the series are "Kofiko Goes to the Kibbutz," "Kofiko in Tel Aviv," "Kofiko in the Army," "Kofiko the Paratrooper," "Chipopo in Egypt," Chipopo in the Congo," and "Chipopo in Alaska."

camp: a family without the unease from There. In those books, there is Sabra-type mischievousness, Palmach-style diction, not a Diaspora-tainted Yiddish kind of Hebrew; the sweat of those working the land streams down with their enjoyment and the calloused hand of the proud farmer wipes it away with his blue *kova tembel*. This is the new Israel, the steadfast, optimistic, young Israel, an Israel free of constant grief, of the pain of loss, not restrained and reserved, not frustrated and complicated, not enmeshed in "that" period, in "Then" and "There." What on earth do they know about being taken off each icy morning, wearing the yellow star, to forced labor in the Large Workshops?

I read on, fascinated by the human members of Kofiko's family, all happy and whole in their one and only identity. They celebrate their Israeliness without the cloud of the Diaspora and its legacy that spreads a heavy shadow of perpetual doubt and sorrow. They celebrate their Israeliness and there is nothing left for me but to rejoice together with them from a distance—for, what can I do, I am the daughter of an *Untermensch*[111] from "There." On Saturday evenings, after the Sabbath, Mother buys us half a portion of falafel. We bite into it, gobbling it greedily, enjoying the flavor of Israeli food. This is the realization of a dream and I am "Here"—a Sabra—Mother's great "victory over Hitler." Only the trace of skepticism mixed with an inexplicable sense of guilt does not leave me in peace: I am too much a Jew from there to really be a Sabra and too much an Israeli to be a Jew. I am *nisht ahin, nisht aher* (Yid., neither here nor there).

---

111 German: sub-human, a term from Nazi racial ideology used to depict "inferior people," in particular the "masses from the East," i.e., Jews, Gypsies, Soviet Bolsheviks, homosexual men, and anyone else not considered "Aryan."

In fourth grade we are small soldiers, "Oferim" (Heb., fawns) of the consolidated Ramat Gan scout unit. A great honor has been bestowed on us to be standing in rows at parade drills, to spend time under the protective shadow of the green and yellow flag; and, at roll call, our eyes shining with excitement, we scream out the scout slogan, "Be prepared." On Saturday afternoons before scout meetings, I would spend time in front of the mirror, folding my tie carefully, threading the ends of it through the leather ring. We wear a khaki blouse or shirt and khaki trousers, and a white linen rope hangs down from my shoulder into my right pocket, and there is also my scout belt on which hangs a scout rope for knotting; I am holding a walking stick, a rod to hold up the scout tent if necessary. I try so hard to look like everyone else from the gang, like the steadfast model Sabra, but I do not really manage to carry it off. Everything is sloppy and awry; my blouse is too starched and ironed, showing how skinny I am, and my pants droop, almost falling off me, as if they had belonged to "my Chaimke," the hapless soldier; even my fastened khaki belt cannot hold them on my waist for any length of time. No, this will not work... it just won't do. *Nisht ahin, nisht aher.*

We set off on a hike, walking in Indian file between narrow crevices, giving each other a hand, assisting one another so as not to stumble on the steep slopes. Whether we are in the Muchraka,[112] the Arbel,[113] on the peak of the Tabor[114] or on the Moreh Hill—any of these journeys into the Land of

---

112 The location on Mt. Carmel where Elijah challenged the 400 false prophets of Baal.

113 Mt. Arbel is in the Lower Galilee near Tiberias.

114 Mt. Tabor is on the Jezreel Plain northeast of Afula.

Israel is the *Ha'apalah*[115] revisited, as if I had been there in a former life. In the lunch break, we sit on a hill covered in pine needles and pass cans of food from one to the other. Using the teaspoon from a set of folding silverware, we eat straight out of cans and we share all the candies each of us has in our backpacks. To be on the safe side. Mother put a chicken leg wrapped in wax paper into my pack, a cucumber with a vegetable peeler plus a small saltshaker. From the experience she had accumulated "There," Mother has learned one should always carry some extra food, provisions for the journey, in case of whatever might happen... and what would happen if... oh, never mind, just pack it in there.

If someone were to tell Grandmother Tzipora that I, her granddaughter and her "victory over Hitler," would be singing and skipping, as do sailors at sea in a jolly operetta, together with the other girls in the "Snonit" (Heb., swallow) group on stage the evening of the scout show, she would have thought her hearing was defective. If she had been told her granddaughter would be sitting back-to-back with Ofer Mizrachi, would be chewing the end of her very short braid and would be singing Russian songs in Hebrew around the campfire on the Rishpon[116] beach, she would have simply laughed. Rishpon is where Aunt Leah first set foot in an Eretz Israel so yearned for, with wonder and joy in her eyes, when she arrived as a

---

115 Hebrew term used for immigration of Jews to Eretz Israel in violation of British restrictions against such immigration. It occurred in two phases: the first, from 1934 to 1942 in the effort to rescue European Jews from the Holocaust; the second, from 1945 to 1948, to provide a home for those displaced Holocaust survivors (She'erit ha-Pletah) languishing in DP camps.

116 A moshav just north of Herzliya.

ma'apila ("illegal" immigrant) from "There." In the dark of night she had descended in haste from the rickety boat, the *Pietro B*, for fear of being discovered by the spying eyes of the British; she had fallen straight into the willing arms of members of the Palyam (the Palmach sea company); by the way, as she did, her shoes fell off into the sea and that is how she had lost the one and only pair she had in her possession from "There"...

If Grandmother Tzipora had been told that at the end of the exhausting journey her granddaughter would be sitting by the main road between Ussefiya[117] and Nazareth in the protective shade of a mature eucalyptus tree, taking off her boots and gray woolen socks, massaging her blistered feet, biting hungrily into a sandwich of green onions and soft yellow cheese spread between slices of thick white bread, enjoying her dessert of a red, juicy tomato, sinking her teeth into a huge cucumber, would she have believed it?

Between trips and hikes, between Scouts' Day and the main summer camp, we would meet every Saturday for scout activities. After troop parade, each group would spread out to one of the corners among the most charming spots in Ramat Gan, Park Abraham; there, her face wearing a serious expression, the scout leader would produce the material she had prepared beforehand for today's activity from a leather-bound writing pad, and work with us on subjects such as the courage of the Lamed Heh[118] and the "Shabbat ha-shechora,"[119]

---

117 A Druze village atop Mt. Carmel.

118 *Lamed heh* equals thirty-five in Hebrew, here referring to the thirty-five Haganah men sent to the defense of Gush Etzion; all were killed on the way.

119 Hebrew: "Black Sabbath," referring to June 1, 1946, when the British arrested 100 Yishuv leaders.

and all of this spoken in the clichés of leadership. We would sing about "Dudu the Palmach member" who had stolen a chicken from a coop, and we would talk about ever-beautiful heroes, about whom there could be no doubt. As if blacking out the Pandora's box within me and for the sake of quieting that voice ticking on and threatening me like a time bomb, I would scream my lungs out singing "*Shu'alav shel Shimson*" (Samson's Foxes), "*Yatzanu At*" (We Left Slowly), "*Hei Jeep*" (Hey Jeep), "*Ha-Esh Mefatzahat Zeradim bi-Demamah*" (The Fire Cracks Twigs in the Silence)—all Palmach songs about rough and tough native Sabras from "Here"…

With these songs I would see myself as a Palmachnik dressed in khaki gym shorts gathered above tanned, solid thighs, worn with a white short-sleeved blouse, a keffiyeh[120] wound around my neck, my hand grasping a Sten gun; I am in an armored car crossing Bab-al-Wad[121] on its way to Jerusalem which is under siege. If only, if only I had been born to the right mother: I wanted her name to be Sara or Devorah and for her to tell me how she, dressed in khaki pants, her hair drawn into a wide braid, pulled out a hand grenade before hurling it into a Qawuqji[122] band… but alas, no! My mother had come from crumbling walls, from the "burning town,"[123] from electric,

---

120 Cloth kerchief worn on the head and about the neck by Arab men.

121 A point on the Tel Aviv-Jerusalem highway where, in 1948, there was fierce fighting between Arab forces and Jewish convoys on the way to blockaded Jerusalem.

122 Fawzi al-Qawuqji, the field commander of the Arab Liberation Army during the 1948 Arab-Israeli War.

123 An association with Mordechai Gebirtig's Yiddish poem "*S'brent*" (It is Burning) written in 1938 in response to the 1936 pogrom of Jews in the shtetl of Przytyk. This song was to become a symbol of the Holocaust and of the annihilation of European Jewry.

barbed-wire fences. I was constantly worried she would go to a parent-teachers' meeting at my school in her sandals; then all would see her twisted big toes that had frozen in her escape from the Death March (and this in addition to the fact that every time she returned from a parent-teachers' meeting, with her face soured from disappointment at my arithmetic grades, she would thunder at me "And for this I have survived from There?").

Together with her, yes, I too would be grasping the very same bundle of few personal belongings and would wander from one region to another with the yellow star on my coat lapel. In my world of associations, the term "heroine" derives from "There" and not as "they," my Sabra friends, saw it (as a humorous, clownish term used by the cool kids, beginning with the stealing of chickens from coops and ending with the bringing of the *ma'apilim* in the dead of night right under the noses of the British). My dark secret was that apart from the Sabra slang I spoke and songs to the Motherland I sang with a parched throat, I had not yet, coming from "There," found my peace in Eretz Israel. To the sound of rattling tracks under the wheels of the death train, I was still seeking temporary refuge from the scene of horror, panting and groping for air like a pursued beast.

I had a home "Here" and a home "There." At school and in the youth movement, a Mapai[124]-oriented Israel with Dosh's[125] caricatures was promoted, and at home my parents whispered in Yiddish about how to make ends meet

124 Acronym for the Land of Israel Workers' Party, a left-wing party and a dominant political force.

125 Illustrator and caricaturist, whose real name was Kariel Gardosh and whose best-known caricature of the Sabra first appeared in 1956 in the *Ma'ariv* newspaper.

to last out the month. It was decided that there was no other way out and that Mother would need to tell the truth to a lawyer who represented the Germans—to tell him that she was in the habit of screaming at night and would awaken dripping in sweat from her horrific dreams about Max the Ukrainian from Stutthof—so we could receive larger reparations that would allow me to be sent to a private math tutor in the hope of improving my grades and of Mother being happy.

Days were piling up like heaps of bougainvillea leaves that had been raked to the sides—to an abandoned area that lay between us and the asbestos walls of the garage housing official vehicles of the Russian embassy— by a broom bristling with pieces of straw. More and more fleshy, deep green leaves were appearing on the carob tree. On a thick branch we—Kookie, Natti, Tammy, and I—fastened a thick rope from which we slid down from the tree-top, shouting "Tarzan on the trees!" In the early hours of the afternoon, with a yellow winter sun tearing a gap through a wall of clouds, sending transparent rays to the earth still saturated with the previous rains, I would practice throwing a pocketknife: I would sketch a circle in the sand aiming to slice pieces off it according to the angles at which the pocketknife struck the ground. After that, I would join neighborhood children, we would all suck oxalis stalks and play jacks and hopscotch. On Friday evenings, Chobachin, the Soviet ambassador, would pace our street for his routine constitutional; as was proper, he wore a gray tailored suit, his arms comfortably joined behind his back. He knew just about every child by name and would greet us with "Shabbat shalom."

There were no strangers in the town. Everybody knew everybody. And if some strange-looking person appeared, we would label him as "crazy," for we knew he had been "There," in the camps. There was that old, toothless, homeless, gentile woman, a kerchief on her head, who was in the habit of sleeping on a bench in the park, all her possessions being two baskets full of rags. Occasionally she would visit our yard to wash her grooved feet under the tap which we usually used for washing the rubbish bin. It was said she had saved a Jew she had loved from "There" from the clutches of the Nazis, they had come to Israel together, he had been killed at Latrun[126] and she, a deranged woman, had remained alone in the world.

On the Saturdays that we did not take a walk to the "Monkey Park" or to the monument commemorating Ramat Gan people who had fallen in the War of Independence, or to the marble bench by the amphitheater on which the poet Hayyim Nachman Bialik had sat. Father and I would go off on the motorcycle bought with reparations from Germany, with me sitting in the sidecar, to the Yarkon River to fish. Father would take the bait out of the saddlebag: he would remove a piece of dough from a plastic bag or a worm from an instant coffee can, attach it to the hook of his fishing rod and sit down to wait; we would be lost in silence like all fishermen. A rusty barbed-wire fence, a narrow strip of beach, rocks formed from thousands of grains of sea sand with evening primrose bushes growing between them on the shore—this is, actually, where the land ended; beyond the horizon was where "There" began.

---

126 A strategic hilltop overlooking the road to Jerusalem. Ten days after declaring the State of Israel (May 24, 1948) the fort was assaulted by combined Israeli forces. The attack failed, leaving heavy casualties. A week later, on June 1, the fort withstood yet another attack even though its outer defenses had been breached. Many of the Israeli conscripts were recent Holocaust survivors and new immigrants who had not undergone rigorous military training.

At sunset, as the sun's rays were still shooting their last moments of light over the water like a dying person refusing to expire, the fishermen would be folding their stools and rods, counting their booty, throwing any unwanted fish back into the water, straightening the black berets over their foreheads and getting ready to go off in the direction of their warm homes. Wearing a blue sweater Mother had knitted me with a matching hat furnished with a bouncing pom-pom, I helped Father carry the fishing gear. And there, once, like a whale opening its jaws, he spilled out an amazing story: Father was born in Lodz, thus he began his story. His family left Poland in the 1920s, and in the late 1930s, went on a bar mitzvah[127] trip, traveling to visit acquaintances on Nalewki Street, the main street of the Jewish quarter in Warsaw, with his mother, Miriam. Suddenly "Abie the Australian," the Irgun killer and he who had conquered Jaffa, was telling me about shops and cafes, traders and porters in Nalewki Street in Warsaw, and that left me a little confused; it was too much for me to take in all at once: for the "There" from Lithuania of forest mushrooms in Kroki, a shtetl in Lithuania—from the ghetto and the Germans at the Flugplatz—now also extended as far as Warsaw and Lodz of Poland.

That is how days passed, filling the house "Here" to overflowing. The olive branches were heavily laden with fruit, and the delicate tamarisk seedlings had grown into strong trees. In winter, the wagon driver would arrive, his cart harnessed to a brown horse, whose back he would constantly strike with a whip, calling *dio* and *hoisse*,[128] Wearing tall rubber boots, a fur-padded peaked cap and leather gloves, he would ring a large handbell, while he called out "kerosene, kerosene."

---

127 Hebrew: celebration of a Jewish boy's thirteenth birthday.
128 Expressions such as "giddyup" and "whoa."

That was just like the *balegoola* (Yid., wagon driver) from Vilijampole, which is, actually, Slobodka.

In her kitchen, filled with a potpourri of aromas of yeast cake and Hungarian goulash, Miriam, our neighbor, a Birkenau survivor, sewed Purim[129] costumes for me: a Mickey Mouse costume, a Dutch girl costume, a flower-seller outfit... For Lag ba-Omer[130] all the neighborhood children would gather to light bonfires in the empty lot next to the building complex housing army personnel: in the center of the lot, a huge bonfire would be built, with smaller fires around it, each surrounded by square bricks piled up in twos, on which a grid was placed for grilling potatoes and boiling water for coffee. Above the central bonfire, a portrait of Adolph Hitler drawn by children, based on what they heard about him in stories, had been stuck onto vertical scaffolding. The holiday celebration would begin after the central bonfire had been lit and the sketch of Hitler entirely burnt. From the direction of the eastern ridges, we could see dozens of bonfires, just like in the time of Bar Kokhba.[131]

Only many years later did Mother tell me about the burning of corpses at the Ninth Fort. It happened when I invited her to join us for a bonfire with my children, Elad and Ariel, in

---

129 A Jewish holiday that commemorates the deliverance of the Jewish people of the ancient Persian empire from Haman's plot to annihilate them, as recorded in the Book of Esther.

130 A Jewish semi-festival, which takes place on the thirty-third day of the Counting of the Oilier, which begins on the second day of Passover; customarily children light bonfires in celebration of it.

131 Simon bar Kokhba: a Jewish leader who led what is known as "Bar Kokhba's Revolt" against the Roman Empire in 132 CE, attempting to establish an independent Jewish state of Israel.

the field behind our house in Jerusalem; from that time on, I have never celebrated Lag ba-Omer.

On the evening of Israel Independence Day, the whole town would congregate and crowd into Rambam[132] Square. Excited and moved, we would watch fireworks of a myriad of colors. On the stage, where the entertainment took place, Yaffa Yarkoni[133] would sing "*Ha'amini Yom Yavo*" (Believe It, a Day Will Come) and "*Ani ve-ha-Savta*" (I and the Grandmother); "The Tarnegolim"[134] would sing "*Shir ha-Shekhunah*" (The Neighborhood Song); circles upon circles of people dressed in their best white shirts would dance to "*U-She'avtem Mayim*" (You Shall Draw Water), and "*Hora Mamterah*" (Sprinkler Hora)[135] to the strains of Elly Netzer[136] playing the accordion. The establishment of the State of Israel was still an amazing miracle. These events were not yet taken for granted. This was a generation whose collective memory was well aware of "Moishike the Palmachnik" in his knitted hat and Moishele the ghetto child. Oh how we honored the country, how much did we love it! We carried it in all its glory on our solid shoulders with unabashed pride.

When summer arrived. Mother would send me off to the kiosk to buy Popsicles and bring them home quickly before they had time to melt. We had a refrigerator with no freezer— actually, it was an icebox. On the way I would get waylaid at Auschpitz's toy shop, checking out what I could buy for ten

---

132 Acronym for Rabbi Moses Ben Maimon (Maimonides), the twelfth-century Sephardic scholar and leader.

133 Popular Israeli singer born in Palestine (now Israel) in 1925.

134 Hebrew: "The Roosters," popular singing group established in 1960.

135 An Israeli folkdance performed in a linked circle.

136 Israeli composer, arranger, and conductor.

agoras: a small plastic baby doll that came with a little bottle in its mouth, a yoyo made of pressed sawdust and covered with red cellophane, coloring books, embroidery threads… Mrs. Auschpitz had a number from Auschwitz tattooed on her arm, and I really made a point of not staring or glancing at it too obviously for fear she would see me looking, but in vain. My eyes would dart around in their sockets and would find themselves focusing on the blue tattooed numbers just as one's gaze would be glued to the limping leg of a polio victim or to the prosthetic arm of an amputee. "Can't you wash it off with soap and water?" I would ask. "Or at least cover it with a band-aid so people won't see it?" Mrs. Auschpitz was white-haired; her blue eyes would moisten. I wish she could have…

And all the way back home, still panting as I made my way uphill, holding the box of Popsicles, I would be monotonously mumbling the two words Auschwitz-Auschpitz, Auschwitz-Auschpitz, Auschwitz-Auschpitz in my mind, like the rattling of a train's wheels.

In the summer seasons when I would not be allowed to take part in the big scout camp or the jamboree, I would go to a summer camp called "Healthy Nation." A truck would collect us from Bialik Street and take us to the Herzlia beach or to the Galei Gil[137] swimming pool, where we would stay until noon. The truck would then take us to a small forest near Kfar Shmaryahu, where we would make lanyards, weave wicker baskets, and sit beneath the pine trees, singing rounds such as "*Ha-Yamim Cholfim, Shanah Overet*" (Days Pass By, a Year Has Gone), "*Hayta Tze'irah ba-Kineret*" (There Was a Young Woman at Kineret), and "*Heveinu Shalom Aleichem*" (We Have Brought You Peace).

---

137 Hebrew: Waves of Joy.

In the upper grades of elementary school, we worked at the agricultural farm on the outskirts of Ramat Gan, bordering on the Paratroopers' Housing Project. (The Paratroopers were the army corps that had adopted Ramat Gan.) On Thursdays a truck would take us through the sloping streets of the Garden City to the farm, to the sound of loud voices ringing from it singing: "Things are not so bad; nothing terrible has happened." At the entrance to the farm, we would make our way between two straight lines of pecan trees, their branches bowing under the weight of their fruit; then, just by the grocery store, we would leap over the truck's ladder straight to the reed-covered booth where we would meet Eli, the instructor. Distinguished by his moustache, Eli would prime us thoroughly prior for each task, whether it be work in the apiary, picking pecans, weeding couch grass in the flower beds, thinning out carrot plants, laying irrigation pipes in the vegetable garden, cleaning out the chicken coops, feeding the sheep, or picking pomelos and persimmons. We rolled up our sleeves and proudly left traces of mud that collected under our nails for many days as a reminder and as unequivocal evidence of the strong connection between the Motherland and us.

On Friday evenings, we would gather at the home of one of our classmates for a "class party" which, once in a while, would also be the host's birthday celebration. Wearing our most festive blouses and shirts, we would sit around tables covered with white sheets singing birthday songs and clapping in time; as the atmosphere warmed up, we would sense the feeling of togetherness. After that, a short film would be projected onto one of the bare walls of the living room, spewing forth onto the surface flickering images, such as Charlie Chaplin and Laurel and Hardy. The birthday child would receive presents like card games to make sets of Israeli wildflowers or of different

Israeli army corps, pick-up sticks, or dominoes and, in return, he or she would give each of us a keychain as we left.

During those years, I played the mandolin in the Ramat Gan String Instruments' Orchestra. A number of times a year, we would perform in retirement homes for elderly people from Eastern Europe, that is, whoever was left from "There." As the concert proceeded, from behind the music stand holding my notes, I would peep into the audience of wrinkled faces and look for someone who might look like my grandmother Tzipora, but to no avail. I think the residents also looked at us, their eyes moist, looking for children and siblings left "There," also to no avail. Grandchildren with no grandparents, grandmothers and grandfathers without grandchildren. That was the situation.

Between Here and There
(June–July 1992)

I have a Star of David on each earlobe, a green and purple enamel Star of David pendant, the identity badge that belonged to Uncle Shlomo from when he was in Dachau, a map of the Vilijampole Ghetto, Mother's prisoner's number from Stutthof, drawings by Esther Lurie[138] (*On the Way to the Ninth Fort:, The Entrance Gate to the Ghetto on Krisciukaicio Street*); with all of those I am traveling There, to the concealed home of memories. This is a journey to cleanse and assuage my childhood fears, and it begins as if it were the waiting room of an operating theater where they will open the chest of memories, awaken the dead, remove my heart and re-implant

---

138 Esther Lurie (1913-1998) was born in Latvia and graduated from the Ezra high school in Riga. She studied drawing and painting in Belgium. She made *aliyah* to Eretz Israel in 1934. She went to visit her sister in Riga and just when she arrived in Kovno, World War II broke out. She remained in Kovno, continuing to paint, and took part in exhibitions from 1939 to 1940. When Lithuania was occupied by the Nazis in the summer of 1941, she was incarcerated in the ghetto with all the Jews, also continuing to paint watercolors there as well as pen sketches that have become a living testimony of figures, sites and events, a testimony to the despair and fear of death that prevailed in the Kovno Ghetto. She survived the Holocaust and returned to Israel.

it in a proper way, so that I will be freed from the subconscious sentence I decreed upon myself—to live my mother's Holocaust childhood.

The process began somewhere in the saga of wanderings I had sentenced myself to, but what is not clear to me is where it will end: not just the story but how I will cope with it—will I be a more complete person? Will I end up more frustrated? Will I have a richer understanding? Will I suffer disappointment? Or perhaps I will shatter into thousands of pieces with nobody to pick them up. Again and again I ask myself why I need to do all of this. For, perhaps I will never recover from the operation and the bleeding web of incisions will remain in my shuddering heart that has been removed and reinserted.

All through those years, my imagination has been roaming to worlds far away, to beyond the mountains of darkness; and now I am on my way there, to see the remains of Slobodka, to seek and find those closest to me, my grandmother, the house in which my mother grew up, to be drawn into the time tunnel, into the black hole of the unknown, to meet my distant past, my roots, myself in a previous life. For, indeed, I am from There—from the fences and the gas chambers. To this day there is no such thing as leaving food on my plate; and when I wander through parks with my children, I look for openings in the fence, alternative escape routes, hidden yards to which I can flee if need be. And who are my best friends? The shopkeepers, the produce sellers, grocers—whoever can provide me with some sustenance. They are the ones to whom I'm obsequious.

I am shaking from fear just from the idea of being There: from the sight of the buildings—endless lines of barracks— from the watchtowers, from the fences; from the Lithuanian gentiles. And now I am going there wearing sneakers, my nails adorned with red polish, what you might call casual, loose pants—I am a contemporary Israeli product inside which evil spirits rage and whisper secrets, accumulating piles of memories from There. I am also stamped—an Israeli product: I use the language with its slang, I am suntanned and can easily get angry; but the truth is that I am from There and nobody will change that. I was born There and I died There. I am the living dead; my laughter is only a courtesy to the other person… actually, just to make them think that; why should I care? But I am from There. Deep inside of me I am a Diaspora Jew, despondent and unfortunate, sad, gloomy, restrained, closed and introverted, a person for whom all has died long ago within her, and here I am traveling to There.

Lithuania personifies at the same time both the best and worst of what could be: it is where everything began and everything ended—communal affability, a rich spiritual life, an atmosphere that is an assemblage of marmalade made of forest grains, the pure white snow of winter, pickled cabbage in the pantry, sponge cake, a hammock in the summer, paddling in the Vilija, and skating on a frozen lake. There, Mother was still a happy person. There, she still had a home, a mother and friends, but she has been uprooted from There. It was from there that her mother was taken and her friends murdered, and it was really There that everything of hers came to an end—including her God. It was there that the ABZ (Irgun B'rit Zion) fell apart and her circle of friends was no more; some of her girlfriends were exiled to Estonia, and Chaim Shapiro[139] was burned to death when the ghetto was liquidated. Everything had finished there

Problems, problems, problems. I am having so many problems. Should I take my Star of David pendant and wear it, or should I not? It could complicate matters for me; it might cause me problems and make trouble for me; I could end up

---

139 See "The Airport," p. 64.

more involved with people's reactions than with what I was seeing and experiencing around me. On the other hand, there is a sense of revenge, a sense of victory. "It is childish to relate to such exterior signs," the little demon within me teases. He has also joined me on the trip.

Different kinds of associations hover around while I pack my suitcase. The bag is bound for the East, Eastern Europe. One is permitted to take only one piece of luggage: that really means taking only what is strictly essential. It sounds so familiar... What do you pack for going to Auschwitz? How do you equip yourself for Ponar?[140] What do you wear in Slobodka? How do you pack for Stutthof? How do you dress at Majdanek?[141] What footwear is right for Treblinka?[142] How much is the entrance fee to the Ninth Fort?

---

140 A mass extermination site near Vilnius, Lithuania, where Jews from Vilnius and the surrounding area, as well as Soviet prisoners of war and other inhabitants who were suspected of opposition to the Nazis, were assassinated by SS men and German police assisted by their Lithuanian collaborators. A great majority of the victims (estimated at between 70,000 and 100,000) were Jews. The mass murder of Jews at Ponar was launched at the end of June or beginning of July 1941 and continued on to the beginning of July 1944.

141 An extermination camp located in a suburb of Lublin, Poland. Close to 360,000 persons from twenty-eight countries and belonging to fifty-four different nationalities passed through Majdanek. Of these, it has been estimated that some 78,000 perished. Sixty per cent of them died as the result of conditions in the camp—from starvation, exhaustion, disease and beating—and 40 per cent (mostly Jews) were put to death in the gas chambers or were executed.

142 An extermination camp in the northeastern part of Poland's General Government. Between July 1942 and the autumn of 1943, a total of 870,000 Jews had been murdered there.

Here is a partial list: rubber gloves (for clearing away hyssop and scrubbing gravestones), an elegant purse (for Krakow), bags (for collecting earth and ashes), bags of earth from Eretz Israel to be scattered over graves There, a warm scarf for Danzig,[143] *yahrzeit*[144] (memorial) candles, pictures from Here, pictures from There, Israeli passport, Lithuanian passport (Grandfather's), walking shoes, running shoes (to use if the need arises to escape), a flashlight and spade (to find the valuables hidden by Leah and Shlomo in the yard by the lavatories beside the house[145]), sections from wills of people who had perished (Yid., *Nekoma*[146]), food!

Those coming to say goodbye ponder over the problem of how to send me off—can one wish someone traveling There a "good time" or a "pleasant vacation"? Or perhaps it would be enough to wish one a "successful trip"?—Success in what? Perhaps in recognizing letters emerging from under the hyssop on smashed graves? In discovering a Lithuanian collaborator? Others have a problem with the very idea of my journey—eyebrows are raised: "To Lithuania, eh?" spoken with a strange glance in my direction. And then, suddenly, I hear that someone has an aunt in Warsaw, an old woman who walks her dog in our street every morning was born in Danzig, and the next-door-neighbor is from Taurage and the electrician... Suddenly everyone is excited, asking me to send

---

143 Today Gdansk, Poland. Stutthof concentration and extermination camp was located 36 km east of Danzig (Gdansk).

144 Anniversary of the day of death of a loved one.

145 See "The Slaughter Begins," p. 47.

146 Hebrew/Yiddish: revenge. This word was written in blood on the door of a murdered Jew in Slobodka. A photograph of this was among the first taken by George Kadish (June 1941) to document the Kovno Ghetto.

regards. Regards where? Regards to whom? For all has been destroyed and all is gone. But people continue to insist, and they ask me to check whether a certain house is still standing and if the cherry tree nearby is still flowering, and perhaps the *gabbai*[147] from the synagogue is still alive… in which case, to send him their greetings.

What a cruel fate, what a tragedy: unlike other nations of the world— the Americans, the Mexicans, the Belgians, the Saudis, the Japanese and the Scots—I, the Jew, am compelled to visit the scattered graves of so many relations of past generations, and this will entail not just a few kilometers or a few hours' travel but packing, making concessions, parting from all of what is mine and from what I am Here and from the self who is now, and in all of those, my heart takes on new life with all the other partings.

What a cruel fate, what a tragedy: I am forced to travel There and take my leave from Here. Other people just say goodbye and go off on a skiing holiday. I am here in Israel for only a few more moments; very soon it is time for the countdown of the final day and then I am on my way. My eyes fill with tears.

Today is Sunday—the first day of the week in Israel—but my last day. Piled in the dim entrance of the apartment are bundles of my belongings in various sizes, standing one next to the other; these include a gray plastic bag into which I have made a point of squeezing some of the elements of my present life Here: my children's drawings, a photo album, collections of Naomi Shemer songs and poems by Yoram Taharlev.[148]

---

147 Hebrew: a person who assists in the running of a synagogue, ensuring all needs are met.

148 Israeli poet, born 1938 to Litvak parents; he wrote almost 1,000 popular songs.

I cling to pictures that will remind me from where I come and to where I am to return. Is it certain I will return? In a small notebook, I have prepared a list of songs for myself: songs of Eretz Israel, songs of Jerusalem, songs of Naomi Shemer—to be played in my head in moments of need...

In the kitchen, I am chewing on my final piece of bread, and sip, slowly and deliberately, together with the coffee in my cup, the entire period to the point that it becomes a doughy, sticky substance of memories, love, a transferring from Here to There and a leave-taking.

At six o'clock the taxi arrives to drive me to the airport. In silence, without ado, all is carried out almost mechanically as if according to some implied division of labor—my right hand takes the gray bag; my left, the suitcase; the backpack is on my shoulder; and the green pouch around my waist. Whatever there was to say has been said yesterday and on the previous yesterdays, and whatever has not been said is lost, a missed opportunity. My eyes conceal tears and do not give anything away. Some minor details: a light gray wooden door, a Yale lock, a broad, iron handle. I turn out the light and the door has slammed shut. In single file, with a sense of mourning, we leave the house: the red-and-black checked suitcase, the gray bag, and I—my head bowed—make our way along the sidewalk and drag ourselves like corpses, and ends of strings and belts hanging out of the case, like so many drooping limbs, get pushed in all directions.

At the airport a severe-faced policewoman checks my passport without batting an eyelash. Weak at the knees, I ride the escalator to the exit gates, the exit gates from Israel, from my home, from Here. In the corridors of the past, memories are busy at work in order to sum up the situation, arguing with the minimal hope that There, the place to which I am going, will merge with Here, and that both homes will finally become one for me.

The airplane takes off. For a split second I still manage to see carpets of orchards and the mosaic of agricultural fields in shades of brown, green, and yellow, a water tower, white Tel Aviv houses, and a network of black roads crossing one another. Still flying at a low altitude, the plane throws a dark shadow over the gravel hills by the sea.

Suddenly, in the blinking of an eye, without any warning whatsoever, the strip of shoreline disappears—that wafer-thin stripe of white sand, with sun umbrellas jammed into its sands on which a few bathers are stretched out. I am amazed at the suddenness with which the land comes to an end. I had been hoping that after going into a cloud and emerging from it, I would once again discover the land below spreading before me its carpets in shades of brown and green. But no! An endless continuum of azure sea, whose waves flicker and dance like ten thousand golden coins, stretches below us and I am surrounded by walls of hollow air and gray clouds passing by me in a flight of unstable bubbles, teasing me in their unbearable nimbleness: they are flying to my home in the East, and I am on my way There. All is empty and my heart also senses the uneasiness of its deserted ventricles cut away from themselves; deep inside myself I can hear my mother's voice, "It took me five years to get away from There, from the scene of horror, and you are actually going There!"

Yesterday, in a casual telephone conversation. Mother begged me to beware of the Lithuanian gentiles ("Those pagan, ignorant idolaters. They are a nation of murderers and you will not come out of there alive"), not to go off into side alleys, not to wander around alone.

Incidentally, in the end I did wear the Star of David pendant.

There (July–August 1992)

The airplane lands, its wheels scraping the landing strip, and grayish smoke sends up a gust of dust from below them. Lithuania is reached only through many tribulations, since there are no direct flights from Israel, from Here to There— Fate wanted me to first go through the Holocaust Kingdom,[149] the largest Jewish graveyard in the world: Poland. What I mean is that to get to the mass graves, I must first go through the gas chambers of Treblinka and Majdanek; and before reaching Kovno, I will be in the Warsaw Ghetto. The little demon within me bursts into fits of laughter, "From ghetto to ghetto," he scoffs. The truth is that it all feels a little strange: I am following my mother's footsteps in the Holocaust from the end to the beginning, from Poland to Lithuania, from Lublin to Kovno via Auschwitz and Stutthof, from freedom to slavery, from what was better to what was worse...

"Where are you?" the little wise guy inside me asks. "I'm Here... hmm... No, I am There..." I am confused. Here has become There and There has become Here. And now I am There, in the place where all my life—like waves shattering as they reach the shore—I have been returning in my dreams.

---

149 This is a reference to Alexander Donat's memoir *The Holocaust Kingdom.*

Just as long as I don't shatter, I think. It feels as if I have been here once, fifty years ago, but all looked different then, less modern. There was no air-conditioned terminal, no conveyer belt bringing you your own luggage. In fact, at that time, they did not give you back the bag you had taken from the home you had left... They took the person to one place, and his luggage—to another. The Poles do not smile at me. I try to make eye contact and to smile as we are used to doing Here (which now is There). Where we are Here (which is now There) they say a smile does not cost money. But Here (which till a few hours ago was There) I see it is not customary to smile, it is not usual to make eye contact, it is not advisable to exchange a few words on the weather. Just take your case, fill in some form declaring what money you have and go on your way—to the ghetto, to the crematorium.

I am in Warsaw. Everything is happening too quickly around me. Here and now it is dark. Symmetrical blocks of housing complexes loom up, and there are wide avenues and parks. Some two million people live in this city, but they are not to be seen, apart from the people traveling on the red trams, their faces dour. Like many Jews arriving in a foreign city, I first have a need to visit the synagogue. From the some 500 synagogues and *stieblach*[150] that had been in Warsaw, only one remains—the Nozyk Synagogue on Plac Gryzybowski. I arrive there in the dim of night and find it difficult to locate the façade which is adorned with reliefs of the two tablets of the Ten Commandments; it is actually hidden from view and is, practically speaking, nothing more than the back end of the synagogue: the entrance door is permanently locked and one has to go in through a small, narrow gate concealed at the side.

---

150 Yiddish: literally, little houses. Refers to small Jewish congregations, typical of the ultra-Orthodox/Hasidic variety.

"Ha, ha. This is the bitter taste of the Diaspora," my little demon whispers.

Close to the synagogue building stands a tall, wide structure with blue neon lights proudly flashing from its roof: "Deutsche Bank."[151] And just like when the Temple stood desolate in its ruins,[152] with jackals and howling foxes wandering through its remains, here too we see large dogs led by their masters into the synagogue yard to take care of their biological functions in the place where the ghetto labor department had once been situated, and where, in better times, the choir, conducted by the famous cantor David Sirota, would sing "*Ha-Nerot Halalu*" (These Candles) on Chanukah, the Feast of Lights. Welcome to There, my inner devil teases me.

Lublin: an industrial city—gray and ugly. It reeks of distress and wretchedness. The façades of buildings are peeling. The Jewish quarter, at the foot of the Zamek (Pol., castle) and outside the city walls, has been completely razed and now serves as a parking lot. Everything here is dead despite the fact that once everything began here—the Liberation, the initial organization of the Brichah movement, no. 8 Lubartowska Street, Beit Peretz, Jewish Committee House, the meeting between the survivors and the Eretz Israel soldiers...

Not far from the city of Lublin, just a few minutes away, stands the Majdanek extermination camp, with its unique odor—the

---

151 The leading global German bank.

152 The destruction of the Temple was a decisive event in the first Jewish-Roman War in the year 70 C.E. The Roman army, led by the future emperor Titus, besieged and conquered the city of Jerusalem, previously occupied by its Jewish defenders in 66 C.E. The city and its famous temple were completely destroyed. This event is still mourned on the Jewish fast day of Tisha B'Av, and the Arch of Titus, depicting and celebrating the sacking of Jerusalem, still stands in Rome

stench of shoes and of the prisoners' striped clothes. It is the smell of death. Evening is setting in. A Polish mother with a toddler enters one of the buildings, she sits him on one of the wooden bunks, or "hutches" as they were called by the prisoners, unhurriedly feeding him some yogurt with a teaspoon. The only birds I have seen are black crows circling above the trenches where people were shot,[153] adjacent to the crematorium.

That night, on the windowsill of my hotel room, there are three sprigs of chrysanthemum in an empty glass bottle that had contained mineral water, flowers from Field no. 3 of the Majdanek extermination camp.

Oh, green Galicia,[154] you look like a picture, frozen and standing still in time. There are tiny wooden huts with low thresholds, with small windows and smoke rising from their chimneys. Endless carpets of herbage are punctuated here and there by forests of dense honeysuckle. Crickets burst forth in rasping strains. There are vegetable patches of cabbages and turnips, cows leading thick-set peasant women, piles of charcoal, and stockpiles of wood for heating, and haystacks dotted around. One sees sheaves of corn in the fields. The ripened grain has already been gathered on the hill slopes and stacked. The noon sun has reached out with its rays. Farmers wearing peaked caps are working their land with primitive plows pulled along by horses. They are plowing and sowing alongside the crematoria.

It is terribly hot, irritatingly so. "August has forever been a terrible month," I am reminded of Mother's words. In August, the Kovno Ghetto had already become a crater of destruction. In August, Nechama and Leah—my mother and my aunt—were already prisoners of the twilight zone, in the

---

153 In November 1943, some 18,000 Jews were killed in the "Erntefest" *Aktion*.

154 Region of much history in eastern central Europe, currently divided between Poland and the Ukraine.

evil kingdom of the Stutthof Extermination Camp. In August, Hungarian women prisoners had arrived in Stutthof simply because there had been no room for them in Auschwitz.

I wander around in my T-shirt, worn-out jeans, and Israeli sandals, and on my shoulders my purple and black backpack containing the green pouch containing my papers and money, a bottle of water, a camera and film, a notebook and pens and pencils as well as a red bandanna.

Here is a dilemma: should I wear the Magen David pendant under my shirt or outside it for all to see?

Then there is the fear of gentiles, the fear of the world around me. I am a Jew traveling alone, wandering around basilicas, lanes, and castles, around cemeteries, the abandoned ruins of synagogues and deserted red brick dwellings where Jews had once lived. My footsteps echo through the city square, the place where Jews, each carrying his or her bundle of personal belongings, had been gathered and taken to some unknown address.

It is freezing cold.

All is gray—I note the facades of buildings.

Everything is dead—even the treetops do not sway.

Apart from ravens and starlings, there are no songbirds here.

Here, there are only nettles and wild berries.

There is barbed wire; there are pine and fir trees.

Iron railway tracks and rail carriages lead to nowhere in particular...

A gentile with flaxen hair and wearing an undershirt peers out at me through the window of his house, a house once inhabited by a Jew. There are drunks ("Watch out for drunken gentiles," my mother's words echo through my head), street musicians, and peddlers with high cheekbones selling their wares with their emaciated hands—selling wedges of sheep cheese. Would these people have hidden me during the Holocaust?

Here I am in the Tatra Mountains: these hills crowd together, peeping out from behind each other, becoming one as a single, continuous, hilly landscape to the end of the horizon. From afar, a windmill with its rotating sails can be seen. While I'm still leaning against a huge, golden wheat sheaf on one of the mountain slopes, diving through azure skies, free of all gloom and embraced by a warming sun, I sketch the escape in my imagination, the escape—the Brichah routes taken from here. This must be the height of optimism. This is where the long haul to the coast of Eretz Israel began. There is a dense, endless forest of conifers. The greenness here is especially green, the pastoral atmosphere refined and so tranquil. There is a deathly silence. Here one can already sense freedom. I am thinking about the *ma'apilim* boat, the *Pietro B*, which made it to the Rishpon beach after the war, and about the joy surely visible in the eyes of Aunt Leah and Uncle Shlomo as they stepped onto the Promised Land of Eretz Israel.

How did Mother manage to climb up those mountains?

How could she ever have crossed the Dunayetz River?[155]

I continue picking flowers to dry and press. Flowers from the places of Mother's wanderings when she was fleeing in the direction of Eretz Israel. At night, in the hotel, I wash my slacks which are stained with flower nectar and imagine seeing Grandmother Tzipora standing on the doorstep of her house in Slobodka, wiping her hands on her apron, offering me a piece of sponge cake and a cup of tea with a cube of sugar, clapping her hands and exclaiming, "Have you come only now? Why has it taken you so long?"

And what will I say?

I should be so lucky as to reach the house on Paneriu Street.

---

155 A river in the Carpathian Mountains.

From Krakow to Auschwitz, in Search of Evidence

It is nighttime in Krakow… the first rays of dawn are peeping through. My hotel room window faces the bridge over the Wisla River which was crossed by Jews who had been expelled from the Old Town to the Kazimierz and, from there to the ghetto in the Podgorze quarter. Those who remained were eventually transported to Belzec, Krakow-Plaszow, or Auschwitz…

The deep, damp, dimmest pit in the depths of the soul, the pit into which all my nightmares and most terrible fears are sunk, is Auschwitz. And I am very soon to be there, in a very short while. In the next few hours, I will stand with my own two feet on Grandmother Tzipora's final stop in life, to where she had arrived in her pink robe and slippers, together with Eisele and the rest of the children from the Kovno Ghetto. I am finally to see the place where Mrs. Auschpitz had the number tattooed on her arm.

I will soon be There—in the place that has been appearing and reappearing in my dreams for so many years. This is the same name inscribed on my innermost receptacle, the "little box from There" that I carry like a millstone around my neck. Wherever I go, my whole life through, this small "box from There" drags behind me, chained to me, its bonds holding me tightly, to the point of pain. And that is how I drag it, my "little box from There," willingly or not, taking it everywhere with me: it is with me at the movies, it is there with me when I am eating a slice of chocolate cake at the Kapulski Coffee Shop, it is with me on a restful Sabbath, never leaving me in peace; it pinches my sack of tears, boring a hole in my heart. That is the nature of this little box of mine. An outsider could never understand that.

Well into the night, I feel my throat is very dry, my forehead and my heart are pounding, my stomach aches and I feel generally uneasy. I am preparing myself for the moment I reach There; I sip water in order to be strong, not to break down. I pack my suitcase as if all were final; who knows in what state I will be after that, after it all? On an improvised clothes line I stretched from where one curtain sails into the other, a shirt and pair of socks hang drying.

The rattling of a distant train is heard.

I have my bag ready: food and drink, tissues, writing utensils, my tourist camera.

Just at this moment, a shot rings out from the other bank of the Wisla River, from the direction of the Wawel Castle. There is a clatter of motors.

Please God, give me strength. I am getting closer to the moment of truth, to the direct confrontation with all the fears, the black holes, the screams and silences, and the grief of death from which are woven and formed the horrific There that I have been carrying deep within myself, a part of my being, for ever and for always.

The transport is about to leave for Auschwitz with me aboard.

May God give me the strength to cross the Sambatyon River[156] with all its resounding waves, and return home safely.

---

156 According to rabbinic literature, the Sambatyon is the river beyond which the Ten Lost Tribes of Israel were exiled by the

He should give me the strength, and also—as Mother says—a drop of *mazel* (Yid., luck) would not hurt.

Auschwitz. It is nothing like I expected. It is a totally impossible scenario. At the entrance to the site there is an ice cream stand, a hamburger stand, a hotdog stand, a flower shop, and a souvenir shop. And in each stall, Poles sit there eager to sell their wares. Like buying a kilo of tomatoes at the market— you can buy a kilo of Auschwitz postcards, a kilo of video films of Muselmenn and burned corpses. Opposite the stalls, one sees the tranquil houses of the town of Oswiecim: a group of children crosses the road, a woman is pushing a baby carriage, there is a group of scouts; members of a mountaineering club from the Beskids mountains are sitting on the grass, having a picnic near the sign announcing "*Arbeit macht frei.*"[157]

In the archive building (which had been a house of prostitution and the canteen for senior camp staff), a Gypsy woman and I, like two people with appointments at a doctor's office, sit opposite each other, waiting our turn, both of us seated on wooden benches that have been sloshed with glossy, white acrylic paint. She is looking for her brother and I, Grandmother Tzipora. She has a number tattooed on her arm, and as for me, my soul is broken and scarred. Only the whirring of a fan can be heard: an old fan from the Communist era. Her face is furrowed from the passing of time, her eyes are sad and

---

Assyrian king Shalmaneser V. Later literature claims that it raged with rapids and threw out stones six days a week, or even that it consisted entirely of stone, sand, and flames. For those six days, the Sambatyon was impossible to cross, but it rested every Jewish Sabbath, the day when Jews are forbidden to travel.

157 German: Work brings freedom.

the number on her arm calls out to the heavens. We have no words to exchange; the corners of our mouths are all that can express anything, not our eyes—we are both looking down. The Gypsy woman is large and heavy and, without uttering a word, I go to sit next to her; only to caress the number on her arm. Fate has brought us together and Hitler has caused us to meet.[158] Perhaps, when Grandmother Tzipora was walking up the *rampa* with the children from the Kovno Ghetto toward the gas chambers, the Gypsy woman's brother was standing by the fence of the "*Zigeunerfamilienlager*"[159] and was the last person to see her in her final moments?

The Polish clerk, pointing to the counter with a finger, gestures to the Gypsy woman and pushes a photograph of her brother's prisoner identification form through a crack in the glass wall. The Gypsy woman weeps in silence. She cries without tears, only her shoulders are shaking. The wellspring of her tears apparently has gone dry since she set foot on the "other planet"[160] decades ago.

---

158 In line with Nazi racial ideology, the fate of the Gypsies became interwoven with that of the Jews.

159 German: Gypsy family camp. The first large transport of Gypsies arrived in Auschwitz on February 26, 1943, when a Gypsy camp was established at Birkenau. The number of gypsies in the Auschwitz "Gypsy camp" is believed to have been about 20,000. Living, or rather existing, in the most indescribable conditions, a great many of them died from starvation, as the result of epidemics, and also from "medical experiments" performed on them, such as were carried out by Josef Mengele on twins. On August 2, 1944, 2,897 Gypsies were gassed as part of the destruction of the Gypsy family camp.

160 See "Here: A Half-Sabra (1954-1968)," p. 154.

A Gypsy woman at the archives
of Auschwitz I. She is looking for
her brother, and the author, for
her grandmother

I am tense. My turn is coming up. Soon I will be touching
you. Grandmother Tzipora. It is a known fact that the Germans
were organized. They filed cards and made lists, categorizing
Untermenschen such as you into lists, noting down transport
numbers and dates and from where each transport had come.
Something of that relating to you must exist here, for most
historians maintain this was the last station in your life. Here
is where your ashes are buried. Now the clerk is approaching,
a woman with light blue eyes and unsmiling flushed cheeks,
her countenance angry-looking—possibly because I have put
her through the trouble of searching more lists, insisting that
she cross-check existing material. But there is no doubt that
very soon I will have some information about you, a lead,
a clue, and then we will make a family occasion of it: we—
Mother, Aunt Leah, I and all our tiny family, all of us who fit
around just one table—will sit together, passing around the

document attesting that here you died, just like people pass around wedding photos.

The clerk gestures me to come forward and I heave myself up off the white wooden bench, slowly dragging myself together with the "little box from There" (or could it be I am dragged after it?). In no time, Grandmother, in no time I will finally know all, and will then. Here and now, do what I have been waiting to do my whole life—I will light a memorial candle; will you, then, perhaps free me, in return, from the burden of the "Box from There"?

The clerk stands opposite me, with the glass wall separating us. Are her hands empty? Indeed, her hands are empty. She is silent and, through her silence, I can detect the irony sending me back to the place from where I came. She has nothing to say to me; she has not the smallest fragment of information for me. I am unlucky. With her demure expression, in which I recognize a smattering of glee at my misfortune, she looks at her watch, hinting that my time there is up; but my feet, firmly planted in that building. Block 24, refuse to leave, not wanting to accept the fact that just then, in the spring of 1944, "the Nazis were less organized," as Mother would say, not having documented their actions. They were already busy retreating, covering up evidence, burning documents and concealing their actions. I weep as I have never wept before. The clerk rolls down the shutters, turns out the lights and shakes the bundle of keys she is holding in the hope that I will take the hint.

How I envied the Gypsy woman then. Later on, I remembered that I had forgotten to ask her name. But, anyway, what difference would it make? "Here your name is the number on your arm," quoting Rudolf Hess, the commanding officer of Auschwitz.

I am at Auschwitz II-Birkenau—the largest cemetery on earth of the Jewish people. I had not imagined that this "other planet" would look so symmetrical, so quadrangular, constructed of so many squares, endless plots, camps, and smaller camps. There are never-ending rows of barracks, between which there are rectangular plots of land on which Appels took place, where they counted prisoners, where corpses were piled up, where people were flogged, and where, lined up, the prisoners were handed rancid soup. There are electric, barbed-wire fences and the silence of death, a silence meagerly cut into tiny slices.

Here, on the *rampa*, Grandmother Tzipora was brought straight to the crematorium in the last moments of her life, in which case there would be no reason for me to enter the area of the BI camp or the BII zone in which the häftlings—prisoners—were kept, those who had made it through selection and had temporarily been given the gift of life.

Here, at the ramp, the train would have stopped along the tracks. Grandmother and the children would have been taken from the wagons, she in her pink robe and slippers, surrounded by the children in the last moments of their lives, they, in desperate need of an adult's reassuring expression, of an adult to tell them there was no need to worry. With her whimsical, serene smile, she is sure to have caressed Eisele, taken his hand in hers, in her other arm holding the baby girl with the apple cheeks and sunken eyes, the other children trailing in her wake like a string of angels rising up to heaven, the little people clinging to the edge of her robe, all pacing down those cursed tracks scattered with bits of stone, walking in orderly pairs toward their unavoidable end. I wonder if the spotlights on the watchtowers were pouring their threatening light down on their small, angelical faces? I wonder whether helmeted SS sentries hurried the toddlers along using the butts of their rifles, shouting "*schnell*," their dogs barking and snapping at their heels? How did those little ones from Kovno march along the *rampa*? In those moments, their delicate foreheads would have become furrowed, and they would surely have understood what was really happening. With Grandmother Tzipora trodding at the head of the line, they would have surely cuddled each other, the bigger children making sure the little ones did not fall, and, in perfect silence and with the honorable appearance of small people bearing Litvak pride, they would have restrained themselves and not wept.

And Grandmother Tzipora, seeing the children wearing expressions desperate for compassion, she embarrassed and ashamed in her robe and feeling the cold badly, would have certainly known what was awaiting her and the children; how would she have taken leave of life in her last steps on the *rampa* before reaching the crematorium? Did she, in her mind's eye, see her three children returning to the empty barrack in the Schanz Labor Camp to hear, "Your mother should never have gone"? Did she perhaps regret this choice of hers—to have gone off with the ghetto children rather than waiting for her own children to return to the building at the end of another day's oppressive work? Might the Rebbetzin Tzipora-Feige Baruchson, in the final moments of her life, have raised her eyes to the heavens in vehement pleas for help; or would she have harbored a grievance toward the Creator? Or did she bitterly clap her hands toward the heavens for having forced her to choose between her own children and those of the ghetto? Or did she perhaps make use of the last fraction of a second left to her to make one single request to God—for her children's lives in return for her life and those of the children who were following her, their hands desperately holding on to her robe?

I am facing the extermination area. This is the dividing line between life and death—I have spent my life trying to visualize this in my mind's eye. It is the twilight zone among a thicket of birch trees. In a peaceful corner between the trees, traces of the gas chambers and crematoria have been hidden away. To which crematorium were Grandmother and the children taken? Were they taken to Krematorium number II, III, IV, or V? Was the prisoners' orchestra playing and serenading their last steps with cloying melodies and jaunty marches?

In the room where they undressed, kindergarten teacher Tzipora is sure to have whispered to the children, bending toward them and helping them to undo buttons, suggesting they first remove their shoes, their trousers and their shirts only afterward, so they would not feel cold. She would have taught her kindergarten class to tie their shoelaces, for later "when we get out of the shower." And just before the door to the gas chamber was hermetically sealed, her last penetrating glance would surely have been in the direction of the Jewish *Sonderkommando*[161] man standing at one side, her thunderous silence breaking his heart forever.

Years after that, I interviewed remaining members of the *Sonderkommando*. I traveled to Holon, to Bat Yam, and to Kibbutz Giv'at Hashlosha; I met them in the studio of the Department of Oral Testimonies at Yad Vashem.[162] I did not give them an easy time: again and again I would ask them if they, by chance, remembered small children and a kindergarten teacher, the latter wearing a pink robe and slippers—from among the thousands of transports that had arrived at Auschwitz-Birkenau. Only one of them once told me, "Small children? Yes. I remember children arriving from Lithuania.

---

161 German: Special Squad of the Jewish slave labor units in extermination camps that removed the bodies of those gassed for burial.

162 The Holocaust Martyrs' and Heroes' Remembrance Authority, in Jerusalem, Israel.

And when we jammed them into the gas chamber they refused to go in, kicking and fighting like lion cubs. And when the door to the gas chamber was kicked shut, they continued knocking on it obstinately with their tightly closed little fists until their voices expired." No. He did not remember a woman wearing a pink robe who had accompanied them. And I refused to shake his hand, just as I had refused those of other *Sonderkommando* men I had interviewed; I would stick my hands into my trouser pockets or vigorously cross my arms for fear that these were the hands that had dragged my grandmother's corpse from the gas chamber to the crematorium, those that had extracted the gold teeth from her mouth, that had cut the hair from her head and crushed her bones...

In spite of the fact that there is no trace of memory left of Grandmother and the children, all that I wish is to leave this cursed and sacred country, but before leaving, I, paralyzed and frozen, decide to enter the area of the BI barracks, to one barrack only, the building which is referred to today as the "Children's Block"—only there!

That is where children of the rebels of the Warsaw Uprising[163] were housed. Non-Jewish Polish children, whose childhood the Third Reich had also taken—though granting them the right to live and allowing—according to hearsay from group guides in Poland—one of the Kapos to draw pictures for the children on the walls of the block, thus creating an illusion, a reminder of their previous good life, instilling within them hope and the joy of life.

There, in the Children's Block, in total darkness, below colorful drawings of children with schoolbags on their backs

---

163 Struggle by the Polish Home Army (Armia Krajowa) from August 1 to October 2, 1944, to liberate Warsaw from German occupation.

on their way to *Szkola* (Pol., school), I chose to light a *yahrzeit* candle in memory of my grandmother and the Kovno ghetto children who had not been as fortunate as the Polish children from Zamosc and Warsaw, and had been taken directly to the gas chambers. I have no talent for drawing, but I so wanted the Kovno children who had "fought like lion cubs" to have their own drawing in this place as well. Tearing a page from my notepad, I took a pencil and scribbled a laughing sun, mountain tops over which tiled roofs were scattered, plowed furrowed fields and date palms sloping downwards toward the Sea of Galilee whose banks were crowded with yellow-weed and star thistles. And then, at the bottom of the page, I added a verse by the Hebrew poet Bialik, lines written a hundred years ago, after the Kishinev pogrom, "Even Satan has not invented the revenge for the blood of a little child." I crushed the note between my fingers and stuffed it into the cracks in one of the stone bunks.

I returned to Auschwitz I and began walking in the direction of the parking lot. I no longer had anything to look for here. From a distance I saw that Yochi, an ultra-Orthodox woman from Bnei Brak[164] whom I had met in Krakow, and her jovial, laughing daughter, Shewy, are about to get into a taxi that will take them away from here. "Hey Yochi, wait a minute. I want to say goodbye to you properly," I called to her. As spontaneously as that... in Auschwitz... they ran toward me. There we stood, under the intimidating watchtower, adjacent to the prisoners' "reception building" through whose gates came transports arriving at Auschwitz (not all of them, only those lucky enough to go through *Selektion*) and in which they underwent the initial dehumanizing stages in their transition from human being to a number in the evil kingdom on that

---

164 An ultra-Orthodox town in the center of Israel.

"other planet." Yochi and her daughter were wearing thick black stockings, long skirts, and long-sleeved blouses in the August heat, Yochi with her *sheitl*,[165] and jolly Shewy wearing a gold Star of David pendant around her neck; and here I was, wearing washed-out jeans and a loose-fitting T-shirt.

"*Oy veh iz mir*,[166] Safirale, we must say goodbye. We hope you find all the missing pieces in your mother's story... we hope you find your grandmother. Take a *siddur* (Jewish prayer book) to safeguard you."

Take a *siddur* to safeguard you(!)—that is what my ultra-Orthodox sisters from Bnei Brak said to me there among the barracks at Auschwitz I, fifty years after the Holocaust. A Jewess wearing a *sheitl* gives another Jewess with a wild head of hair a prayer book to help her as she continues her troubled search in the plains of Poland and Lithuania, to give her the strength to complete the mosaic puzzle

One thing we must admit regarding Hitler is that, contrary to the situation prevailing in Israel, he did not differentiate between religious and secular people.

"Grandmother Tzipora, you who have been peeping down at me through openings in the sky all these years, did you see that?" I cried out. Poles with picnic hampers walked past me, as did Japanese people who had come from the other end of the world to "see exotic things"; there were also some immaculate-looking Americans sympathizing with me, even offering me a can of Coke...

God should only give me strength. May I not fall down here and now, may I not shatter into a thousand pieces. A burning, stifling, Polish sun peeped through a covering of dust,

---

165 A wig worn by Orthodox women.
166 Yiddish: an exclamation expressing something like "Oh, woe is me!"

blinding my eyes and not managing to dull my pain. The entire Auschwitz camp was shaking from my cries.

The air was congealing from the heat wave and the silence. Nature was unconscious. The heat was suffocating but without the additional soul of the Israeli *khamsin*.[167] A killing heat. A dead heat. Everything here was dead. Desolation. "It was with the coming of Autumn, he loved her so."[168] I dragged my secret ammunition out of my sack and hummed softly to myself. Only my tears were streaming spontaneously down my face, smudging my eye makeup into a black, sticky mess. That's me, I'm a *Zydowka* (Pol., a Jewess).

Later I remembered I had not picked flowers to dry and press. I looked for some flowers, but there were none there. There are no flowers in Auschwitz, only white poplar trees, gray sand, and small pieces of stone.

---

167 Hot, dry weather.
168 From "*Tzipporim Nodedot*" (Wandering Birds), a song written by Yoram Taharlev.

Stutthof, in Mother's Footsteps

I am alone.

I am on my own on the train, on my way to the Stutthof extermination camp.

I am traveling the same rail route taken by millions of Jews to the unknown. They were taken there to their deaths, and I am going there in the hope of being released from the fetters of There: to be cleansed of fear, to remove the pain, to become purified of anxiety, to be rid of the load of my burden. I need to see the camp, to feel the ground under my feet, to touch the barracks and to add one more shard to the never-ending mosaic of There and Here.

I had sat down in the wrong car, not in my proper seat, and the conductress walking through the train, checking tickets during the journey, drew my attention to the fact and made me move to carriage number 29. How embarrassing! Everyone gazed in my direction: little girls with braided hair, sitting on their mothers' knees; country folk wearing caps; nuns and refined young girls with prominent cheekbones, small noses and flaxen-colored hair fluttering in the breeze. There were satchels, baskets, and packages. The smell of cheap vodka mingled with that of pork sausage was wafting through the air. Everyone is watching me as I trudge along with my backpack in the footsteps of my family's fate. I am convinced they know

I am Jewish—my hair is dark and curly, my nose protrudes and my eyes... my eyes are like those same eyes that gave themselves away There and Then, revealing themselves to be those of Jews trying to find refuge on the Aryan side; they are sad eyes.

The door of one carriage slams behind me and the door of the next opens. Perhaps I will find a little respite in this car... even for a short while... I grip my bag tightly, and it serves as a protective layer between myself and the train. My head lolls toward my shoulders, my eyelids close, and I dream about heaps and heaps of numbers, in simple arithmetic: fifty sealed and marked cattle or freight cars multiplied by one hundred Jews per wagon—a "transport"—in other words a "load" of 5,000 Jews bound for extermination. And so on and so forth...

"And sometimes the Jews even paid for the train trip with their own money, paid to go there to die." I am aware of this in my dream.

And, in my dream, I am a little girl on my mother's lap, and Mother is singing me a song about a train puffing along, about being the most loved girl in the world.

Along the Baltic Sea, between Danzig and Gdynia, between Gdynia and Sopot, the forest begins to thicken. The area becomes less populated, the silence interrupted only by the squawking of crows. Wherever there are crows, lots of crows, I guess there was an extermination camp. That is the detective in the little demon inside of me; that little fellow has taught himself and me to pay attention to such things: to identify mounds covering piles of human ashes, mass grave pits in forest clearings, rail tracks and freight cars from There and Then...

I decide to wander in the forest following the crows, just like Hansel and Gretel. Mature trees in the forest give off the scent of pine. Fir branches bother me, piles of pine needles hinder me, and I tread my way on cow dung. Tree tops conceal the sun, turning the world gray. Only the mushrooms and tiny flowers around tree trunks smile at me, indicating, "You are on the right track."

Indeed, am I?

Suddenly I see an iron bar jutting out from some thorns, with another one parallel to it. There is a narrow space between the bars, both being connected by a wooden railway tie.

What could this be?

I bend down toward the metal bars, pull up some weeds and thorns, using my hands to brush away clumps of sand; my heart begins to race. This is unbelievable—could these be the narrow railway tracks over which Leah and Nechama had been brought in open wagons from Tiegenhof to Stutthof? I decide to walk along them and, if these are the tracks, I should reach Stutthof, should I not?

Totally alone, I walk on and on. Time seems to be turning into eternity.

Here I am alone in a dense forest in the north of Poland; alone in a time warp together with the women from Kovno being taken to Stutthof. All alone here, I begin thinking of their humiliation—their dehumanization—their loss of humanity. Humiliation can be the worst of all human suffering, in particular the humiliation of being a Jew in the period of the Third Reich. "We would envy the dogs," my mother's words echoed in my mind. Humiliation was the diabolical, terminal disease of the scheme determining the "Final Solution of the Jewish problem." The humiliation of being transported in open wagons, just like sand and gravel in a wheelbarrow, like they transported rusty scrap iron, like they usually transport coal here in Poland.

Didn't Mother and Aunt Leah feel the cold around their ears when they were being transported? Perhaps because of that, Mother has begged me to wear a sweater and a woolen undershirt beneath my blouse all these years and to have a hat with me to cover my ears.

A wailing wind cuts through the silence of the forest, and, in my mind, I hear the Israeli navy entertainment troupe's song "*Im Zeh Tov o Im Zeh Ra, Ein Kevar Derech Hazarah*" (Whether good or bad the track, there's no way going back…) and I trudge on over the narrow iron railway tracks, panting and totally exhausted, my throat dry and parched from thirst, the straps of my backpack cutting painful grooves into my shoulders, my body hurting and drained. Droplets of sweat bead on my forehead due to the dampness from the Baltic Sea. I am physically tired and emotionally worn out for fear I might never get to the place I want to reach and from the worry that if I do, then what?

The forest is becoming greener and less prickly.

The forest is becoming, so-to-speak, more refined.

Little by little, the view of mighty trees are replaced by fragile saplings. Here and there one sees thin, bare trees, their bark dry, their needles gone. The sun skips and hides behind the treetops.

The forest is wrapped in the silence of death, a silence of the kind kept for cemeteries whose gravestones have been pilfered.

The screaming of ravens has been replaced by the twittering of other birds. The treetops are noisy. I have reached the edge of the forest. The ground is covered with carpets of grass, and strawberry and raspberry bushes are growing here in abundance. The railway tracks are disappearing, becoming buried in earth. So where do I go from here? Where am I? It is so beautiful, so quiet and tranquil here, like in a convalescent home… a convalescent home? Actually, originally, even before its establishment as a concentration camp, the Stutthof site was a convalescent home and sanatorium for the elderly…

And then, with no warning, the signpost "Waldlager Stutthof"[169] looms up right before me...

The Forest Camp of Stutthof... a lake meets my eyes, a lake in whose green-tinted, translucent waters huge goldfish drift, in whose waters pure white water lilies bloom. A red brick house is hidden between large tree branches. A chimney protrudes from the tiled roof. Window panes, clean and gleaming, are adorned with floral curtains. There are pink and orange geraniums on each window sill. This place is so pretty and elegant, so quiet and pastoral; surrounded by pine, fir, and oak forests as far as the eye can see, its edges graced with a vivid green carpet of flowering blueberry bushes. That is surely what the Garden of Eden looks like; all that is missing here is to see angels... and here I was expecting to see barbed wire, watchtowers, and endless rows of barracks...

I hear a voice from behind me saying, "You are treading on the grass in the area of the private house belonging to the camp commander"; I turn around to see a woman extending a skinny hand to me, her arm draped in lace and chiffon; she gives my hand a delicate, limp shake. "And I am Janina Grabowska, director of the Stutthof Museum." There is a very large amber brooch on the round collar of the white, starched blouse she is wearing. "She is so frail," I think to myself, "She could never have passed *Selektion* There and Then"...

So this is it: the Stutthof Concentration and Extermination camp has become a museum, and the Holocaust of the Jewish people—just one stratum in a series of eras. That being the case, my mother is a museum item, an archeological exhibit.

She would be an "Untermensch" in the eyes of the Germans.

She would be an "object" to the Poles.

---

169 German: Forest Camp.

Janina Grabowska, director of the Stutthof Museum, with the author

And she would be thought of as "soap" and as "sheep led to slaughter" in the opinions of some Israelis.

I am treated with the greatest respect at Stutthof. I am offered the hospitality extended only to the daughter of a Stutthof "graduate" ...

"Be my guest," Janina says, bidding me to walk through the "Gate of Death" before her.

"Thank you," I reply politely.

So much for ceremonial courtesy right by the gas chambers...

The protective vest I wear in such moments is purely academic: you might call it a "scholarly garment." I show interest in the period of the gas chambers, inquire as to management of the crematoria, discuss Stutthof and its similarities to Dachau, the first concentration camp. I focus my camera on the locks of barrack buildings.

"And where is the New Camp?" I ask, without allowing my voice to reveal any emotion. "For you surely know that the Kovno women were brought there."

"Yes, of course," Janina answers gently.

And then she takes me to the huge, endless, green outdoor area, now dotted with flowers—apart from them, nothing is left—and tells me that this is the New Camp; that, on the liberation of the camp on May 9, 1945, the Red Army was forced to burn down all the wooden barracks due to a terrible typhus epidemic that had spread among the prisoners who had not been sent on the Death March.

"Ha, ha," the little demon within me rejoices at this misfortune. "Not one building of the barracks has remained for which to mourn. You have undergone this whole obstacle course in order to see a yard… an empty yard. You could have stayed home (that is, "Here") and gone to the Jerusalem YMCA playing field; there, at least, you have the ground markings for soccer games"…

This is the same little demon that has spent all my life asking me, "What is wrong with being Here, that you consistently have to think of There?"

I do not answer, as befitting my good upbringing from home. Children of the Second Generation do not answer back.

I walk on and on, rubbing my hands, saying to myself that perhaps the fact that not one block is left to weep over symbolizes the drama of my life. Kind Janina takes my hand. She hugs me and wipes away a telling tear from my cheek. She manages to send the little demon away. "I want to show you something," she tells me in the discreet tones of a mortuary employee as we stride along like those people crossing the Red Sea, on dry land in the direction of the electrically wired fence, toward the extermination area. A bronze Star of David suddenly appears before my eyes, a huge Star of David, astounding in its size. It must reach up halfway through the sky.

"*Dobje* (Pol., good)—fine" she says to me. "This is for Mother and Aunt Leah."

After the tour of the camp, Janina, with her sharp eye and keen, understanding heart, invites me back to her office— in what had been the camp's military headquarters—for refreshments.

The tea trolley is covered with a lace cloth, and on it there are pitchers of tea and coffee, carbonated mineral water, and apple juice.

"Do have an apple," Janina says, offering me one from a gold-leaf rimmed porcelain bowl from which rosy-cheeked apples beckon. "They are from the *Lagerkommandant's* (Ger., camp commander) own tree, the tree right next to his house. Do have one!"

Star of David in Stutthof near the gas chambers

"Thank you, but no," I decline politely. How could one possibly eat the fruit of a tree whose roots imbibed the milk and blood of the prisoners, whose fruit was nourished by fertilizer made from their crushed bones?

Heat and humidity waft across from the Baltic Sea. The air itself, in fact, is a film of sticky particles of water. I am dripping with sweat. My curly, Jewish hair becomes frizzy, whereas Janina's hair is perfect—each hair in place. She wipes the perspiration from her shiny forehead with the coquetry of a lady in a powder room as she walks along mincingly on her wafer-thin high heels—my athletic shoes, their laces unraveling, are covered with mud mixed with small bits of stone, and thistles stick to their soles from walking along the railway tracks. From our shoes, you can see the difference between us: she manages a museum and I am trying to manage Mother's and my own private journey between There and Here; for Janina, Stutthof means a day's work from eight to three, and, to me, it means my whole life. And those who spend their whole life walking do not walk on high heels...

Janina proceeds to put on a pair of heavy, brown-rimmed glasses and excuses herself—she has to answer an important phone call from Warsaw.

All that is left for me is to wander alone around headquarters.

This museum is like all museums. Just as in the Science Museum, I touch the camp commandant's table to convince myself into believing it is that—a heavy, wooden table with family pictures of his wife, his dog, and his children under the glass on top. There is a photo album made as a gift for Himmler[170] on his visit to the Stutthof camp in

170 Heinrich Himmler was the Reich Leader (*Reichsführer*) of the
      SS, head of the Gestapo and the Waffen-SS, minister of the
      interior from 1943 to 1945 and, next to Adolf Hitler, he was
      the most powerful man in Nazi Germany.

1941; on black rectangular pages, the letters "SS"[171] are inscribed in Gothic script and a white ribbon ties the black pages of photos together. In the same room, there are some wonderfully comfortable, leather upholstered armchairs in which the commander's staff could sit when sitting deciding who and how many people would be sent to the gas chambers.

From a window in the building of the main headquarters I am looking over the Old Camp. In the distance I see the crematorium chimney; closer, there is the interior courtyard of the main headquarters. Opposite, I see the parade area. In my mind's eye I see Mother and Aunt Leah standing there, their chests held stiffly high: one person thin and tough, the other short and petite, both rigid with fear—the fear of the *Selektion*, fear of Max, in fear of being discovered as sisters, both together, of having each other.

Roles are now reversed. I am now in the shoes of the murderer, sitting here in the meeting hall: I am seated on a leather armchair, my elbows resting on the glass table cover, a glass of apple juice in one hand, observing the victims.

From the other window I look at the refined surroundings of the house, at the grass, the flowers, and the lake. Opposite the home, one sees the kennels where SS soldiers trained and groomed the murderous camp guard dogs, where they pampered and loved them. Adjacent to the kennels, the Gate of Death presents its threatening aspect. That must be exactly how the entrance to hell appears—not especially tall and not especially solid, but right here is where life was divided

---

171 German: Schutzstaffel or Protection Squad. Originally guard detachments formed in 1925 as Hitler's personal guard. In 1929, under Himmler, the SS progressed to become the elite units of the Nazi party.

into "before" (or, as Mother would say "when we were still somewhat human beings") and "after."

I return to the first window, in which the camp and its facilities are reflected: the hothouses and flowerbeds the prisoners looked after, the central kitchen block, the wooden living quarters, and the Old Camp. I can see Max in his black shirt rushing across the parade ground, ruthlessly lashing out at the Kovno women with his whip. German shepherds snarl at little girls who miraculously survived the Children's *Aktion* of the Kovno Ghetto and arrived here with their mothers. It seems to me as if the dead have woken, and the echo of their screams is shattering the silence of the air.

After that, I go again to the window that looks out over the house, the lake, the apple tree, the rabbits, the deer, and the squirrels. When Leah and Nechama were there, SS-*Stürmbannfuhrer* Paul Werner Hopper served as commander of the Stutthof Extermination Camp. Was it from here that the commander saw his wife picking forest grains, shaking out the rug, cheerfully waving to him, pointing to her watch and hinting to him to come home for tea and to relax on the balcony to the strains of music by Wagner and Strauss? And, of course, it would be important for the children to see their father at least once a day. The family circle is important.

Did he have an iota of compassion? Might he have regretted his actions, even for a fragment of a second? Did he beg God's forgiveness for the fact that he had become a monster? Or could it be that he would take his rifle to shoot at prisoners who happened to come into the view of his field glasses, as did Amon Goeth, the psychopathic commandant of the Nazi concentration camp at Plaszow?

Oh, the potted plants, the flowers, and the chiffon.

Do observe the chiffon fabric, the flowers, and the potted plants.

That is, indeed, what Stutthof is, right in front of the Gate of Death.

Now that I have arrived here in Poland, what am I supposed to feel at the edge of the European continent, at the end of the world, at the outer limit of life?

Should I have a sense of satisfaction, of joy, of revenge, of victory?

I wrap myself in a protective vest of silence—for what will I say and what should I tell?—I cannot even manage to recall one song from my secret ammunition of songs I have brought with me from "Here" (which is now There). My thoughts are silenced; they have stopped dead at this point.

In the meantime, Janina Grabowska has finished her phone call. I am saved from the intensity of my passing thoughts and, then, my eye lights on a drawer—a heavy, iron drawer of the kind often used for filing papers. I ask her permission to open it. "Yes, yes, all right," she answers me as you would a child. I open the drawer. Inside it, hundreds, thousands, perhaps tens of thousands of cards are placed in exemplary, organized, uniform order, in amazing symmetry: mute cards, the personal cards of Stutthof prisoners. They are adjacent to each other, one behind the other, as if on roll-call parade, like people lining up for bread, like prisoners in the line waiting to enter the "showers." It is as if my fingers are caressing the dead.

My poor, miserable ones, for how long has no Jew visited you? How long has it been since you have had the right to be caressed with the touch of human kindness?

I will take out just this one card. Janina is not looking; Janina will not know. She excuses herself and rushes out to meet someone important at the train station and she leaves me alone in headquarters. I am here on my own in the main headquarters of the Stutthof Concentration and Extermination Camp.

The last rays of sunshine skip around the walls of the room; the quivering of dying—a last sunset, and I am alone; alone with the cards of the dead and of the "living dead." I touch the typed numerals and numbers of those who once were people. I am touching death, touching destruction, touching the bureaucracy of the devil.

One card attaches itself to my perspiring fingers, beckoning to me to redeem it from its frozen state. Somewhere in the middle of the drawer, it is crowded in between the huge number of cards, pushing in front of all and jumping out of line. I fish it out with my fingers, pulling it out, refusing to believe my eyes:

JUDE
Prisoner number 44134
Name: Nechama Baruchson
Born in Kovno

Other details recorded on the card are that Nechama Baruchson was born May 25, 1925, was taken into the camp on July 13, 1944, and that she spoke German, Lithuanian, and Hebrew.

In the evening I dine in the company of Janina and her husband at the Teachers' Hostel in Sopot. One sees the German influence everywhere: windows, gleaming and clean, are adorned with lace curtains—did Mother, hiding, peep out from behind such a curtain when axe-wielding Lithuanians passed through the lanes of Slobodka? There is a pure white starched cloth on the oak table—could it be that this was a confiscated tablecloth, perhaps the same cloth Grandmother would spread on her Sabbath eve table, placing on it Sabbath candles, challah loaves, and wine for the blessings? We sit on solid, rustic-looking wooden chairs on whose backrests a piece in the shape of a heart has

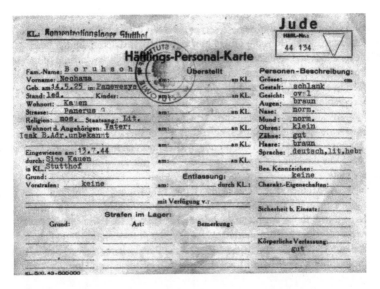

Stutthof Camp personal prisoner card for Nechama Baruchson

been sawn out—and the heart on the chair reminds me of your bleeding heart, Mother, when they took your sister, Leah, from you; the inscriptions in Gothic script above door-frames remind me of those displayed in streets during the Reich—"Dogs and Jews forbidden to enter here" or "Aryans only"—and the small rugs in passageways between rooms, hallways reminding me of Max the Murderer who would stand at the entrance to a barrack, using his whip to strike at the little Jewish women prisoners on their way to roll call. The one waitress here serves the soup with a ladle matching a porcelain tureen; her hips are girded in a white, starched apron, on her head she wears a lace cap, and she performs a typical Prussian curtsy in front of me, in front of the daughter of an "Untermensch." Mother, I am consuming a double portion of soup—yours as well, the portion you never got in Stutthof—is that acceptable?

We are offered grated carrot, slices of tomato on which finely chopped onions are sprinkled, potatoes, sauerkraut and crispy, somewhat sweet pastries that have been baked on the premises. Here, not far from the Stutthof camp site, I, the daughter of Prisoner number 44134, pile more and more food onto my plate.

As Mother says, "This is my victory over Hitler."

I am at the Baltic Sea, on the pier at Sopot. I am walking along the long cement path to the northernmost beach of Poland. I feed the swans. The sea is like a colorless layer of marble at low tide. Small waves crash onto the shore and die. Everything here is dead. Here Poland ends; here the world ends. But for me, this is not the end of my travels. The way home is still long, but where is home? There (which now is Here) or Here (which now is There)?

At Home, in Kovno

Very soon the clock will chime five times and then we will meet. Grandmother and I will meet in Kovno.

We will meet in Slobodka, in Paneriu Street.

It is midnight. I am sitting in a carriage of the Russian night train on the Warsaw-Vilna line, arranging my possessions by the light of a flashlight. I am preparing myself for the meeting and taking stock, first of all, making order among the memories I have collected from Here (usually referred to as There).

From the Tatra Mountains I have some dried flowers in a paper envelope; from Auschwitz-Birkenau, bags of ashes and earth and the *siddur* I received from Yochi.

From Stutthof I have a stone chip from the main-kitchen barrack, a spiky, rusty bit of barbed wire, and I have Mother's prisoner's card (number 44134).

And there are the memories I have brought from There (normally referred to as Here): my secret arsenal of songs and pictures of my loved ones.

I will reach home dusty and tired from the burden of my wanderings, and she—Grandmother Tzipora—girded in her apron and clapping her hands, will be mumbling in Hebrew with a Yiddish accent "My *Maideleh*,[172] it has taken you a long

---

172   Yiddish: Little girl (term of affection).

time, but you have finally arrived." After that, I will mount the creaking wooden stairs to enter the house. Grandmother will insist I take off my overshoes and move closer to the fireplace; she will serve me a steaming, hot cup of tea with a slice of her own homemade sponge cake. And I will laugh with tears of joy I have never known before, and with the laughter of freedom I will say to her, "Actually, all through these years, I have known that you were alive." And after that, my eyes shining and glistening, I will spread pictures of all the uncles and aunts, the children and grandchildren on her wooden kitchen table, and then I will sing *"Be'Eretz Lahadam"*[173] to her from my secret arsenal of songs. She will look down, will mutter something about little Eisele in the children's roundup, and we will then change the subject and talk about something else: about the fact that everyone says we look alike, that we have the same character traits.

That is how it is going to be very soon... at home... in Kovno.

The train speeds ahead with its green carriages, a train constructed from cold, alienated iron, a train with no aesthetic appearance whatsoever; its paint peeling off, it is old-fashioned and rusted, groaning its miserable way around each corner. The carriages are heated by coal. One cannot open the windows, with their dirty, loosely hanging curtains now pulled off the curtain rail along which they should have glided; and the filthy toilet is just a black hole in the floor. Dirt is piled up in the narrow corridors.

---

173 Lahadam in Hebrew is acronyms of *Lo Hayu Devarim Me-olam* (Things Never Happened). The song *"Be-Eretz Lahadam"* was written by Naomi Shemer (1930–2004), hailed as the "'first lady of Israeli song"; she was one of Israel's most important and prolific songwriters.

And at the end of the carriage, like an oasis in the desert, is a narrow cubicle boasting a huge samovar and next to it a heavily built, elderly woman wearing a floral kerchief, a dark blue pinafore, and tattered slippers. Sighing, she pours piping hot, dark-hued tea into crystal glasses as if performing some religious ceremony of great importance. After that, she comes out to serve the tea: on the shiny tray there are cups of tea served in beautifully decorated, silver-plated glass holders and, in each cup of tea there is a silver spoon. It is pure silver. Each passenger is served tea in a crystal cup inserted into a silver-plated glass, a silver spoon with which to stir it, and three cubes of sugar. In total darkness, as we enter a long, black, threatening tunnel from which there is no way back—to the USSR that has recently collapsed, to behind the Iron Curtain, among Ukrainians laden with sacks of onions, Armenian tradesmen with yellowed teeth, peasant women holding sacks, packages, and luggage in their wrinkled hands—I feel like delicate Lara, the heroine in *Doctor Zhivago*. This is a surrealistic sight, in which all these unfortunate people from the degenerate, collapsed Communist regime, all the downtrodden, all those physically and mentally crippled, those missing limbs and teeth, their faces furrowed in wrinkles, their bodies giving off a bad odor, all of them (I, myself included) are sipping tea as if at some private garden party at the court of Catherine the Great's palace, each of us holding a silver-plated glass, dropping sugar cubes into our tea one after the other, stirring it slowly, staring into the cup for a while, only after which, slowly, oh so slowly, we sip the very sweet liquid, inspiring in us all the illusion that life is sweet.

The train's whistle sounds and the train grinds to a sudden halt; it becomes clear that border police and railway porters are present. There is much commotion and noise. In the small hours of the night, the train gives up the ghost, screeching loudly. For several hours we are stuck in the same place, in the same carriage, and, when I clean the window with my breath to try to see where we are, I cannot make out a single thing. In the hermetically sealed carriage, we have been drawn into a silent, black sleeve and the loneliness within gnaws away at me, digging painful furrows: I am There and I am rushing toward the northeast, into the center of There, to Lithuania, in a train which, at this moment, is not going anywhere. In a narrow cabin consisting of four beds of narrow planks, with the company of a Ukrainian drunk, a peasant woman groaning under the insufferable burden of her life, and a toothless, ancient woman, I curl up on the upper pallet, my teeth chattering from the cold, from fear, from anxiety, from total exhaustion. I must not shut an eye; I must watch my suitcase. I do not yet see the flickering light at the end of the tunnel...

Outside the carriage, on the platform, vigorous footsteps can be heard, after which the silence of night is punctured by the pounding of hammers: they are striking the train and derailing it... "They are changing a set of wheels," those who understand what is going on explain to us. Railway workers crawl under the carriages. We are at a station close to Bialystok in Poland, and before the border crossing into Grodno in Belarus they change the carriage rings, separating the train from the engine, attaching the train to another engine, as the tracks from here on are of a narrower gauge. "They also detached the carriages from the engine at the station close to the Treblinka Extermination Camp," I remember hearing said in oral testimonies of Holocaust survivors.

Quite a few hours after that, hours that seem to creep by like an eternity, still in the black sleeve in which no star can be seen to flicker and in which no flashlight or spotlight penetrates the pitch blackness, the train stops dead once more. We have reached the border crossing: there is barbed wire and there are military buildings, spotlights, laborers in oil-stained work clothes. The carriage doors are thrown open. Khaki-clad mustached soldiers, wearing black leather boots and peaked caps adorned with Red Star pins, burst in. "Passport," one of them barks in my direction, stamping his foot angrily and spitting to the side. I drag out my Israeli passport from the pouch strapped around my waist, a passport testifying to the fact that I, among those present, am a Jew... The soldier continues roaring, ordering me to leave the carriage and accompany him. The hundreds of pairs of eyes belonging to passengers in the carriages glance at me pityingly and out of curiosity through the windows and follow the Belarus soldiers, their arms primed, surrounding me, leading me along the railway platform. I hop along the platform in my Israeli sandals and scenes of my life flick through my mind— the image of There (which is usually Here) as well as pictures from the previous days Here (usually referred to as There); and these pictures are accompanied by thorns and thistles, rocky ground, iron railway tracks, barbed wire, chimneys... and like the person sentenced to death who has been granted one last moment of life, I ask my children's forgiveness for the fact that I have been taken from them, from Mother since I did not complete retracing her steps with my own two feet; and from Grandmother whose death I will never be able to decipher nor give her a symbolic and fitting burial. Tears stream down my cheeks.

That soldier who screamed at me to get out of the carriage is also shouting at the other soldiers; they look down, accepting his authority. We arrive at a small wooden hut at the end of the platform, and, there, he and all his soldiers encircle me. He stretches out his hand in my direction shouting "Dollars, dollars," and this time I dig my purse out of my pouch, in which there are dollar bills, some 150 dollars; this would amount to two months' salary in Godforsaken places like Grodno and Bialystok. Luckily I have stashed my money in various places: on my right ankle, under my sock, under my armpit, on my stomach. The bills I had in my pouch pass from hand to hand, from soldier to soldier. With wonder in their eyes, the soldiers stare at the bills in the light of the only lamp there, peering at George Washington's portrait in the dead of night, on the railway platform at a station close to Grodno in Belarus. "The Jews are rich, all of them," they mumble, looking at me. The officer shouts at me, stamps his foot and raises a threatening finger at my camera, "No photography. Photography—sabotage"; he returns the passport and money to me, allowing me to return to the carriage.

On the platform, on my way back to the carriage, I thank God. The glances of the soldiers, passengers, and rail workers hurtle toward my back. A great silence now engulfs the carriage on my entry. Bent and wrapped up deeply within myself, I curl up in the corner of my bed on the upper plank, put the bills back into the purse in my pouch, grope for my faithful camera, thinking to myself: the last time I came across the word "sabotage" was in reference to the partisans who had placed dynamite charges on the railway tracks to blow up the Reichsbahn train transporting ammunition and soldiers to the Wehrmacht units on the Eastern Front.

And I? What do I have to do with sabotage?

The first signs of sunrise penetrate the horizon adjacent to the moon, which is still present in all its paleness, together with streaks emanating from the floodlights puncturing the sky. The attendant, in her blue robe and tattered bedroom slippers, goes from carriage to carriage, checking to see whether the doors are properly locked so that the journey can proceed. A damp coldness penetrates to my bones. On the opposite line, a freight train passes through the station—its wagons a brown-red color, sealed... just like then... could it be that those were the ones they used then to transport Jews to destinations of extermination!'

This is a twilight zone; it is the transition from Here to There. Borders are unclear, worn away and blurred. Sometimes I am Here, and sometimes—There.

With each rattle of the train we cross borders: geographical borders, emotional borders, borders indicating the transition from one era to another, from one planet to another.

Around me, people are speaking with rolled *r*'s and I cannot tell whether they are speaking Polish, Russian, or Lithuanian. In the course of the last half day of my rail journey, destination signs have changed again and again: Warsaw, Praga, Bialystok, Grodno. Each name has plucked a different string, each of which has been torn, its sound silenced. "There" has become closer, has become demanding.

The train slows down, its journey, I sense, having become endless. The iron hoops have rubbed against the rails, causing rasping whistles similar to those of loud, heartbreaking wails—Li-ta, Li-ta, Li-ta.[174] And I stand there as if hypnotized, my face stuck to the carriage windowpane, staring at the landscape flying past. Gradually, the green, dense forest scenery, through which we had been traveling for many hours since leaving Grodno, fades away and turns gradually into small bits of thicket, then fields dotted with stacks of hay and with country women milking cows into large, aluminum buckets; the scenery is changing, becoming that of a more populated area crowded with wooden huts with tiny vegetable gardens with scarecrows, tomato bushes, and sunflowers. The train

---

174 Hebrew: Lithuania.

continues on its tortuous, slow journey, entering an industrial area of factories, smoking chimneys, sewage and piles of scrap iron, then traveling through a complex network of railway tracks; finally, it groans, chokes, and stops at a station. This station is "Vilnius," actually Vilna.

The doors open and I am unaware of the fact that the patch of thicket sloping toward the train station is none other than the death valley of Ponar— the mass extermination site where seventy to one hundred thousand people, the great majority of them Jews, were murdered.

I have arrived There. I am standing in There alone, with my bags, on the platform. Nobody is waiting for me at the station, and no woman is waving to me with a light blue handkerchief. I cannot see one Jewish face—no Hasid, no Mitnagged,[175] no wagon driver, nobody belonging to the intelligentsia, no yeshiva student and no member of the Bund movement, no pioneer woman with a certificate for Eretz Israel, and no student girl with a stack of books thrown into a bag, no little girl with braids, and no tiny, mischievous boy wearing a skullcap. I hear no fluent "cultured" Hebrew and no vivacious literary Strashun[176] Yiddish. And all this amazed me, even though I knew, of course, from all the years I had spent between Here and There, that Lithuania was the country of bloodshed and was consequently *Judenrein* (Ger., cleansed of Jews).

---

175 Hebrew: opponent of the Hasidic movement.
176 Mattityahu Strashun (1817-1885) was a rabbi and scholar of Vilna. The Strashun Library of rabbinical and other works, often spoken of as the largest library of Jewish learning in the world and which Strashun gave to the community, became an important landmark in Vilna.

I was also astounded by the fact that, after so many years in the company of my own personal Holocaust survivor (my mother), who had given me "private lessons" on the subject, that I had still refused to completely comprehend the reality of the total destruction of the community, its complete annihilation. I still have difficulties in accepting the Holocaust as an established fact.

And thus, my feet planted on the entrance platform to There, my eyes damp, I look around, observing people walking back and forth, and try, in vain, to find a Jew among them, even just one who has survived.

"Welcome to There. Where do you go from here?" the evil little demon inside me protests, fixing his disparaging eyes on me. At the end of the platform, a gentile woman is selling salted pretzels piled onto a wooden stick. That is all that has remained from Yerushalayim De Lita.[177]

"Beware of Lithuanian *goyim* (Heb., gentiles)," Mother's words reverberate and echo in my head, and 1 take her advice this time and conceal the Star of David I have under my shirt.

Suddenly the sky blackens, a gusty wind rises intensely. From beyond, a dull roar of thunder is heard and heavy rain begins to drench me.

The heavens are weeping.

A railway employee in blue work clothes comes up to me and puts my luggage on a wheelbarrow. He is missing a few teeth, his breath smells of alcohol, his shoes are worn out, having no laces, and his age arouses my suspicion: if he could have been a youth, then... That little demon I take with me

---

177 Hebrew: the "Jerusalem of Lithuania." Vilnius from the eighteenth century was comparable only to Jerusalem in Eretz Israel as a world center for the study of the Torah, and for its large Jewish population.

actually enjoys the sweet joy of vengeance directed at the
Lithuanian gentile who is carrying my bags and also the *siddur*
I had received from Yochi at Auschwitz, my writing pads and
notebooks written in the language of the "*Zhids*."[178]

Later, in the hotel which is lacking the most minimal touch
of human hospitality and kindly warmth, I dine all on my
own in the dimly lit restaurant. I eat blintzes with sour cream,
herring (the pickled fish which is such typically Jewish fare),
and brown rye bread, it being called "Kaunas" bread, (that is,
"Kovno" bread, about which I am later informed). I do not
feel comfortable with the other people who are eating here:
a group of tourists from Kielce,[179] the Lithuanian basketball
team, thick-necked German tourists... and my bad little
demon protests and teases me, "You have gotten two for the
price of one: both Lithuanians and Germans around the same
table." I finger the Star of David pendant hidden from all eyes
there, enlist my Jewish sense of black humor together with
Israeli cynicism and answer the little demon heavyheartedly,
"Yes and the tourists from Kielce have been thrown in as an
extra... "

In the wee hours of the night, between the pillows, the quilts
and the starched bed linen, the creaking wooden furniture,
and the rug whose corners have been worn away, I sink deep

---

178 A derogatory term for Jew.

179 On July 4, 1946, thousands of incited Poles burst into the
     building of the Jewish Committee at 7 Planeti St., carried out
     a pogrom on some 200 Jewish Holocaust survivors gathered
     there and killed 47 of them. The false rationale behind the
     pogrom was the story of an eight-year-old Polish child who had
     disappeared three days before and who, on his return home,
     claimed that he had been abducted by Jews with the intention
     of killing him.

into my mother's childhood, hearing the murderous ticking of time: soon the grandfather clock will strike five and then we will meet.

After my journey of so many days, Grandmother's long-gone hand pulls the bedclothes over me, her voice whispering in my ear, "Good night, my *Maideleh*… we will meet…"

And the day did arrive! At 3 a.m. I got up to prepare myself for the greatest journey of my life. I washed the laundry that had accumulated and put my suitcase in order. What should I take on the journey to the center of There?

I would need road maps—a map of the outskirts of Slobodka at that time, a map of the Vilijampole district of today, a map of the Kovno ghetto and a map of the city of Kovno; drawings by Esther Lurie and memorial candles.

With my pack over my shoulders, the pouch round my waist, and the rolled-up maps in my hand, I mounted the yellow bus that travels from Vilna to the central bus station of Kovno. The driver, smartly turned out in the kind of clothes worn in the sixties—Terylene trousers and tie—greeted me with a facial expression lacking all emotion as I got onto the bus. Hanging on the front window of the bus was the Lithuanian flag of red, green, and yellow stripes, and a huge sticker on which "Lietuva" was printed in large letters.

I am the only Jew here. Around me, all are Lithuanian gentile men and women, and all examine me, fixing their eyes on me. I am viewed as a foreigner, a tourist, not from Here, a J-E-W-E-S-S. They see my nose and my dark, curly hair. I might possibly remind the older people of other Jewish passengers they had known before the "Jewish catastrophe," as they call the Holocaust in Lithuania. Some of them look the age to be suspect, and some of the others are surely the children and grandchildren of those who had murdered Jews. How is one supposed to know? This is a game of Russian roulette with the devil. Perhaps the edge of this man's coat is touching my bag, perhaps he is breathing on me, or he might be looking at me from behind with a murderous expression.

I sense fear. What an unfathomable fear has come over me. This is a tease of fate like a butterfly fluttering near the flame of a candle.

These are the "Lithuanian gentiles" I have heard Mother talk about all my life. These are the Lithuanians from the Lietukis Garage,[180] from the Fourth Fort,[181] from the Seventh Fort,[182] the Lithuanian "partisans."

I am amazed to see that they actually look like human beings. We are all standing in the bus, holding onto the iron railing and swaying together in the direction the bus is traveling. I examine the people's hands, their yellowish-green veins, their nails. The passengers are wearing sweaters because they feel cold, they sigh from tiredness, and they look out the window. And that is a striking discovery for me—to see the "Lithuanian

---

180 The Massacre at Lietukis Garage took place on June 27, 1941: while crowds of spectators and many German soldiers looked on, Lithuanian partisans killed sixty-eight Jews at the Lietukis garage in central Kovno, battering most of them to death with iron bars.

181 On August 18, 1941, in what came to be known as the "Intellectuals *Aktion*," SS, police units and their Lithuanian auxiliaries shot hundreds of Jewish professionals at the Fourth Fort. Einsatzgruppe commander SS-*Standartenführer* Karl Jäger reported that units under his command shot more than 1,800 Jews at the Fourth Fort on this date.

182 On July 6, 1941, acting under orders of the SS, Lithuanian auxiliary police units shot nearly 3,000 Jews at the Seventh Fort, one of the nineteenth-century fortifications surrounding Kovno.

gentiles" as elderly people, as mothers, secretaries, students, as business people...

Would they have fired at me fifty years ago? Would they have torn me apart with their axes? Or would they perhaps have hidden me in their barns?

The road from Vilna and Troki winds through dense forests. Every mound, every slope, every place where the forest is sparse and withered arouses my suspicion as to whether it could be a mass grave or, perhaps, a pit where people were shot dead. For that is how the complete Zezmariai[183] community from nearby perished. As my mother put it, they "went" as victims and were shot dead into mass graves; those taken in the *Aktionen* died in the gas ovens. "I am going, you are going, and she is going" the despicable little demon within me garbles the song sung by the Tarnegolim in my head—"I love, you love, and she loves"... just horrible. "Right, left, just one pit after another... "

This region is all pits, pits, and more pits. If Poland is the land of railway tracks and trains, Lithuania must surely win the title of "champion of the pits"; and the victims dug the pits with their own hands. They stood at the edge, were shot dead in perfect order, and fell into the pit as one man. The Germans fired and the Lithuanians covered up the dead. And sometimes the Lithuanians fired as well as covering the dead. Lithuania is the largest pit into which humanity has ever fallen: there were

---

183 This was approximately one kilometer south of the Kovno-Vilna road. Before the Holocaust, some 200 Jewish families lived in this town, known for its bond with Eretz Israel. All the town's Jews were shot and buried in pits which had been previously dug on August 27–28, 1941, in the nearby Strosiunai Grove.

small pits in Babtai,[184] many huge pits in Ponar, and trenches in the Forts. The larger the pit, the larger the community that once existed and is no more.

According to road signs, there are fewer kilometers to go: Zasliai, Kaisiadorys, Kruonis, Rumsiskes, and, finally, Kaunas, which is, in fact, Kovno! My eyes are met with a city of scenic beauty surrounded by water and mountains, the Vilija and Nemunas rivers cross it and, beyond their banks, lie the Aleksotas mountains and the "Green Mountain."

Equipped with my maps, I walk over the bridge joining the old town of Kovno and Vilijampole, crossing the Vilija River into Slobodka. Rabbi Nathan Tsvi Finkel, referred to as the "Grandfather from Slobodka," used to say it had been built to be crossed in only one direction—from noisy Kovno to the Slobodka of yeshivas, for the Knesset Yisrael yeshiva was situated there. Slobodka's young people walked across that bridge on their way to the city's various educational institutions: to the technical high school, the arts high school, the Schwabe school, and the Yavneh school; Jews banished from all parts of the city crossed it, moving in the direction of the Slobodka Ghetto, dragging with them a line of farmers' wagons loaded with only a few household items they had accumulated over the course of their lives. Clothed in rags and accompanied by their guards—armed Germans and Lithuanians— ghetto inhabitants who worked in the Jewish Brigades in town also crossed the bridge.

With the bridge behind me, something absolutely amazing happens: I reach Slobodka and know exactly where to go!

---

184 The 316 Jews of a neighboring town, some 25 kilometers north of Kovno, were murdered in the forests by the mayor, Justinas Janoshaus, and his friends and were buried in the grove next to the town in pits that had been dug by local citizens.

From Jurbarko Street I turn right into Krisciukaicio Street. Like a lost son returning home, I walk along calmly and serenely, identifying the ghetto gate from afar, and I know where the path leads without consulting a map.

Rabbi Averbin, the ritual slaughterer of Slobodka, lived at number 4; he was Chayena's father. Chayena, my mother's best friend, drew the illustrations for the *Ha-Nitzotz* (The Spark) magazines of the ABZ, copying issues in her old-fashioned, curved script to produce a number of copies.[185]

I approach the yard next to the main gate of the ghetto to which ghetto inhabitants, wrapped in old, torn rags, the yellow star on their chests and backs, surged to forced labor in the mornings in frost and rain, accompanied by the Germans and Lithuanians who would abuse them. I imagine I can hear the noise of the thousands of them, Flugplatz and Brigade workers, standing in dense rows which had merged into one group, waiting for the order to set out for the town through the gate for another long, fatiguing day's work.

And here, are the first houses of the ghetto... Linkuvos Street, Krisciukaicio Street, and Ariogalos Street—the same sky, the same earth, the same wooden huts and patches of earth planted with tomato bushes, sunflowers, and pear trees. I had come home. I have no strategy left but to put the maps away.

---

185 From September 1941, *Ha-Nitzotz* (spark) was the magazine of the ABZ movement; its editor was Avraham Tiktin. Some thirty issues of *Ha-Nitzotz* were published in the period of the ghetto. In the days of Russian control, the magazine was printed and duplicated by Shapirograph, and later on in the period of the ghetto—due to a lack of technical equipment—dozens of copies were written by hand by candlelight, with the use of carbon paper, by members who had legible handwriting.

The buildings in Slobodka are small, depressing, and crowded together; the wooden huts, almost half sunken in the earth, as well as their sloping tiled roofs and vegetable gardens, welcome me with a wink of the eye, as if to say, "We have been waiting for you to come. Welcome, welcome home."

I walk along Paneriu Street, passing number 15, number 13 and number 11... and here is number 9 Paneriu Street—the *house*, the house itself. Here is the house in all its mighty glory. It is a wooden hut. A mulberry tree leans over it from the right. Branches of weeping willow droop onto its walls from the left. The arms of weeds consume its sides, and it is mute in its silence, as are its brown-colored walls constructed of wooden beams. There are double-glazed windows, some of the upper ones being tiny: they are only for the purpose of ventilation and small so as not to let in too much cold air. Somebody moves the lace curtain aside from inside the window of his apartment and peeps at me from one side, concealing himself. There is deathly silence, a thunderous quietness. Other than the drumming of my steps on the sidewalk, which slopes down to the unpaved road, one sees nothing and hears no living soul. And the house, in its misery, looks at me, and I—from the other side of the road—put my wanderer's staff aside, inhale the air into my lungs and just look at the house to which I have been gravitating all these years. So here I am standing, minute by minute, for at least one hour, for a number of hours, opposite the silent house, observing my mother's life. The sun has finished warming Paneriu Street, has finished drying the puddles left by yesterday's rainfall, just as it had dried the streams of blood running here at the end of the first week of the occupation, after the Lithuanians had used their axes to smash the heads of Jews who had been living here for hundreds of years... The yellow sunlight is peeping out from beyond the dark orange house roofs like petals of the

The author in front of the house at 9 Paneriu Street

sunflowers in the adjacent garden. The sun will soon be setting
and I am still standing here opposite the house: some magnetic
force is anchoring me most firmly to the ground, gluing the
soles of my sandals to the paving stones of the street; I am
afraid to move, afraid to blink, for if I do for a fraction of a
second, the house might disappear and never return again.

A soft breeze blows among branches of the trees, but there
are no birds here...

I am beginning to get a feel for the tragedy which was,
all in all, a collection of small details—the well in the yard
from which Leah and Nechama will never again draw water
and the doorframes no longer bearing mezuzahs.[186] And I am

---

186 A piece of parchment in a decorative case attached to doorframes
     of a Jewish home. On the parchment is the "*Shema*," beginning
     "Hear O Israel, the Lord our God, the Lord is one."

beginning to understand that even if I stand here for many more hours, for several days, there is nobody in that house who will come out to meet me. That is a fact: Grandmother no longer lives here.

Weak at the knees, I walk in the direction of the backyard. Pink and white flowers peep miserably out from a pile of scrap iron. The yard was and still is where the lavatories are situated—small, locked wooden sheds spread around an open, sandy lot, with miserable stalks of grass adorning its mounds; each family living here has its own shed with a lavatory. In the dead of night, here in some place, despite the Nazis' threats, Aunt Leah and Uncle Shlomo buried the watch Aunt Leah had received as a bat mitzvah present, Grandmother's Sabbath candlesticks, and a few gold rubles. Should I dig and look for what is left, if anything? An intimidating dog, whose black fur is dotted with rust-colored spots, is tied to a laundry line in the yard and barks at me threateningly, baring its teeth. "Beware of Lithuanian gentiles," Mother's words echo in my mind. And I wonder whether that dog's ancestors had sunk their teeth into the ankles of children being thrown onto trucks in the Children's *Aktion*...

At the side of the building I see a staircase with the kind of wooden stairs I had pictured in my dreams and my imagination all these years from Mother's stories... wooden stairs leading up to heaven. With trembling legs I ascend the creaking, wooden stairs alone, going into the dim, damp stairwell. Nobody is waiting for me any more—not even Grandmother whom I had so believed I would see at the threshold of the house, wiping her hands on her apron and welcoming me— her long-lost granddaughter—clasping me to her bosom.

In measured steps, following the diagram Mother had sketched, I make my way to the flat itself and knock on the door, the frame of which shows no signs of where a mezuzah had been. A somewhat short, Lithuanian gentile man opens the door, his eyes, appearing frightened, darting around in their sockets, his mouth exuding a strong smell of vodka. "A certain rabbi lived here many years ago…," he says unwillingly and spits sideways.

"Yes, I know. I am that rabbi's granddaughter," I say, glancing at him directly and, in a burst of Israeli chutzpah, I make my way inside, without being invited to do so, entering a house whose every wall is crying out to me, sending out emaciated, anonymous arms in my direction. It is clear to me that I am standing in the hall, opposite the kitchen, and to the left is the living room which was also used by Grandfather when he sat with yeshiva students. To one side of the living room, beneath the sloping roof, was the little, narrow bedroom used by the two sisters—Leah and Nechama; on the other side—the main bedroom. Shlomo slept in the living room.

The Lithuanian man at the entrance to the apartment on 9 Paneriu Street

This is a tricky situation: the granddaughter of a victim is standing there together with a son of a nation of murderers! The victim is afraid the murderer might carry out another murder, and the murderer is concerned the victim might have come with the idea of avenging the blood of her forefathers. And so they continue to stand in front of each other; only, this time, the victim is determined to triumph—for the sake of all those who were overcome. So the victim stands opposite the murderer, a man standing there whose breath reeks of vodka, who has lowered his glance to the cracked, wooden floor, and the victim, bearing a look of abhorrence, overcomes her pain and... chews gum in the face of the murderer, in scorn and outright arrogance, her hands thrust into the pockets of her jeans. Please pardon me, Grandfather—noble rabbi of great repute; pardon me, Grandmother. This is not the upbringing I received at home, rather that of a drowning person who is grasping at a straw and who needs to gather all the strength she might have—I gathered courage and adopted a rather cheap body language, the gum in my mouth being the straw that was saving me from drowning...

The victim was now quietly stepping from one room to the next. In Grandfather's room, where he would sit—a tall, black-bearded man, pondering the Bible or studying Talmud and carrying on interesting, never-ending discussions with his students—there are no longer any sacred books, and pictures of the Vilna Gaon[187] and Rabbi Israel Salanter do not hang there. Its walls are now painted blue and adorned with icons, crosses, pictures of the Madonna and Jesus as well as stuffed

---

187　Eliyahu ben Shlomo Zalman was one of the most outstanding rabbis of recent centuries. He is commonly referred to in Hebrew as "'Ha-Gaon he-Chasid mi-Vilna"—the Saintly Genius from Vilna.

deer and foxes that had been hunted in nearby forests. The bedroom is locked, while in Leah and Nechama's small, narrow room there are two beds… the beds are made… pillows, quilts, and white sheets… as if waiting for the sisters to come home…

I take my time making my way toward the kitchen. In times gone by, in an earlier life, that is the place where Grandmother would have spent most of her days. Here is where she would have pickled cabbage, made jams from berries, baked challah for the Sabbath and made gefilte fish. Suddenly, a huge gentile woman looms up, a heavy-set woman with tightly closed lips and flashing eyes, her entire visage expressing hatred. Her short, gaunt husband stands beside her, his head lowered; he cowers in the corner, obediently waiting for her to utter something. She is wearing an apron… wiping her hands on it… just as Grandmother would have done at such a moment if she were still alive. She now plants her huge, red hands on her hips, using her body to prevent me from entering the kitchen. There is something provocative and humiliating about her steadfastness, but, at the same time, something wretched and quite absurd.

The tables have turned: now the murderer has the upper hand and he is cruel and abusive toward the victim, he threatens to hurt her, with the victim frightened and twitching, seeing moments of her life flickering before her eyes just now. These are images from There (usually considered to be Here)— images of blue sea and sky, of yellow-weed plants. The victim realizes that this is the moment of truth—the moment she has been looking forward to more than anything—only she ends up losing control, is drawn into the whirlpool of There, swept away from her protected shore, soon to be sinking into the dark depths of a sea, never to return to the yellow-weed and blue skies of There (normally referred to as Here).

Beyond the gentile woman's wide shoulders, I spy a razor-sharp butcher's knife at the side, on the wooden chopping board in the kitchen, and Mother's words resound in my mind more than ever, "Beware of Lithuanian gentiles." However, I am aware that if I have not been able to follow Grandmother's footsteps until now, then this I should stake out with my two sandaled feet. I take a rolled-up dollar bill from my pouch and thrust it into the bony hands of the murderess to bribe her into letting me enter the kitchen; she moves aside, but just a little.

For the first time in my life, I understand the double meaning of the Hebrew word *damim*:[188] that is why entering my grandmother's kitchen was only possible by payment... the angel of death had stood like a wedge between the victim and her granddaughter at the entrance to the twilight zone and had demanded a ransom. Is my safety guaranteed? Any moment now she just might wring my neck with her own two hands.

The kitchen is a small cooking corner; it contains a small cupboard and a rickety wooden table. Strips of bacon hang down from the ceiling and there are burnt saucepans and unwashed dishes in the sink. A pile of damp laundry is spread over some small wooden stools. All of this is in a kitchen that was once so gleaming and scrubbed and which, in better days, knew of different aromas and flavors. And then, before the mesmerized eyes of the murderous race, the victim's granddaughter hauls out a *yahrzeit* candle, places it on the shaky wooden table, lights it, and weeps loudly. "*Yitgadal ve-yitkadash shemei rabba...*"[189] The voice of my

---

188 *Damim* in Hebrew means both blood and money (particularly in biblical usage).

189 Kaddish: Aramaic meaning holy, the mourner's prayer, said at funerals and memorial services as well as part of the synagogue service. It is actually a magnification and sanctification of God's name.

grandmother's blood cries out to me this very moment from the walls of her kitchen, "My *Maideleh*, it has taken you so long, but you have finally arrived."

I am sorry to be leaving the house. I am once again burdened with the familiar sense of longing for the home There (generally referred to as Here) as well as to this home, in the country that is There. And, once again, I grasp the wanderer's staff with all my might, following Mother's course with the goal of learning about Grandmother's fate. The Lithuanian couple is happy to be rid of me. After I leave, they are sure to blow out the memorial candle I had lit in honor of Grandmother's soul, shortening the life of its wick... how symbolic that is.

A Cow on the Airfield

Continuing on my way, trudging heavily, I crossed Paneriu Street in the direction of Vezeju Gatve ("Carters Road"), to the corner of the "Yeshiva Street." Where the yeshiva was located, the mighty stronghold of Hebrew teachings and the light of Lithuanian Jewry, foreign winds now blow. From there, the voice of Torah and prayer are no longer heard. The building of the acclaimed Slobodka Yeshiva, which had served first as a storeroom for confiscated books and later (on January 14, 1942) as the place where the ghetto cats and dogs were killed, was then cleaned up and renovated, becoming the cultural center of the ghetto. There literary and poetry evenings, lectures and symposia took place, and Purim and Chanukah parties were celebrated, and that is where concerts and musical performances were given.

On 20 Tammuz 5703 (July 23, 1943) at the end of a concert in memory of Theodor Herzl, the whole ghetto audience rose to its feet weeping and, to the accompaniment of the orchestra, sang, or should I say, cried out "*Hatikvah*": "We have not lost our hope!"

And, so, the glory of the world has passed and is no more. I am reminded of the will of the "old, dolorous sexton of the Slobodka Yeshiva": "When you are free, tell your children of our suffering and murder. Show them the graves and the inscription at the

Ninth Fort."[190] Mother had managed to go free and had told me of all her suffering. Now I am here, in her footsteps, among the scattered graves. I must also never give up hope!

Making my way northward in the direction of Demokratu Square, I pass by the corner of Paneriu and Dvaro streets where the wooden bridge had joined both quarters of the ghetto, the Large Ghetto and the Small Ghetto, and my thoughts turn to the Austrian Jews from Vienna who were transported past the ghetto, along this same road, and taken away, with their sporty knitted garments and colorful socks, their Tyrolean hats, carrying backpacks on their shoulders, as they passed by the barbed-wire fencing of the ghetto, they asked ghetto residents, standing on the other side, where the Kovno Ghetto was... and, on that same day, they were shot dead at the Ninth Fort.

And so my feet drag me to a place where cubic, communist-style housing complexes stand out, the same shard from There, from where all my childhood heroes had come: Dr. Elkhanan Elkes, Ika Greenberg, and Yehuda Zupowitz. I reach the center of the ghetto that was burned down when it was liquidated. Here is where the Ältestenrat was housed, the "Large Blocks," the "Small Blocks," the place where Nahum Meek was publicly hanged[191] after being accused of attempting to escape from the ghetto

---

190 The song "The Will," better known as "In the Slobodka Yeshiva," was written by Avrom Akselrod, who had drawn inspiration for it from Abraham Goldfaden's well-known Yiddish lullaby "*Rozhinkes mil Mandlen*" (Raisins and Almonds), transforming the original image of a mother singing of her son's future into a prophecy that the Jews of the Kovno Ghetto would one day be liberated. The song urges Jews to "tell of our history/Tell your children of our hellish pain."

191 Nahum Meek, the only Jew hanged in the Kovno Ghetto, was publicly executed on November 18, 1942.

and of firing a pistol at a German sentry; Eizik Serbenitzky's pharmacy—he had had a secret radio, transferring information from the front to the Underground by way of it, and Demokratu Square.

Demokratu Square, the very square of the *Aktionen*. In this public square, the victims of the *Aktionen* were collected, here is where the *Selektionen* took place, and from here, the victims would be taken to the Ninth Fort. Jewish policemen assisted in keeping order, a regiment of the Lithuanian police guarded them, and German sentries surrounded the square. On October 28 and 29, 1941, in the Great *Aktion*, Gestapo Sergeant Helmut Rauca had stood there, all spruced up in his black SS uniform, a heavy pistol on his belt, pointed the whip in his hand at the lines, and ordered them to start moving; with the flutter of a finger, he had determined the fate of the people passing in front of him—"*links, rechts, links, rechts*" (Ger., left, right). There were family members who could not take the decision to part from their loved ones, to be torn to pieces—and all of them went to their end together… It was thus with the Kaplan family, Mother's next door neighbors from Paneriu street. The mother and her daughters had wept and refused to part from the father, joining him on the side of those selected to die, just to be together right up to their unavoidable end…

It was cold. Light snow had begun falling. And Rauca was conducting the *Selektion* with great composure, separating family members from each other, sending young people to the line on the left and women and children to the line on the right, and while doing this he smoked a cigarette, drank coffee, and bit greedily into a sandwich wrapped in waxed paper.

It is cold. It has started raining. Dalia,[192] the Lithuanian interpreter, insists we find shelter and sit somewhere to rest. I am stuck to the muddy ground opposite the red wooden house from so long ago which, amazingly, looks exactly as it appears in Esther Lurie's aquarelles; raindrops bounce into a puddle that is forming around me, they drip down onto the ghetto map in my hand, soaking my notebook, which is becoming a mess of ink blots. The heavens are crying for the mothers who were separated from their children here; for the children who were separated from their parents; for the families who had trained themselves in what to answer when asked so as to make the right impression; for the elderly who had pinched their cheeks in order to look younger; for those gaunt people who would hold themselves more upright and push out their chests in order to look healthy and robust; for the fathers who put stones in their sons' shoes to make them look taller; for the wretched, bent people who, in the last minutes of their lives, made an effort to impress the angel of death that they were blessed with every intention to work. And, in their grief, the streams of tears had split into channels, flowing and cleansing and drowning the heartrending screams of mothers and the pleading of weeping children; the water drains into the edge of the road in the southern part of the square, where a supermarket has recently been erected and, next to it, an automated teller machine adjacent to a small bank. For, indeed, this was the place where the ghetto Jews would sluggishly move into line, beads of sweat dripping down their foreheads despite the snow and cold, in tense hope of discovering where Rauca had decided to place them—on the potato shelf of the "Untermensch" type still fit to be eaten or on the shelf of the rotting.

---

192 Lithuanian: fate, luck. The name of the Lithuanian goddess of weaving, fate, and childbirth.

The rain has stopped and an unreliable sun is returning and dancing out from its hiding place in the sky. Housewives are walking lengthwise and widthwise and along the diagonal paths that cross the square; they are laden with baskets of dark, sour "Kaunus[193] bread." There are children honking on their bicycles, workers in blue overalls jumping over the puddles on their way to the automated teller machine, their expressions glazed and void of feeling. This is Demokratu Square: it is the supermarket square of life, where people's lives were traded like banknotes in a teller's hand.

From Demokratu Square I proceed, walking toward the right, to the location of the wood-chipping factory (this was considered the "good labor Brigade") and, from there, southward along the Vilija River. I imagine seeing the resistance leader Chaim Yellin secretly meeting with representative members of all the underground groups in the ghetto—Zionists and Communists alike—seeking to establish contact with those who had remained from the Lithuanian Communist party as well as with Soviet partisans who were becoming active in the area. I imagined I was hearing the horrendous screams of the Slobodka Jews who had been murdered and drowned in the waters of the Vilija River at a time when ultra-nationalist Lithuanian "partisans" were accelerating the pogroms against Kovno's Jews. From all the years I had been studying and living Esther Lurie's drawings, I remembered that ghetto vegetable gardens ran along the river bank and that Eshel[194] youth made sure that no one dug up

---

193 Lithuanian: Kovno.

194 Hebrew acronym for the "Irgun Le-Shmirat Ha-Ganim" (Organization for the Protection of Gardens) organized by Chaim Nachman Shapiro, head of the Education Office and ghetto cultural affairs, to ensure no person would unlawfully remove produce from the ghetto gardens.

potatoes and carrots or picked the cucumbers and tomatoes before they were ripe. And now I am here, in the place where ghetto residents had worked the land for their survival.

I reach the edge of the ghetto, where the cemetery is located, the graveyard in which the last rabbi of Kovno, Rabbi Avraham Duber Shapiro, had been buried.[195] I proceed to Jurbarko Street, outside the ghetto, where the venerable rabbi of Slobodka, Rabbi Shlomo Zalman Osovsky, had been very brutally murdered by Lithuanian nationalists accompanied by mobs of ordinary Lithuanians. Entering Jewish Slobodka with axes and saws, on June 25, 1941, they carried out their savage butchery, decapitating people and sawing them into half, taking their time in doing so to prolong their victims' agony. Moving from house to house, they reached Rabbi Zalman Osovsky's home while he was studying a volume of the Talmud, bound his hands and feet to a chair, sawed off his head and left him "sitting" in the rabbinic chair at his desk, his Talmud text open before him, and they placed his head on the windowsill...

I continue walking in the direction of the Nemunas River Valley, to the old Jewish cemetery of Slobodka that was mostly destroyed, and I trace a mass grave in which 800 of Slobodka Jews were buried after having being slaughtered by the Lithuanians in the pogrom which took place during the first days of the Nazi occupation. Alongside the cemetery there is the orphanage where the pediatrician Dr. Petras Baublys, a Righteous Among

---

195   Rabbi Avraham Duber Shapiro (1871-1943 [22 Adar 5703]), president of the Lithuanian Rabbinate and a representative of the Jews of Lithuania, was the last Chief Rabbi of Lithuania. He died in the Kovno Ghetto after a long illness. In 1979 his bones were moved to the Jewish Cemetery in Aleksotas.

the Nations,[196] had sheltered Jewish children until permanent places of refuge could be found for them. He remains a precious ray of light in a sea of despair.

I could easily have continued roaming the streets looking for acquaintances and relations in the narrow lanes of Slobodka, wandering for many more days in the hope of meeting people who might have remained behind there—Dr. Shifra Yatkonsky the dentist; Chaim Shapiro who was an ABZ commander of the Ma'apilim regiment; and blond little Eisele who had been taken away in the Children's *Aktion*. But the little demon inside me was poking fun at me cruelly, "That's it. Enough; it is gone and lost forever! " referring to Block C, the meeting place of the ABZ friends, the laundry workshop where Chaim Yellin had worked, "*De groisse Werkstetten*,"[197] and all the rest...

Sad and grief-stricken, I pace around the streets and squares of my town, the town for which I have been yearning all my life, wandering among the rows of buildings standing quietly and mute. A heavy stillness emanates from the small windows. Pears and apples glisten on trees and, in one yard, a mother and her baby are sitting on a bench between the cherry trees. The sky above has grown pale. A thin film of fog is enveloping the wooden fences standing there as silent as shadows. I have not met a living soul from Kovno of There and Then.

Tired and broken, treading the yellowing leaves underfoot but with desperate stubbornness, I continue searching for those laughing faces of girls with black braids, the pupils in school uniforms, stands laden with newspapers in Hebrew and Yiddish, the enticing smell of cholent,[198] silver candlesticks on a snowy

---

196 In 1977, Dr. Petras Baublys was recognized as a "Righteous Gentile" by Yad Vashem.

197 Kovno Ghetto terminology: the "Large Workshops."

198 A traditional Jewish stew, simmered overnight.

white cloth, the whispering of evening prayers coming from the direction of the *beit midrash*, I continue looking for the Slobodka with its streets and lanes scrubbed in all readiness for a festival day on which Jews gather, congregating on the banks of the Vilija for *Tashlich*,[199] and for Sabbath lights flickering from inside the houses.

But now everything here is Lithuanian. What is awful is that Slobodka is no longer Jewish in its soul. Slobodka is the Vilijampole of today: a poor suburb, a bereaved town, abandoned and void of Jews. The city of Torah has disappeared. Silence reigns in the street where the yeshiva was. All is empty, an endless space. The buildings stand on their foundations, but their tenants are gone. Lithuanian men and women wander around below the trees that are bending under the heavy load of their fruit, people go about their business in their homes, they shop in the stores, and they walk from street to street, from corner to corner, as if nothing had happened. In their yards, they are already piling up logs for heating; lace curtains flutter in the wind. A new world has come to be in place of the world of yesterday which has gone up in smoke. There were Jews in Slobodka but no more. The ghetto has gone down in a sea of flames and the ancient Jewish quarter has become *Judenrein*. Yet, the traces of a world gone are before the eyes of those who have known of them from the past, and for those people, the Slobodka quarter is no longer, yet it is still present—in their hearts.

I cross the river once again. This time I am off in the direction of the "Altstadt," to the Old City of Kaunas. I have reached the old Kaunas Castle where the Vilija River flows into the

---

199 Hebrew: casting off, a long-standing Jewish practice performed on the afternoon of the Jewish New Year, whereby the previous year's sins are symbolically cast off by throwing bread crumbs and the like into a body of water—a lake, river, or sea.

Nemunas. The Lithuanian flag, with its yellow, green, and red stripes, flutters in all its glory over the remains of the tower; a gnawing sense of alienation together with a paralyzing chill penetrate my bones. I have left Slobodka on the other side of the river and am now in Kaunas, a completely Lithuanian Kaunas.

At the outbreak of World War II, Kovno had a Jewish population of 35,000-40,000, about one quarter of the city's total population. It had a rich and varied Jewish culture and was a center of Jewish learning: supplementary to the yeshiva in Slobodka, one of Europe's most prestigious institutions of higher Jewish learning, there were forty synagogues, Torah study centers and *kollels*,[200] many Yiddish schools, four Hebrew high schools, daily newspapers and journals in Hebrew and Yiddish, almost 100 Jewish organizations including a ramified network of cultural institutions, economic independence, social welfare and health care as well as associations and parties of all political streams. It was also an important Zionist center and had scores of Jewish-owned businesses. Could it be that all this has been obliterated from the face of the earth as if it had never existed?

I have reached the "*Fisch Mark*" (Yid., fish market) This place once bustled with life. On market days, gentile peasant men and women, wrapped in their shawls, brought eggs and strings of bagels. I walk through nearby streets that had been inhabited by Jews and, in those days, were even called by names that attested to their Jewish character ("*Brick Gas*" [Yid., Bridge Lane], "*Yatkevar Gas*" [Yid., Butchers' Lane]), but I will never again meet the Jewish artisans and tradesmen standing at the thresholds of then shops, offering their wares... In the din of buses and trolley cars,

---

200   Institutes of advanced studies of Talmud and rabbinic literature for married Jewish men.

in the market square opposite the "Hasidish Kloyz,"[201] I long to hear a little Litvak Yiddish and see Grandmother Tzipora doing her shopping there—a futile hope. Today it is an asphalt-surfaced square with a fountain that sprouts no water; Lithuanian women wearing head scarves bustle around with their baskets, and I eye them with my piercing glance, wondering where they had been at the time of the Holocaust.

The Yavneh School looks drab, bare, and mute. Its walls are peeling and its windowpanes are shattered. The joyful voices of girls coming out from Mrs. Chaya Chwas-Levin's lesson are no longer heard, and pupils are not rushing home to the Green Mountain or to Vilnius (Vilna) Street. Instead of that, I suddenly feel the arm of a Lithuanian ruffian descending on me, his large hand covering the lens of my camera; he rams the camera into my face, pushing me roughly off the sidewalk as he curses me in vulgar language. "Hey, you were not careful enough of the Lithuanian *goyim*," my nasty little demon teases me. The air is alive with hatred. Anger mists my eyes. I do not know what has hurt more—the traumatic experience of being struck in the face, the spectacle of tough hooliganism, or the burning insult, that moment of humiliation.

I have reached the building which had been the *Kauno rotuse*—the Kaunas Town Hall of those days; dating from the sixteenth century and familiarly called "White Swan," it is now used as a wedding hall. Here, the Lithuanian "partisans" would collect the Jews they had snatched off the streets and from houses at the outset of the occupation, at a time when there was no longer room in the municipal jail (the "Yellow Prison") on A. Mickeviciaus Street and in the police stations, imprison them in the building, and herd them to be executed at the Seventh Fort.

---

201 Small synagogue and house of study affiliated with the Hasidic movement.

Close by, standing abandoned and neglected looking, are the Bikur Cholim Hospital that had been considered one of the largest and most modern hospitals in Lithuania and is now derelict, the Rabbi Yitzchak Elchanan Spektor Orphanage, the Jewish old age home, and Dr. Frumkin's "Beit Ha-Bri'ut,"[202] the Kovno Jewish well-baby clinic, established by OSE,[203] constituting a silent testimony to a community that was prominent, not only spiritually, but also in charitableness and in its sense of moral duty, a community that had known how to support its needy.

And here is the central boulevard of Old Kaunas, Laisves Aleja (Liberty Boulevard), a pedestrian street and for a long time the city's main commercial district, one and a half kilometers long, that was paved in the second half of the nineteenth century. Jewish workers, traders, artisans, members of the free professions and scholars, each person with his own special attributes would hurry on his way, hastening to evening prayers at the synagogue or to dip in the *mikveh*,[204] a newspaper with Hebrew letters dancing on its pages tucked under his arm. At the "Jewish crossroads," where Vilna, Mapu, and Zamenhoff streets met, people would assemble to have a vociferous conversation in colorful Yiddish or Modem Hebrew.

In the afternoon hours, thousands of Jewish students with satchels would throng here—in their various uniforms, wearing the hats specific to each school—walking home between the

---

202 Heb., Health Home.
203 French: Oeuvre de Secours aux Enfants (Children's Aid Society). A worldwide Jewish health care and children's welfare organization, founded in Russia in 1912. In 1933, it transferred its headquarters to Paris.
204 Hebrew: a bath house designed for the purpose of ritual immersion in Judaism.

buildings through the main street, each in the company of friends, and all speaking Hebrew!

On the Sabbath everything would be closed, as all the shops and businesses were owned by Jews. And, then, it was the accepted thing for each family to take walks through the main boulevard. People would meet acquaintances and the sound of Hebrew would ring through the side streets. Only the few buildings that still stand hint at what had existed then: the Avraham Mapu Library, which from 1908 contained thousands of Hebrew and Yiddish books, serving as the main source for promoting modern Hebrew culture and for strengthening a sense of national pride, is actually a library today too, but its books are in Lithuanian... for Lithuanians; the Hausman Shul (Yid., synagogue) today houses the Kaunas Regional Archives; the synagogue on "Yatkevar Gas" is now a pottery school, and what had been from 1921 the "Central Bank for the Furtherance of Cooperatives in Lithuania" is now a zoology museum. "Have you murdered and also taken possession?"[205]

In a concealed corner of Laisves Aleja, with Dalia looking at me in total astonishment, I put down my bags for a moment, smooth down my clothes, take out my pink lipstick, tidy up my hair and spray a few drops of perfume on myself. It is important for me to look like an especially "pedigreed Jew" here. With my back held erect and my neck taut, I begin my walk along Liberty Boulevard, crossing the road again and again, going back to stride its length another time, too—once along the sidewalk on the right, then on the left-hand sidewalk. "This is a small obligation to my mother, the 'Untermensch' who was led here, along the road, to forced labor in the Flugplatz," I explain to Dalia who is, by now, begging me to stop all of this.

---

205   1 Kings 21:19.

I continue walking until I reach the modern quarter of the city, known as "Neuer Plan."

Kestucio Street is attractive and elegant, its buildings new, spacious, and modern; the Reali Hebrew Gymnasium—now the Lithuanian Academy of Music—the Tarbut School, situated in the lot behind the science high school, and the clinic and residence of Dr. Elkhanan Elkes, chairman of the Ältestenrat, were all situated here. All of a sudden, a raging rain comes pouring down. The heavens are overflowing with a torrent of water; the sidewalk has become slippery and shiny. Striking down on my head are huge drops, the size of glass marbles, of a strength demanding an answer to their aggressive question, "Why did you come here?"

I enter one of the nearby yards. Saturated with water and sadness, I sit under a stone arch that connects two buildings. Streams of water are flowing down at a tremendous pace, and I am here alone on Kestucio Street, 40 meters from Gestapo headquarters and some 100 meters from the Lietukis Motor

Dalia the Lithuanian in Slobodka

Garage at Vytauto Prospektas, where, in broad daylight on June 26, 1941, a large group of armed Lithuanians brought sixty-eight Jews, abducted from their homes and from the streets in the vicinity, to the garage yard. At first they forced them to gather up garbage and feces in their bare hands and then they savagely battered them to death. The local population watched the "performance" with alacrity and clapped enthusiastically after the murder of each victim or when the intestines of a victim had exploded as the result of water forced down his mouth from hoses used for washing cars. After the massacre, the leading killer (Juozas Luksa) took out his harmonica and began playing the Lithuanian anthem. The assembled crowd had joined in joyously.

In exhaustion or despair, or perhaps a miserable combination of both, a question arises in my heart as to God's intentions, "Why do they have what we do not?" Why do the murderers have water and rivers, forests and fruit trees, and why does Nature, in its abundant colors, laugh and smile fortune upon them? And why do the victims have a blighted country, with the water level of the Sea of Galilee below minimum for so long? This is a simple question. I was not asking why on earth one and a half million Jewish children had perished; I was not asking about the fact that a third of the Jewish people had died in the Holocaust. I was only presenting the Creator with a question as to the problem of water, linked incidentally with the murderers, to victims and His mysterious ways. And then, at once, the rain stops and the inconsistent sun is smiling, and I think I see a rainbow behind one of the clouds. Between the sidewalks, two squirrels squeak to each other and passersby eye me curiously.

In an attempt to reconstruct the route walked daily by the forced laborers who were taken from the Kovno Ghetto to the Aleksotas Airport, passing by the Schwabe Hebrew Gymnasium, the facade of which is still impressive, but in whose walls now dwell a different spirit (today it is a school of textile design),

I cross the Nemunas Bridge in the lower town and walk up in the direction of the Flugplatz. Above green mountains and densely verdant hills, I stop to gather my strength at the place where Avraham Mapu, the first modern Hebrew storyteller, had looked out onto Kovno's narrow lanes, the crystal-clear waters of the Nemunas and the Vilija and the beauty of the green mountains surrounding it, and received his inspiration for the first Hebrew novel, *Ahavat Zion* (The Love of Zion), awakening in his readers a strong yearning for Eretz Israel.

But what a disappointment it is when I am refused entry to the airport area, now used as a Lithuanian Air Force base and fenced off as a classified military area. "But my mother built it," I tried to protest. "Here she lost her jawbone and her teeth," I say, raising my voice, stamping my foot and refusing to leave. "Beware of Lithuanian *goyim*," I hear a duet of Mother and the little demon within me chanting their warning. "But, nevertheless…" I say to myself, ignoring their voices, for I absolutely cannot return without sizing up with my camera the landing strips that thousands of the Kovno Ghetto's forced laborers, with Mother among them, had spent three years paving with their own hands for the German Air Force, the Luftwaffe. And so, equipped with a good deal of daring (a potpourri of Israeli character and Litvak stubbornness), I stand in a concealed spot among tree branches and, using my zoom lens, photograph the wing of an airplane and the horizon meeting the endless cement runways that were left saturated with the sweat of the Jews of Kovno; and here, my eyes rest on a cow greedily devouring the grass that is growing between the cracks in the asphalt cracked from the Jewish blood that had flowed here.

While still in Aleksotas, I feel it would be fitting to visit the Jewish cemetery, which dates from the nineteenth century. The graveyard is enclosed by a stone wall and is, indeed, a place of verdant tranquility. Above the wall, white and gray gravestones can be seen. The silence of death abounds, only to be punctuated by the whistle of a train from the nearby station, the sound shattering the air. (At that station, Mother and Aunt Leah were loaded onto railway wagons on their way to the Stutthof Extermination Camp.) I wandered around among the graves, which presented a sad picture of today's Lithuanian Jewry: the grave of a music-loving tailor next to a man named Yakov, whose life had been cut short before finishing a game of chess, and signs of assimilation—on many of the gravestones one can see a portrait of the person buried there. Lithuanian artists have engraved these portraits from photographs provided by the family of the deceased. But how moved I was when, all of a sudden, among the entangled branches, my eye chanced upon a memorial monument honoring the Rumsiskes[206] victims; and far from the perimeter of the graveyard, between weeping willow trees, there is a mass grave where the bones of the last of the Jews from the Kovno Ghetto are buried, those people who were taken from the *malines* where they had hidden when the ghetto was

---

206 A town approximately nineteen kilometers southeast of Kovno. Before the Holocaust, some fifty Jewish families had lived there. In September 1941, the Jews of the town were shot dead, among them Rebbetzin S. L. Grosovsky (Tzipora-Feige Baruchson's sister), widow of the last rabbi of Rumsiskes; she was killed together with her four children, at one of the three mass graves in the environs of the town. The town was totally burned down during battles between the retreating Germans and the Russians' freeing it in July 1944. Rumsiskes was sunk in the depths of a man-made lake—the Kaunas Lake—and just a few kilometers from it, a new town was built and given the same name, but no Jews live in it.

being wiped out in July 1944,[207] among them Chaim Shapiro, the Ma'apilim regiment commander of the ABZ and my mother's friend from their youth. In their honor, I recite the "Sicarii with the Yellow Star," and there, for the first time, after many days of feeling profound grief, I finally allow myself to shed tears.

Landing strips of the Flugplatz that Nechama paved in the Aleksotas suburb

---

207 In the final stage of the destruction of the ghetto, after transports had left for Germany, the Nazis conducted a meticulous search of the deserted streets of the ghetto and threw hand grenades into any building that aroused their suspicion, finally blowing up all the stone buildings and burning down all the wooden buildings. Many of those hiding in the *malines* died in the grenade explosions, were burned in the flames, or were forced to leave their hiding places, only to be shot on the spot—or were put on the last transport to leave for Germany.

End of the Road: From the Ninth Fort to Estonia

In the Schanz (Lithuanian place name, Sanciai) neighborhood, a large industrial zone belonging to Kovno located at the bend of the Nemunas River, I was as close as one could get to my grandmother in the last moments of her life.

With the help of a map, I made my way to Schanz as evening was falling, with the purpose of finding some clue as to what had happened. I managed to locate Rabbi Yakov Shmukler's *beit midrash*, where he and the other Jews had been forced to take all the Torah scrolls into the yard and burn them with their own hands, as well as the bridge over the river on which Jews from the Schanz Camp were led to the Aleksotas railway station when the ghetto was liquidated—the bridge from which Mother had thrown her knapsack in her attempted escape.

I finally reached a military zone and found myself standing outside a Russian army base—evidence of the latter part of Soviet occupation. A Russian soldier came from a booth and gestured to me to go away. And when I remained standing there, pleading to him in sign language to allow me to enter the camp area, he lowered an iron barrier in front of me, on which the Soviet red star was prominently displayed. "Nyet" (Rus., no), the same soldier said yet again. But I, aware of the fact that I was just not going to leave without managing to visit the place from which my grandmother had been taken away, remained standing there at the metal fence; out of Israeli chutzpah and Litvak stubbornness, I enlisted all the Russian I knew and said "Nyet, nyet." And, miraculously, after my refusing to budge, an hour later he raised the barrier and here I was wandering around a Russian army base, looking for my grandmother, walking around in between jeeps, tanks, and barrels of explosives belonging to the army that had freed my mother from the claws of the Nazi monster fifty years earlier.

Suddenly I heard footsteps. Turning around, I saw the same Russian soldier who had raised the barrier for me and allowed me to enter the base was now chasing after me. "I had a Jewish girlfriend who made *aliyah* to Israel," he said. "For her sake, come with me and I will show you the blocks into which the Germans crowded the Jews many, many years ago."

And he was to be my pillar of light!

I reached the place where the blocks stood and everything was just as it had been then: barbed-wire fences, the barracks built from red bricks like horse stables, and the remains of pallets; even the walls were still painted the way the Nazis had done them: yellow at the bottom, white at the top, with a blue stripe between the two colors...

And there, in that very place, in one of the barracks, among the frames of the pallets—with the Russian soldier standing next to me, with Dalia the Lithuanian and Russian interpreter with us—I once again lit a memorial candle for my grandmother, placing under it a note written on a page torn out of my notebook; "Grandmother Tzipora (Feige) Baruchson. Till today I have no idea what happened to you or where you were murdered—was it in Auschwitz? Or was it at the Ninth Fort? When I reach the place where you were killed I will know it for sure, for the earth there will shake under my feet. Until that happens I will know no peace. May God revenge your death! Your granddaughter who also bears your name, Safira."

Considering I do not know how to pray, I told her about her two great-grandchildren, my children, Elad and Ariel, each of whom could be assumed to represent a memorial candle for a Jewish child from among those taken in the same *Aktion* in which Grandmother perished.

The path from the ghetto valley to the Ninth Fort on the mountain top, through which tens of thousands of Jews from Lithuania and western European countries had passed on their way to being killed, is a moderately steep climb among tall trees planted at the side of the road, meadows, and flowers. It had been dubbed "Death Path" and also "The Path of Torture." Long convoys of people had slowly climbed from here, endless lines of them surrounded by armed soldiers, the people hesitatingly budging the path as those doomed to die. Everything is green; it is as green now as it was then. The Kovno houses run along one side of the slaughterhouse.

This is where the way ends and here is the fortress, the Ninth Fort, in a rustic setting, the last stop in the funeral procession of

The Russian soldier at Schanz with the author

those condemned to death. A mound is dug into the mountain slope, barbed wire coils atop the surrounding wall: this wall of death is pitted from bullets that were fired at irregular intervals, and, after that, in bursts of machine gunfire. And from the mound extends an expansive plateau—the massacre site. There are those who claim that some 300 children, victims of the second day of the Children's *Aktion*, were shot dead and burned here. Is Grandmother Tzipora's soul, the soul of she who had accompanied the children, also here among the treetops? How can I trace her among the scars of the fourteen firing trenches sealed with slabs and covered with grass to cover up the facts, distort evidence, and deny the Holocaust?

While amazed at the sight of a lake at the foot of the fortress that, indeed, does not appear on maps of that time, and which is also not mentioned in testimonies of those who burned the bodies, the woman managing the site tells me that it is an artificial lake that was dug to give the place an atmosphere of tranquility. The Ninth Fort, the site of the murder of tens of thousands of Jews, has actually become a popular picnic spot visited by young Lithuanian couples and their babies on Sundays after they have attended Mass in the church. They sit on the banks of the lake there, point their faces toward the sun, spread a blanket on which they take out food from their hampers, and row boats on the lake. They do not hear the murmurs of souls among the branches of trees which have imbibed vitality from the dead, and they do not see the eyes of Gertrude, a Jewish child who was brought here on a transport from Vienna, peeping down at them.

Close to the lake, there is a museum, imposing in its façade and its architectural design, for the Lithuanian victims of both the Communist and Fascist regimes: it represents the rewriting of history, the distortion of facts, the denial of the Jewish Holocaust and relegating it to be forgotten.

It is intensely cold, the kind of chill and dampness that freeze bones. A strong wind blows down to topple me. "Perhaps it is time to give up and return home," a small voice within me pleads. I bend down to collect some dark, black clumps of earth from the huge mound, possibly the center of where they burned the corpses, and I pick some star-thistle flowers to press, a souvenir for Mother, Nechama "the company commander" of ABZ, a huge picture of whom I had chanced upon in the fortress at an exhibition called "The Tragedy of the Lithuanian Jews"; there you see her surrounded by young ABZ ghetto youth under her leadership.

On that very day, I felt that a large hole had been bored into my heart. I did not look again for Jews in that clean and beautiful city, with its well-kept center, its new buildings, its towers, its wooden houses, its wide streets, its modern, asphalt-paved roads, its churches and cathedrals. With a sense of bitter grief, sorrow, and pain for Kovno, for its lost crown, I chose to complete my visit at the "Choir Shul,"[208] the one and only synagogue that survived and is, today, not a place of Torah study but one designated only for prayer. In better days, it had been known for its high standard of cantorial singing, and it is told that a concert once held there had included sacred Hebrew music as well as classical pieces; even well-respected Christian personages—people with high municipal posts, from the police and the army—had come to hear the cantor singing. Very soon after the liberation, it had become a meeting place for the few people who had survived the Kovno Ghetto.

I arrived there at twilight to say a prayer for Grandmother Tzipora's pure soul, for Mother—the victim who had survived

---

208 Yiddish: the Choral synagogue. The one remaining synagogue in Kaunas dates back to 1871; it is also known as "Ohel Ya'acov."

the Holocaust—a burial prayer for the home that had been destroyed and the orphans' Kaddish for the Jews of Kovno.

In the sanctuary, with its cracked floor, sat whispering in Yiddish about a *minyan* of Jews—just a handful of survivors, so different from those who had known the glorious Lithuanian Jewish community. On the wall, there is a picture covered in a layer of dust, a picture of Rabbi Avraham Duber Shapiro. Only the use of Hebrew, now for prayer, forges a few rays of light. I retired into a dim, private corner at the rear of the synagogue and sat there deeply withdrawn into myself. Yishayahu, one of the few Kovno-born people to survive the Klooga[209] camp in Estonia, asked me to send him a Hebrew calendar upon my return to Israel. On exiting, peering behind the synagogue building I saw a monument to the children of Kovno who had perished in the Children's *Aktion*—it showed a group of stars rising to heaven, arms raised upwards crying out for help, and I rather think I also saw the hand of an older person protectively closing in on the hand of an infant, in memory of my grandmother.

It is evening. My strength has run out and I am unable to return to the dullness of the hotel to be alone among tourists from Kielce and Germany and Lithuanian basketball players. In the large square of the Old City of Kaunas, from which one enters the streets of the Old City at the heart of which are rows of shops in whose entrances Jewish shopkeepers once stood; next to the White Swan, the municipal building from where the Lithuanians had abducted Aunt Leah when she was standing in

---

209 The Klooga camp, subcamp of the Vaivara camp in northern Estonia, near Tallinn, was created in the summer of 1943 and was one of the large labor camps in Estonia. It held some 2,000–3,000 male and female Jewish prisoners, most of whom had arrived in August and September of 1943 from the Vilna Ghetto; a minority had come from the Kovno Ghetto and elsewhere.

line for bread, taking her to the Seventh Fort during the first week of the occupation, Lithuanian gentiles, the likes of whom Mother had been speaking about all these years, were now flocking to the church from all directions. They were dressed in their festive clothes (it was Sunday), excited and enthusiastic at seeing the bishop, to kneel in front of him, to offer him prayers of thanks as he sprinkled holy water on them. Dalia the Lithuanian and I the Litvak are seated in an exclusive restaurant in a damp basement, eating vanilla ice cream. This is my "last supper" in Kovno…

I am sitting here imagining that, from all sides, the gray faces of shrunken Jews hiding in the *malines* in the basement are peering at me, their teeth rigid from fear of being discovered by Nazi troops and their Lithuanian collaborators. While having a farewell drink with Dalia, I sense I can hear the voices of Jews who have been caught in the *Aktionen* and are being escorted to the trucks to go off to the unknown. "Dalia," I mumble, my eyes filling with tears, "I find it difficult eating here; I am choking. Let's leave. The eyes of victims are staring at me through the walls." And Dalia, who has been serving as my "mouth," urges me to stay, "Imagine you are in a bustling place where cultural and spiritual life once abounded. Think of the good that there was prior to the bad. You are here and that is your victory, that of your mother and of your grandmother." Could that be so?

Rumor had it that the transport carrying my grandmother and the children had passed through Estonia.

I bought an air ticket to Tallinn and, in the early hours of the afternoon, I reached the small airport of a small country that had only just been freed of the shackles of Communism and wanted to prove its Lithuanian national spirit to the world. The Vilnius Airport is situated close to the railway station, adjacent to the Ponar murder site. Everything here is close to death!

I look at my watch. I have ten minutes before boarding the aircraft. Much to my surprise, the landing strip is deserted; there is no airplane there. "This is the last call for people traveling to Tallinn, Estonia, to board the aircraft," a loudspeaker declares in faulty English. But where is the airplane? I ask a ground hostess I happen to see and she points to a "toy" plane on whose nose somebody has painted "Air Estonia" in light blue and white. Could this be the plane? Dumbfounded by its size, I burst into hysterical laughter, imagining the newspaper headlines: "Killed in an accident in a toy airplane"…

Gripped with fear and tired as well, I am engulfed in feelings of uncertainty: to what extent and, actually, why should I continue my journey there?

I have children, a home, and family. Perhaps this is the sign that I should leave Here and get home safely. The little demon within me launches his objection, "You have just been home to Slobodka, have lit a *yahrzeit* candle in Schanz, you have visited Auschwitz-Birkenau"; he is the same little demon who ridicules me for the "Second Generation" hump I bear on my back. "Your mother wanted you to be a proud Sabra and that is all. The children need you with them at home." That little demon, wicked and loathsome as he is, knows how to pluck the strings of one's guilt feelings, "Anyway, you will not bring Grandmother and the children back to life. They are DEAD now. They were annihilated and turned to piles of dust and ashes. Do you understand that? It is time you return to dealing with matters of life and leave the dead in peace… And if you are at the airport anyway," the demon adds, "come on, buy a ticket and go back HOME."

"But my home is Here," I answer him in a feeble voice, "and I need to know what happened to Grandmother. I have not yet completed the mosaic. I need finally to bury her and light a *yahrzeit* candle in the place where her soul rose up."

Having no other option, my little demon tags along behind me to the airplane. I take the opportunity to check the standard of the landing strip with my feet. Mother having paved such a runway for the German Luftwaffe at the airport in the Aleksotas Quarter of Kovno. I walk toward the toy aircraft. Lithuanian maintenance workers walking on both sides of me, and Mother's words ("Be careful of the Lithuanian *goyim*") echo in my mind. With one hand I grasp the Star of David pendant around my neck and, in the other hand I hold the *siddur* I had received from Yochi in Auschwitz.

In Israel, I will be able to tell them I had flown in a UAV (Unmanned Aerial Vehicle), I chuckle to myself in my black Jewish humor. But how does one get into this toy which is all of six meters long? A Lithuanian airport employee growls at me and waves his hand, gesturing me to bend down below the aircraft; one gets in from there, from beneath the plane. Just as long as he does not hit me; one punch was plenty for me, when my face was struck as I was standing opposite the Yavneh Gymnasia in Kovno...

I bend down. A six-rung ladder leads up into the plane whose engines are thundering into high heaven as if it were at least some luxurious Concorde aircraft. Inside, I count ten seats, and on them, all perfectly organized, there are cages of chickens, cases of Vodka, two strong-looking men with Baltic faces, and myself. "*Shema Yisrael*"... my lips murmur, "I should just return safely."

The most unbelievable thing then happens: the airplane manages to take off over Lithuania. I see thick forests, small wooden huts, lakes, and stream beds; even from above, from a bird's eye view, it seems I spy mass graves and firing trenches within bald patches in the forests. The airplane swoops down between the clouds and sways like a nutshell in the air pockets. God, I do not wish to end my life this way.

Within this whole surrealistic performance, an air hostess approaches me, suddenly appearing from among the chicken coops, and serves me a bag of salted nuts and a glass of bubbly champagne. To whom should I drink, for all are dead?

Tallinn is beautiful—a harbor town on the Baltic Sea, southwest of the Finnish Gulf—a city of castles and palaces, spires and towers, of antique clocks and massive stone buildings in Gothic style. Eighty kilometers of sea divide it from Finland, that already being a part of the "West."

However, my heart is not free to enjoy beauty and tourist attractions; I have come here on a very specific mission, and that is all!

So I travel to Vaivara and am, as it were, at the end of the world—in northeastern Estonia. Here, there was a concentration camp serving more than twenty labor camps from all over Estonia and a transit camp through which some 20,000 Jews passed from the Vilna and Kovno ghettos as well as from Latvia. There are those who claim that the transport of the Children's *Aktion* from the Kovno ghetto also passed through here.

In close proximity to the Vaivara railway station there are endless expanses of long, green, grassy stalks, thick forests, purple and yellow flowers, blue skies, a yellow sun... so now, where does one go? A lone horse is grazing in the meadow, a lowing cow is heard. Estonian country folk wearing black rubber boots ride past me on bicycles, a small girl wearing a pale blue, floral skirt with a huge, white, silk ribbon in her hair, holds her mother's skinny hand; an elderly man comes limping along in a field, a cane basket in his hand.

And here, in the heart of this endless grassy plain, there is a rock. Chiseled into the rock is a Star of David, with the dates 1943-1944 beneath it; the next line down, reads "Vaivara Koonduslaagri" written in Estonian. This is the place. I stop by the rock and some local people gather around me, one of whom speaks a little English. An elderly man, his voice overflowing with emotion, sheds tears and tells of how there was a children's camp here, where 200 children had been housed. "They were from Lithuania," says the old, blue-eyed man. "They were shot to death in the adjacent forest and burned in the crematorium there," his finger now pointing in the direction of a cowshed about a quarter of a kilometer from where we are standing. So perhaps my grandmother was also with them in the last moments of their lives, I reflect. At the foot of the rock with the Star of David on it, with the words in Estonian that I cannot understand, apart from "Vaivara" and "Lager," I set down a *yahrzeit* candle to the astonished looks of the country people leaning on their bicycles and holding straw baskets. There is utter silence. Tears stream from the old man's eyes, unaware of himself; and, in the eyes of those assembled there, I surely seem like a member of some strange, foreign tribe who has come to their village totally by chance, bending over at the foot of the rock and lighting a memorial candle for a grandmother and children who had possibly arrived here from Kovno. And, just as the wicked little demon in me is teasing and planting doubt in my heart—"Perhaps, it is not certain"—an elderly Estonian woman, wearing the traditional embroidered white blouse with puffed sleeves and a skirt of woven fabric, walks up to me and hands me a notepad, whose cover is worked in her own embroidery, with the message inside, "You must never forget Vaivara."

That night, I hear a hesitant knock on the wooden door of my hotel room in Tallinn and, when I ask in English, "who's there?" my voice shaking, an old man answers me in Yiddish in frail tones, "My girl, do open the door." Since the days of the Holocaust one does not get to hear Yiddish, certainly not here in Estonia; for, as early as January 20, 1942, at the Wannsee Conference,[210] Reinhard Heydrich, chief of the Reich's Security

---

210   Meeting held at a villa in Wannsee, Berlin, on January 20, 1942, to discuss and coordinate the implementation of the "Final Solution of the Jewish Problem."

Main Office (RSHA), had declared Estonia to be "*Judenfrei*" (Ger., free of Jews).

Curiosity gets the better of me and I open the door just a very little. There, in front of me, I see an elderly Jew with a paunch; his stomach almost hits my astounded eyes. There is a kindly smile on his face, and he asks me, in wonderment, if I am really a "Sabra fon Eretz Israel." It is after midnight, not exactly a convenient time to examine to what extent I am prickly on the outside and sweet on the inside... I tell him I am "fon Israel," and the Jewish man, whose name I cannot reveal for obvious reasons, cries like a child.

He is holding a rolled-up sheet of paper some meter in length. Breathing with difficulty, he opens it out for me to see in the dim corridor. I recognize the map of Estonia on which hundreds of coordinates have been marked, of prisons, POW camps, concentration camps, extermination camps, and murder sites.

"I was an officer in the Red Army and was among the first liberators to enter the Klooga Camp a few short hours after the massive slaughter.[211] I will never forget the sight that met my eyes: countless heaps of bodies of prisoners who had been burned between layers of long tree trunks," he tells me, crying vehemently. "Since then, I have never known peace of mind. Nowadays, they are trying to hide the facts, to deny them. Only

---

211 Early on September 19, 1944, as the Soviet army advanced through Estonia, Klooga was surrounded by German and Estonian SS men. Toward midday they began to take groups of prisoners from the camp to a nearby forest for execution, beginning with the men's camp. Some of the men tried to hide inside the camp, but most were found and shot. Others tried to flee from the execution site. Approximately 2,400 Jews and 100 Soviet prisoners of war died in this slaughter. A few days later, on September 28, when the Soviet army liberated Klooga, they found the corpses of the slain stacked for burning.

a week ago, Estonian SS officers who had served in the Third Reich openly held a picnic here and the beer flowed like water. Neo-Nazi groups exist here quite openly."

Photos he had taken secretly spilled from the pocket of his faded suit: pictures of swastikas sprayed on public telephone booths, skinheads with swastikas tattooed on their arms saluting to each other with an outstretched arm... "You must get this map out of here and take it to Yad Vashem," he said. "At great danger to myself, I stole it from the National Archives of Tallinn. You will see camps marked that no one knows about. There are camps to which Jews from Vilna and Kovno were expelled, from Latvia and Transylvania and from Theresienstadt, and the camps where they were killed." I am silent; only the little demon inside of me is annoying me, "Now you have really complicated matters, haven't you—smuggling out state property and an item that testifies to Estonia's involvement in the destruction of European Jewry. The Estonians will catch you with it, and if they do not—the Lithuanians will; and that will be the end of you."

I could not refuse his request and I did not have the wherewithal to argue with my despicable little demon; and so it remains to tell that, on that night, we both, S. and I, lit symbolic memorial torches for the Jews who had perished there—at Lagedi, Klooga, Ereda, Goldfilz, Vivikoni, Asari, Kureme, Soski, Vaivara, Narva, Kunda, Kivioli, Auvara and Ilinurme; and there and then I unraveled the lining of my suitcase and inserted the folded map of the Jewish camps of Estonia into it.[212] From my secret arsenal I dredged up the song, "Whether good or bad / There is no turning back..." And I fervently wanted to be back home, in Jerusalem.

---

212   It is now in the Yad Vashem Archives.

Between There and Here (August 1992)

The night train from Vilnius to Leningrad. Dalia's face is tanned from the sun and wet with tears. I am leaving Lithuania. Through the window I see Dalia standing on the station platform wiping away her tears and waving her handkerchief at me. Who would have believed it? A Lithuanian woman is crying over a Litvak woman. Black smoke rises up. Dalia's silhouette is rapidly shrinking and fading. The station platform disappears, the railway carriages are very slowly passing by Vilna's sad and silent houses, buildings crowded together and, seemingly, pushing each other aside, then to be left behind.

Leaving the factories, we are out of the city limits and enter an area of fields. The last of Vilna's lights have disappeared behind us, and we are approaching a vast forested area with lakes, green slopes, and wooden huts, which accompany us silently on the wayside. Inhaling the fragrance of the fields, choking back tears, I take my leave from There. It is not we who are passing by fields and forests but the fields and forests that are passing us by: fields of grains, barley, oats, flax, and buckwheat. Tall electricity poles chase us with their lights. A heavily loaded coal train approaches from afar. Villages and towns appear and then vanish. Here and there a small house becomes visible, but it also disappears, until we suddenly find ourselves in a train that is stateless. Lithuania and the entire There spin into the darkness and so does my mind, together with them. One by one, the carriages cross the border, leaving Lithuania, and all is behind me. Darkness finally falls, wedging itself between myself and a Lithuania that is no longer visible at all, removing it from my vision.

We have already crossed through Latvia and it seems to me we have arrived in Russia. Outside, it is pitch dark and a gentle rain is falling. We stop at remote railway stations along the way. Downtrodden-looking people board the train: mothers holding the skinny hands of their children, middle-aged people dragging behind them their rolled-up bundles in burlap bags, in plastic bags, in suitcases whose sides are coming apart and have been tied with rope, young people holding brown paper bags containing bottles of alcohol to drown their sorrows. In the crowded carriage, each human being withdraws into himself, spending time with people who are as isolated as they are, not exchanging a glance with a living soul until, burdened by passing time and the distress of loneliness, we establish a kind of covenant among ourselves; minimal smiles curl the sides of mouths and we nod at each other.

In Leningrad—the city that has returned to its pre-Revolution name, St. Petersburg—one discovers impressive architecture, churches with spires built with 400 kilograms of pure gold, museums, water canals crossing the city, well-kept gardens, lawns, bronze statues... I can now continue to be a tourist until reaching the Moscow airport.

Wretched people live in this city: drunkards, beggars, hooligans, street musicians, twelve-year-old Gypsy mothers carrying babies swathed in rags, people selling Russian Matryoshka dolls, people selling shirts with the insignia of the KGB (that replaced the NKVD), people selling flags of the Former Soviet Union, people selling fur-brimmed hats, street artists. They all seem sad and I find it painful looking at them. How many hungry people could one feed here, if some of the gold-plated spires could be smashed and melted down, exchanging the gold for bread, milk, eggs, and vegetables?

Leningrad, Petersburg—how unbearable your face is. On a corner of the sidewalk, on Nevsky Prospekt Avenue, like some ironic contradiction, there stands an attractive, middle-aged woman with a noble yet bony, starved-looking face; wearing a gray head scarf and a gray sweater, her eyes dull; she displays a jar of instant coffee, begging passersby to buy her single item of merchandise.

There is a line to buy tobacco, a line to buy bananas, a line for cans of food. At a bread shop, shop assistants stand there, dressed in white uniforms. The line is long and getting longer, despite the fact that the shelves have been empty for a while.

This is a miserable country.

I find seeing this poverty hard. I no longer have the strength to cry for other people's troubles. I give out throat lozenges to pale-looking children who are eating smoked fish tails wrapped in newspaper, their large, sunken eyes encircled by dark rings. This is all I have left to give them.

It is Sabbath evening on the St. Petersburg-Moscow train. We are approaching the longed-for city—getting closer to the El Al airplane that will finally take me home. Slouched and silent in a corner of the carriage, bundled up in layers of sweaters and a padded coat, my fantasy takes me to the Israeli flag painted on the wing of the plane. "*Shalom aleichem malachei ha-shareit malachei elyon*,"[213] I haul out Sabbath melodies from my secret arsenal of songs. I do not have any Sabbath candles in my bag. All I have left are *yahrzeit*

---

213 Hebrew: "Peace upon you, ministering angels, messengers of the Most High, of the Supreme King of Kings." A traditional song sung Friday night at the beginning of the Jewish Sabbath.

Dalia the Lithuanian and Safira
the Litvak next to the Vilnius–
Leningrad train

candles which I had hoped to light at the exact place where Grandmother had been murdered, but that was not to be.

From the great railway station in Moscow, train tracks branch out to the whole, wide world. There are endless tracks and hundreds of carriages, a blast of smoke and the shouting of humans. The Moscow River flows lazily, just like the Vistula, the Bug, the Vilija, the Nemunas, and the Neva rivers. Everything flows on. Everything comes to an end. All streams make their way to the sea; everything finally ends, and the cycle starts again.

Outside the Pushkin Museum, I see a few tough-looking men with beards like those of the Pravoslav priests; they are dressed in black uniforms, black boots, and brown leather belts and wear the black, yellow, and white armbands of the "Pamyat"[214] movement. They shout at me, "Get off the bench. For Russians only." I adjust my watch to Israeli time.

---

214 A Russian ultra-nationalist organization identifying itself as the "People's National-patriotic Orthodox Christian movement." It has been accused of racism, xenophobia, and antisemitism.

In the time remaining until the flight, I will go to the Israeli Embassy. That seems to me to be the most fitting place to end my journey. Hundreds of Jews are gathered at the entrance to the embassy; they are there to obtain the necessary papers for the privilege of coming Home. There is commotion and disorder. "From Slavery to Freedom" is posted on the opposite wall. There are posters showing Haifa and Tel Aviv; but where is Jerusalem? I am not bothered; I know it is in the hearts of the people crowding here.

With unconcealed pride I stand in the line marked "Israeli citizens," allow my Star of David to show, and push my way to the counter, requesting them to stamp my passport. "I am closing a cycle of events," I tell the clerk who, consequently, gives me a strange look.

Toward the end of my trip I have a difficult dilemma; with one picture left on the film in my camera, what should this last photo be? And then, as if in a dream, I see an army truck zooming out of one of the Moscow side streets and, in it, smiling Russian soldiers... Just as it was then. There, in the north of Poland when the Russian soldiers freed Mother and Aunt Leah in January 1945...

And that was my last photograph.

Here (September 1992)

That's it. I have returned home. Home to Here. The pair of shoes that has measured There in steps, with mud stuck to its soles, is left orphaned. The shoes have paced out my wandering from the Slobodka Ghetto to the Flugplatz at Aleksotas and the Death March paths; they have soaked up droplets of dew that dripped from the weeds that had soiled the walls of the Slobodka house. I will never in my life wear them again!

In the kitchen in Jerusalem, all the family is sitting round the table eating some refreshing watermelon; the rest of my family is on the window sill in bags of dust and ashes from There—from Auschwitz-Birkenau, from Stutthof, from the Ninth Fort, from Rumsiskes, from Ponevezh,[215] from the

---

215 In that region in the north of Lithuania, there had been some 10,000 Jews before the Holocaust. The "'Grand Yeshiva" at Ponevezh (Lith., Panevezys) was among the largest in Lithuania and it had produced great and well-known rabbis of Torah study. The Jews of the town were taken out to be killed in groups of 200 and were murdered, mostly at the hands of the Lithuanians, on August 26, 1941, in the Pajuoste Forest, approximately eight kilometers east of Panevezys, adjacent to the village of Pajuoste. Around 8,000 of the Jews from Ponevezh and the neighboring towns were killed in the forest, among them Tzipora-Feige Baruchson's father, Shmuel-David

Pajuoste Forest, from Pumpenai[216]… and placed next to them are dried flowers from the Majdanek Extermination Camp and from the Tatra Mountains.

Most of the songs played in my mind all through my wanderings are no longer sung; they have been totally erased from the Israeli awareness of Here; their beautiful words have lost their value over the years.

Totally immersed in the yesterdays of the past, pictures of rough roads still flash through my mind, as do those of deserted houses, shops that were owned by Jews, wooden huts in which Jews had lived, the gray walls of the empty

---

Chayet, and his son, the banker Avraham Chayet, who was killed with his wife, Gita, and their three children.

216 A town in the north of Lithuania, close to Ponevezh, where some seventy-five Jewish families had lived before the Holocaust. On July 15, 1941, all the Jews there were forced to leave their homes and were gathered in the homes of six local Jews, one of them being the house of Rabbi Meir Yitzchak Chayet (the last rabbi of the town and Tzipora-Feige Baruchson's brother), that was a kind of ghetto surrounded by barbed wire. There they were all held together in filthy conditions and without food. They lived in fear, were beaten, robbed, and sent to forced labor. Rabbi Meir Yitzchak Chayet was tortured to death in his house on August 26, 1941: the Lithuanians falsely accused him of swallowing gold coins, threw him to the ground, beat him and trod on his stomach till his intestines spilled out. A local Lithuanian related that it was a slow, intensely cruel death, with his wife, Gitel, and the three small children looking on. After that, the Pumpenai Jews were taken to the Pajuoste Forest where all were shot to death—men, women and children—next to long pits which were then used as mass graves. The bodies were covered with dirt, despite the fact that some of the people were still alive.

batei midrash (study halls), barbed-wire fencing, the barracks, the skeletons of the pallets at Schanz... railway stations... the Jewish Committee House in Lublin where the Brichah was organized, and Stutthof—the most beautiful extermination camp on the face of the earth...

From now on, life will look different: while waiting in line at the post office I will think back to the line at the Auschwitz Archives, a thicket will remind me of the bald parts of a forest covering mass-killing trenches, a wooden hut will remind me of a barrack... I will forever remember my own private "righteous among the nations" who saved me from falling into the abyss of a loss of faith in humanity: Janina Grabowska from Stutthof; the Russian soldier at Schanz; Dalia J., my Lithuanian interpreter who had served as my "mouth" in Kovno. These people were the pillars of fire that lit my way. Amid the sea of evil and sin on the scorched earth of There, these people were revealed to me as pure, white lilies springing up between the ruins and debris. These few saintly individuals, allowing a small glimmer of light to penetrate into Mother's words "Beware of the goyim..." had personified the triumph of humanity over cruelty and, in their company, I could wear my Star of David pendant in comfort and enjoy a sense of oneness of all mankind.

My journey of wandering between There and Here has ended but has not been completed; I am still lost and perplexed. I have not found my peace of mind. My disappointment is growing deeper and becoming permanent. Still my common sense tells me that Grandmother Tzipora was murdered at Auschwitz-Birkenau, but the curtain of doubt has not been raised, and I do not know for sure to where she was taken, from where, or when and how she was killed.

I had left one home in order to visit another. With the perforated identity of a little from Here and a little from There, in my unflagging search to know what had happened to Grandmother, with my aspiration to close the circle and complete the endless puzzle, I have traveled beyond the mountains of darkness to rummage There for my deepest roots, to get to know the nucleus of my identity, to follow the footsteps of Mother's hardships and suffering during the Holocaust, and to be in the very places where my grandmother had been, the grandmother whose name I bear, until she was taken to her unknown end. I traveled There to be touched by her in some small way, in case she should look out on me from one of the clouds for a fraction of a second, or should be discovered among the wooden huts of Slobodka, or by the barbed-wire fences of Birkenau. I traveled There to remember events in history, people and important moments, to render it all for eternal memory.

I planned this journey of mine for many years, since I was caught and held in a place between two worlds—the post-Palmach world of Eretz Israel that had rejected me for not being a pure Sabra and the world of There, from which I had requested to be saved. As a small girl hearing my friends' voices— they were Sabra children of Sabra parents— resounding from the playground, I remember myself choosing to stay in my room to study Esther Lurie's paintings for hours: *The Young Woman with the Yellow Star of David, On the Way to the Ninth Fort*. Beneath the pastoral atmosphere of water colors, I sensed the sadness that hovered over those colorful landscapes: an atmosphere of despair and the fear of death. (In time, fate led me to meet the esteemed artist Esther Lurie in her Tel Aviv home. I had come to her as an interviewer on behalf of the Department of Oral Testimonies under the auspices of Yad Vashem; we consequently became friends and I visited her several times. She would serve me lunch and talk in detail of her deteriorating health. On one of the visits, she presented me with a canvas of *The Young Woman with the Yellow Star* she had drawn especially for me, complete with dedication;

all through the years, I found a likeness to my mother in that painting and it remains dear to me).

As the years go by, I have moved from reading *Tamara's Diary*[217] and *The Children of Mapu Street*[218] to *The Destruction of Kovno's Jewry*[219] and *The Black Book*,[220] while constantly jotting down the dates of the *Aktionen* and the names of their perpetrators on small pieces of paper, gathering shards of stories over time, clinging to the past, and, in the small hours of the night, studying the map of Vilijampole, as if I were wandering through the lanes of Slobodka; for wherever I go, I return to Lithuania, or, to be more accurate, to Kovno or, should I say, to Slobodka, to the house at 9 Paneriu Street. That is how I move from house to house, between There and Here, from Jerusalem to Lithuania and from Lithuania to Jerusalem.

I have looked for my grandmother in the places where she had lived—it seems to me I was there in periods and times prior to the Holocaust, before the gaping chasm was torn into the heart of humanity, leaving us, the Jews, scarred and bleeding; bleeding for eternity. I have visited the places where she was last seen, where she might have been murdered. I have roamed

---

217 Tamara Lazerson, *Tamara's Diary: Kovno 1942–1946* [in Hebrew], a twelve-year-old girl's story of life in the Kovno Ghetto.

218 Sarah Neshamit, *The Children of Mapu Street*, a novel about how the war had disrupted the lives of four children, once residents of Mapu Street in Kovno.

219 Leib Garfunkel, *The Destruction of Kovno's Jewry* [in Hebrew], an account by the deputy chairman of the Ältestenrat of events in Kovno from before the establishment of the ghetto through its liquidation.

220 Ilya Ehrenberg and Vasily Grossman (eds.), *The Black Book*, a collection of eyewitness testimonies, letters, diary entries, and assembled histories of towns and ghettos of Soviet Jews.

to unknown stations, searching for tranquility. I crossed rivers and forests. In the length and breadth of a ground saturated in the blood of my brethren and drenched in profound hatred, I journeyed for days and nights on trains, crossing the skies in airplanes. I rubbed shoulders with people from other worlds, trying, in vain, to glean some kind of splinter of a clue or just a smidgen of reference. I have strayed among the pits and gazed at the walls of death; I was jabbed by barbed wire; I have crawled through sewers in filth and stench and rolled down steep slopes; and my senses have become dulled from so much anguish. I have climbed, fallen, and climbed again; however, the more fervently I took the path that moved further toward a haven of serenity, the further serenity moved away from me.

Sometimes, at night, I wonder whether these things did not really happen, but the grooves in my shoulders from my pack, the cracked skin of my feet, and the bruise mark I received as a token of remembrance when close to the Yavneh Gymnasia are proof that I have, indeed, returned from There.

I am now back home in my daily routine of everyday tasks. In the morning I cross the street on my way to the grocery store to buy a loaf of fresh bread, crowding in there with a handful of people who have been at synagogue at the Shacharit (morning) service, all reading the daily newspaper headlines written in large Hebrew letters. To me, all this is a miracle after everything Mother has told me, and also after the painful glimpse of things I have seen There. It is amazing to me that I am able to wear my Star of David pendant peeping out of my shirt and that my feet, in their clogs, come up against the small stones on a thorny Jerusalem roadside. People nod their heads and say "Shalom"[221] and "Good morning" to me in the

---

221 Hebrew: Hello; also means "peace."

sacred Jewish language. I can have as much bread as I want and a goodly sun sends us its warming rays.

It is only in the small hours of the night that I am reminded of my yearning for Slobodka, asking myself "Who will visit the grave?" and "Who will go to the house?" Lost and straying, with a sense of perpetual estrangement, I know that I will forever move back and forth between Here and There and between There and Here; and, no matter where I go, I will eternally remain faithful to my roots... and that is the whole story! Again and again I will be in Kovno and from There I will yearn for Jerusalem, and that will go on endlessly. A weakness in the notion itself, that the story is incomplete, is awakening in me. The mosaic has not been completed and the mighty heap of memories awaits me around every corner. Will I break down in the end; will I come to my senses and learn to free myself of the burden of my disappointed love for Slobodka that never leaves me? I believe that will not happen. The dying out of a home can continue over a great many generations, and yearning for it lives on in the second and third generations, both emotions clashing painfully.

It is well known that clods of earth are mute. They tell no story and supply no answers. You will only find the memory of destruction in earth that is saturated with blood, trembling with no hope of peace, with flocks of screeching black crows flying above. In hours of depression and doubt, when asking myself what will be and to where all this will lead, I take my missing grandmother for a walk to show her the abundance of cyclamen and poppies at the foot of the olive trees on the edges of the Valley of the Cross.[222] Home is here! The Divine Spirit is here.

---

222   A valley close to the Rehavia district of Jerusalem. According to the legend, Lot came to live here after being separated from his daughters and planted cedar, cypress, and pine seeds, which germinated and grew together to form the tree from whose wood Christ's cross was made.

The author laying a memorial wreath in commemoration of the Lithuanian community, in the Ohel Yizkor (Hall of Remembrance) at Yad Vashem (Holocaust Memorial Day, 1993). To her left (in the second row) is former Knesset member Dov Shilansky, a native of Siauliai, Lithuania

Can one call a journey such as I took successful? Would it be considered a kind of victory?

The oppressive load of the journey still weighs heavily on me and is troubling and I suppose it will continue to be so... perhaps forever... until, at the end of the days allotted to me, I will go to heaven and, there, I will finally meet my grandmother. And there she will whisper to me "My *Maideleh*..."